What to Bring to the Rental Shop

- A pen
- Your height, weight, and shoe size
- A credit card for the security deposit
- A driver's license
- The pair of socks that you plan to wear for skiing
- Gloves
- A distraction, such as a newspaper, a Walkman, or a book
- A friend

A Checklist for Your First Day on the Slopes

Be sure to have the following items with you when you leave the parking lot:

- Two pairs of waterproof gloves
- A knitted hat
- Sunglasses
- A pair of ski socks
- A not-too-warm jacket
- Long underwear
- Ski pants
- Sunscreen
- A credit card
- A driver's license

Skiing For Dummies®

Your Responsibility Code

The rules of skiing, by the National Ski Areas Association:

- Always stay in control, and be able to stop or avoid other people or objects.
- People ahead of you have the right of way. It is your responsibility to avoid them.
- You must not stop where you obstruct a trail or are not visible from above.
- When starting downhill or merging into a trail, look uphill and yield to others.
- Always use devices to help prevent runaway equipment.
- Observe all posted signs and warnings. Keep off closed trails and out of closed areas.
- Prior to using any lift, you must have the knowledge and ability to load, ride, and unload safely.

What to Include in Your Carry-On Bag when Flying

Here's what I pack in my carry-on bag, listed in order of importance. I wear my ski jacket and fleece on board. (Your items may differ somewhat.)

- Ski boots
- Contact lenses
- Knee brace
- Ski pants
- Gloves
- Socks
- A set of thermal underwear
- Hat
- A change of underwear

Trail Designations

- Green circle: Easiest
- Blue square: More difficult
- Black diamond: Most difficult
- Double black diamond: For experts only

...For Dummies®: Bestselling Book Series for Beginners

Praise for Skiing For Dummies

"*Skiing For Dummies* accomplishes a rare feat: It embodies a spirit of fun and adventure while dispensing truly valuable advice about and insight into the skier's world. With his breezy, almost offhand manner, Allen St. John cuts through the jargon and explains the sport, its gear, and its characters in clear and direct terms. Every operator's manual should be this simple — and accurate.

> — Rick Kahl, Editor-in-Chief, *Skiing* magazine

"Once you try skiing, you'll get hooked, but starting out can seem complicated. Picking up this book is the first step toward demystifying the sport."

> — Billy Kidd, Olympic medalist and former World Champion

"From the rental shop to avalanche awareness all the way to injury prevention, Allen St. John reveals why everyone should learn to ski. It's fun, safe, and the best way to spend a winter's day!"

> — Dan Egan, extreme skier and author of *All Terrain Skiing*

"I give this book 'Two Tips Up!'" The research displays true ski vacation scenarios that constantly transpire. Not only does the first-time vacationer NEED to read this for a headache-free vacation, but the veterans will find some new hints and tricks that will preserve time better spent catching first tracks."

> — Trace Worthington, seven-time World Freestyle Skiing
> Champion and two-time Olympian

"This sport isn't as hard as people think — so stop throwing poles into trees and screaming obscenities. Think simple, dummy . . . and read this book, for you too can achieve skier enlightenment."

> — Kristen Ulmer, voted best female skier in North America by
> recent *Powder* and *Skiing* magazine surveys

"Unlike many ski writers, Allen St. John remembers what it's like to be a beginner, and the result is a book that tells first-timers everything they need to start having fun on the slopes. But *Skiing For Dummies* is also filled with savvy advice and insider's tips that any expert can use — from booking a perfect vacation, to finding great snow, to skiing better on any terrain and in any kind of condition. Take it along on your next ski trip."

> — Kim Reichhelm, two-time World Extreme Skiing Champion and
> founder of Women's Ski Adventures

"Finally, a book on skiing that's not full of irrelevant technical gobbley-gook. *Skiing For Dummies* is fun, easy to read, and tells you what you need to know to have more fun on the slopes. What more can you ask for?"

> — Tim Pietrick, COO of Booth Creek Properties, former President of K2, and former member of the Professional Ski Instructors of America Demo Team

"Allen St. John packs in everything you need to know to have a blast — and avoid looking like a dork — on the slopes. This book is more useful than a good lawyer and more fun than a Three Stooges marathon."

> — James Kaminsky, Co-Editor, *Maxim* magazine

Skiing FOR DUMMIES®

by Allen St. John

Foreword by Jonny Moseley

IDG Books Worldwide, Inc.
An International Data Group Company

Foster City, CA ◆ Chicago, IL ◆ Indianapolis, IN ◆ New York, NY

Skiing For Dummies®

Published by
IDG Books Worldwide, Inc.
An International Data Group Company
919 E. Hillsdale Blvd.
Suite 400
Foster City, CA 94404
www.idgbooks.com (IDG Books Worldwide Web site)
www.dummies.com (Dummies Press Web site)

Library of Congress Catalog Card No.: 99-65860

ISBN: 0-7645-5161-2

Printed in the United States of America

10 9 8 7 6 5 4 3 2 1

1O/QT/QZ/ZZ/IN

Distributed in the United States by IDG Books Worldwide, Inc.

Distributed by CDG Books Canada Inc. for Canada; by Transworld Publishers Limited in the United Kingdom; by IDG Norge Books for Norway; by IDG Sweden Books for Sweden; by IDG Books Australia Publishing Corporation Pty. Ltd. for Australia and New Zealand; by TransQuest Publishers Pte Ltd. for Singapore, Malaysia, Thailand, Indonesia, and Hong Kong; by Gotop Information Inc. for Taiwan; by ICG Muse, Inc. for Japan; by Intersoft for South Africa; by Eyrolles for France; by International Thomson Publishing for Germany, Austria and Switzerland; by Distribuidora Cuspide for Argentina; by LR International for Brazil; by Galileo Libros for Chile; by Ediciones ZETA S.C.R. Ltda. for Peru; by WS Computer Publishing Corporation, Inc., for the Philippines; by Contemporanea de Ediciones for Venezuela; by Express Computer Distributors for the Caribbean and West Indies; by Micronesia Media Distributor, Inc. for Micronesia; by Chips Computadoras S.A. de C.V. for Mexico; by Editorial Norma de Panama S.A. for Panama; by American Bookshops for Finland.

For general information on IDG Books Worldwide's books in the U.S., please call our Consumer Customer Service department at 800-762-2974. For reseller information, including discounts and premium sales, please call our Reseller Customer Service department at 800-434-3422.

For information on where to purchase IDG Books Worldwide's books outside the U.S., please contact our International Sales department at 317-596-5530 or fax 317-596-5692.

For consumer information on foreign language translations, please contact our Customer Service department at 1-800-434-3422, fax 317-596-5692, or e-mail rights@idgbooks.com.

For information on licensing foreign or domestic rights, please phone +1-650-655-3109.

For sales inquiries and special prices for bulk quantities, please contact our Sales department at 650-655-3200 or write to the address above.

For information on using IDG Books Worldwide's books in the classroom or for ordering examination copies, please contact our Educational Sales department at 800-434-2086 or fax 317-596-5499.

For press review copies, author interviews, or other publicity information, please contact our Public Relations department at 650-655-3000 or fax 650-655-3299.

For authorization to photocopy items for corporate, personal, or educational use, please contact Copyright Clearance Center, 222 Rosewood Drive, Danvers, MA 01923, or fax 978-750-4470.

is a registered trademark under exclusive license to IDG Books Worldwide, Inc. from International Data Group, Inc.

About the Author

Nicole Esposito

Allen St. John is a contributing editor at *Skiing* magazine, where he writes about gear, resorts, travel, trends, and instruction, as well as writing the Brain Dump column. In 1996, he won the Harold Hirsch award for Excellence in Magazine Writing awarded by the North American Ski Journalists Association.

He is also a member of the Professional Ski Instructors of America and has contributed to its magazine, *The Professional Skier.*

His writings about the sport have appeared in many national publications, including *The New York Times Magazine, Los Angeles Magazine,* and Conde Nast *Women's Sports and Fitness.* He also writes frequently for *The Wall Street Journal, The New York Times Book Review, Maxim, Men's Journal,* and *The Village Voice.* His previous book projects include Major League Baseball's *American and National Leauge Pocket Almanacs* and the hardcover edition and CD-ROM of Tim McCarver's *The Way Baseball Works.* Most recently, he is the author of *Bicycling For Dummies,* also published by IDG Books Worldwide, Inc.

He lives in Upper Montclair, New Jersey, with his wife Sally, son Ethan, and Alison the brown dog.

Dedication

To the Waack family: My mother-in-law, Catherine, who showed me why skiing is the best family sport there is; my father-in-law, Richard, who still makes the smoothest Arlberg turn in all of New Hampshire; my sister-in-law, Nancy, whose friendship has brightened so many of my ski days; and of course my wife, Sally, my favorite chairlift partner.

ABOUT IDG BOOKS WORLDWIDE

Welcome to the world of IDG Books Worldwide.

IDG Books Worldwide, Inc., is a subsidiary of International Data Group, the world's largest publisher of computer-related information and the leading global provider of information services on information technology. IDG was founded more than 30 years ago by Patrick J. McGovern and now employs more than 9,000 people worldwide. IDG publishes more than 290 computer publications in over 75 countries. More than 90 million people read one or more IDG publications each month.

Launched in 1990, IDG Books Worldwide is today the #1 publisher of best-selling computer books in the United States. We are proud to have received eight awards from the Computer Press Association in recognition of editorial excellence and three from Computer Currents' First Annual Readers' Choice Awards. Our best-selling ...For Dummies® series has more than 50 million copies in print with translations in 31 languages. IDG Books Worldwide, through a joint venture with IDG's Hi-Tech Beijing, became the first U.S. publisher to publish a computer book in the People's Republic of China. In record time, IDG Books Worldwide has become the first choice for millions of readers around the world who want to learn how to better manage their businesses.

Our mission is simple: Every one of our books is designed to bring extra value and skill-building instructions to the reader. Our books are written by experts who understand and care about our readers. The knowledge base of our editorial staff comes from years of experience in publishing, education, and journalism — experience we use to produce books to carry us into the new millennium. In short, we care about books, so we attract the best people. We devote special attention to details such as audience, interior design, use of icons, and illustrations. And because we use an efficient process of authoring, editing, and desktop publishing our books electronically, we can spend more time ensuring superior content and less time on the technicalities of making books.

You can count on our commitment to deliver high-quality books at competitive prices on topics you want to read about. At IDG Books Worldwide, we continue in the IDG tradition of delivering quality for more than 30 years. You'll find no better book on a subject than one from IDG Books Worldwide.

John Kilcullen
Chairman and CEO
IDG Books Worldwide, Inc.

Steven Berkowitz
President and Publisher
IDG Books Worldwide, Inc.

WINNER

Eighth Annual Computer Press Awards ≥1992

IX WINNER

Ninth Annual Computer Press Awards ≥1993

WINNER

X WINNER

Tenth Annual Computer Press Awards ≥1994

XI WINNER

Eleventh Annual Computer Press Awards ≥1995

IDG is the world's leading IT media, research and exposition company. Founded in 1964, IDG had 1997 revenues of $2.05 billion and has more than 9,000 employees worldwide. IDG offers the widest range of media options that reach IT buyers in 75 countries representing 95% of worldwide IT spending. IDG's diverse product and services portfolio spans six key areas including print publishing, online publishing, expositions and conferences, market research, education and training, and global marketing services. More than 90 million people read one or more of IDG's 290 magazines and newspapers, including IDG's leading global brands — Computerworld, PC World, Network World, Macworld and the Channel World family of publications. IDG Books Worldwide is one of the fastest-growing computer book publishers in the world, with more than 700 titles in 36 languages. The "...For Dummies®" series alone has more than 50 million copies in print. IDG offers online users the largest network of technology-specific Web sites around the world through IDG.net (http://www.idg.net), which comprises more than 225 targeted Web sites in 55 countries worldwide. International Data Corporation (IDC) is the world's largest provider of information technology data, analysis and consulting, with research centers in over 41 countries and more than 400 research analysts worldwide. IDG World Expo is a leading producer of more than 168 globally branded conferences and expositions in 35 countries including E3 (Electronic Entertainment Expo), Macworld Expo, ComNet, Windows World Expo, ICE (Internet Commerce Expo), Agenda, DEMO, and Spotlight. IDG's training subsidiary, ExecuTrain, is the world's largest computer training company, with more than 230 locations worldwide and 785 training courses. IDG Marketing Services helps industry-leading IT companies build international brand recognition by developing global integrated marketing programs via IDG's print, online and exposition products worldwide. Further information about the company can be found at www.idg.com.   1/24/99

Author's Acknowledgments

Skiing is a social sport, and there's a community of people who helped make this book happen. Thanks first of all to my acquisitions editor, Stacy Collins, who brought me into the IDG Books family and lent her unqualified support to both this book and *Bicycling For Dummies*. Thanks to my agent, Mark Reiter of IMG, who helped turn a magazine writer into a book author. I also have to thank my project editor, Nate Holdread, who kept his eyes unwaveringly on the prize and turned my (at times virus-infected) files into a real-live book; copy editors Donna Love and Kathleen Dobie, who polished my prose to a high gloss; and Sally Onopa, whose illustrations help my words make sense. And my technical editor, Jerry Beilinson, who possesses that rarest of combinations: An eye for detail coupled with an unrelenting grip on the big picture. He's a wonderful writer in his own right, a good friend, and a much better skier than he lets on to be. This book wouldn't be half as good without him.

Big thanks to all my friends at *Skiing* magazine — Rick Kahl, Bill Grout, Helen Olsson, Lindsay Diforio, Mike Miracle, Janice Finnell, Bevin Conn, and Charlie Glass — as well as the magazine's alumni team — Dana White, Josh Lerman, Lee Carlson, Hollis Brooks, and Paul Prince. Much of what I know about skiing I learned at *Skiing Trade News* — working with Iseult Devlin, Patricia O'Connell, Elaine Marotta, Torry Colichio, Jeff Rich, Jim Deines, and Greg Reilly — and this book stands as testament to those long nights. I'd like to thank my friends in the ski industry, who provided information, insight, and in some cases, the photos that illustrate this book, including Tim Petrick and Julie Maurer at Booth Creek Properties, Skip King at American Skiing Company, Ed Pitoniak at Intrawest, Jean Marie Gande at Rossignol, Bruce Barrows and Bill Irwin at Elan, Stuart Rempel at K2, Mike Adams at Salomon, Mark Dorsey at PSIA, and Michael Berry at NSAA.

And of course I'd be remiss without mentioning my skiing friends, including John Dostal, Dan Rusk, Mary Grunmeier, Barbara Witt, and Craig Hockenberry, with whom I've shared many a chairlift and many a philosophical discussion about what exactly it takes to make a ski turn.

I also have to thank my editors, who helped me make my mortgage payment every month: Jim Kaminsky at *Maxim;* Kyle Creighton at *The New York Times Magazine;* Lucy Danziger, Dana White, Alex Seigel, and Vicki Lowry at *Women's Sports and Fitness;* Michael Anderson at *The New York Times Book Review*; Jeff Csatari at *Men's Journal;* and Miles Seligman at *The Village Voice.*

And lastly, a thanks as high as the top of Arapahoe Basin goes to my family. My wife Sally made this book possible in more ways than I can count, from taking me skiing for the first time, to posing for illustrations in 90 degree heat, to keeping the fridge stocked, the bills paid, and Alison the brown dog fed while I logged week after week of 18-hour days. My son Ethan has been tagging along on ski trips since he was 10 weeks old. But last winter, as he watched the snowmobiles play hide-and-seek, the groomers push the snow up the mountain, and Mommy, Daddy, Nana, Papa, and Nancy go "keying," his two-year-old wonderment helped me remember what's so special about playing in the snow. And to the littlest St. John — ETA February, 2000 — who brought a special joy to this project's final few weeks, I can't wait to meet you.

Publisher's Acknowledgments

We're proud of this book; please register your comments through our IDG Books Worldwide Online Registration Form located at http://my2cents.dummies.com.

Some of the people who helped bring this book to market include the following:

Acquisitions, Editorial, and Media Development

Project Editor: Nate Holdread

Acquisitions Editor: Stacy Collins

Copy Editors: Kathleen Dobie, Donna Love

Technical Editor: Jerry Beilinson

Acquisitions Coordinators: Jonathan Malysiak, Lisa Roule

Acquisitions Assistant: Allison Solomon

Editorial Manager: Leah Cameron

Editorial Assistant: Beth Parlon

Production

Project Coordinator: Regina Snyder

Layout and Graphics:
Brian Drumm, Angela F. Hunckler, Kate Jenkins, Barry Offringa, Brent Savage, Janet Seib, Michael A. Sullivan, Brian Torwelle, Mary Jo Weis

Proofreaders: Mary C. Barnack, Nancy Price, Rebecca Senninger, Toni Settle

Indexer: Joan Griffitts

Special Help
Tracy Barr

General and Administrative

IDG Books Worldwide, Inc.: John Kilcullen, CEO; Steven Berkowitz, President and Publisher

IDG Books Technology Publishing Group: Richard Swadley, Senior Vice President and Publisher; Walter Bruce III, Vice President and Associate Publisher; Steven Sayre, Associate Publisher; Joseph Wikert, Associate Publisher; Mary Bednarek, Branded Product Development Director; Mary Corder, Editorial Director

IDG Books Consumer Publishing Group: Roland Elgey, Senior Vice President and Publisher; Kathleen A. Welton, Vice President and Publisher; Kevin Thornton, Acquisitions Manager; Kristin A. Cocks, Editorial Director

IDG Books Internet Publishing Group: Brenda McLaughlin, Senior Vice President and Publisher; Diane Graves Steele, Vice President and Associate Publisher; Sofia Marchant, Online Marketing Manager

IDG Books Production for Dummies Press: Michael R. Britton, Vice President of Production; Debbie Stailey, Associate Director of Production; Cindy L. Phipps, Manager of Project Coordination, Production Proofreading, and Indexing; Tony Augsburger, Manager of Prepress, Reprints, and Systems; Laura Carpenter, Production Control Manager; Shelley Lea, Supervisor of Graphics and Design; Debbie J. Gates, Production Systems Specialist; Robert Springer, Supervisor of Proofreading; Kathie Schutte, Production Supervisor

Dummies Packaging and Book Design: Patty Page, Manager, Promotions Marketing

◆

The publisher would like to give special thanks to Patrick J. McGovern, without whom this book would not have been possible.

◆

Contents at a Glance

Cartoons at a Glance

By Rich Tennant

"Very impressive. However, I don't think being able to tap dance in a pair of boots necessarily constitutes a proper fit."

page 7

"This is the 5th time down the slope you've claimed a sudden urge to make a snow angel. Why don't you just admit you're falling?"

page 99

"Okay—here they come. Remember, it's a lot like catching salmon, only spit out the poles."

page 277

"Well, it's partially their fault for putting a restaurant that close to the chairlift."

page 259

"The simulated mogul function isn't working, so every once in a while I'll sneak up behind you and try to knock you down."

page 175

"We did a lot of altitude training before coming out here. It wasn't easy either—there's only one roof-top restaurant and bar where we live."

page 223

Fax: 978-546-7747 • **E-mail:** the5wave@tiac.net

Table of Contents

Foreword

● ●

*M*y love for skiing runs deep, deep into my long underwear, where I used to pee as a child because I was having too much fun to go into the lodge. Growing up as a weekend skier, I was not discouraged by the fact that I didn't get out of school early every day to hit the slopes. Instead I was forced to appreciate every second I spent on skis. My day did not stop when the skis came off. The mountain lifestyle and atmosphere surrounding ski areas should be enjoyed as much as the sport itself.

From back in the day until now, the skill level at which someone skis is irrelevant to the amount of enjoyment one can have. With the right attitude, every snow day will be memorable. Some of my most memorable moments as a skier have been off the hill, like when my two older brothers and I threw snowballs at the traffic filing out of Squaw Valley on a Saturday afternoon, until smart Jonny drilled one at a sheriff. While fleeing, we sank up to our waists and were easily apprehended and returned to Mom and Dad — guilty.

Think nothing of the cold or the foreign things on your feet, but instead think about effortlessly gliding down mountains using only the power of gravity to reach incredible speeds, experiencing g-forces, and flinging yourself off incredible jumps to do death-defying stunts! You are only a short read away from the world in which I dwell. If I only had such a book growing up as a young hot dog skier, maybe I would easily have two gold medals by now.

For the young as well as the young at heart, few sports allow an 80-year-old man and an 8-year-old girl to ride the same chairlift to the top of a mountain, schuss their way with the same fluidity through trees and over humps, and by the end of the day enjoy a cup of hot chocolate together in the lodge, reminiscing about the great day they had. This happens, so if you want it and more, read up! And when you're done, don't forget to take me up on that hot cocoa . . .

Jonny Moseley, Olympic Gold Medalist in Freestyle Mogul Skiing and International Skiing Superstar

Introduction

● ●

*Y*ou've heard the buzz. Skiing is like flying without wings. It's like floating through the middle of the world's biggest white sale. It's the most fun you can have with your long underwear on. Yes, there's more than a grain of truth to all this.

But as with most things that sound this good, there's a catch. If you head to the slopes without knowing your way around, chances are you'll end up cold, broke, and frustrated. That's the reason why more than 80 percent of the people who try skiing once never come back. Maybe, once upon a time, you were one of them. That's where *Skiing For Dummies* comes in. This book is your personal trail map to the wide, wonderful world of skiing.

This isn't an instruction book — although it does provide some quick, easy ways for you to improve your skiing. This isn't a guide book — although I do include some insider's information about the nation's top ski areas. And this isn't an equipment buyer's guide — although I do tell you how to find the gear that'll help you ski better. What you're holding is a survival guide, the paper and ink equivalent of an expert friend to guide you every step of the way.

Why You Need This Book

Anyone can ski. Four-year-olds can do it. Ninety-year olds can do it. And you can do it, too. No matter what your level — whether you just got psyched by seeing Picabo Street at the Olympics and are thinking "Hey, I'd like to try that," or you're a true expert — you'll find a wealth of useful stuff in this book.

The good news is that skiing has gotten easier and more fun. The equipment is better than ever, with boots you can wear all day and easier-to-turn skis. Fast lifts that let you cram a full day of skiing into half a day. Snowmaking system guarantee that after saving up for a vacation for a year, you won't end up skiing on mud.

The bad news is that the world of skiing is also filled with more options than ever, and if you're familiar with Murphy's Law, you understand that it means more ways to screw up. I'm here to help.

In the process of logging thousands of days at resorts all over the world, I've learned a thing or two about how to make a ski vacation work. I can tell you where to go, what to pack, when to find the best snow, and how to get down the mountain efficiently so that you don't spend four of your five days sitting in the hot tub, soaking away your sore muscles.

How This Book Is Organized

I understand that you're not going to curl up in front of the fire with this book and read it cover to cover. It's not *Angela's Ashes,* after all. More likely, you're going to pick it up, flip through it, read the section about buying equipment, graze the list of top ski resorts, and photocopy the *Top Ten Skiing Slang Terms* list and post it on the fridge.

I designed *Skiing For Dummies* so that if you don't understand a term, go to the glossary in the back. If you need info on a particular subject, head to one of the two detailed tables of contents in the front of the book. Save your exploring for out on the mountain.

Part I: Gearing Up

Remember when you were a kid and the two most magical words in the English language were "snow" and "day?" Playing outside, making snow angels, sliding down your driveway on a garbage can lid? Well, with skiing, you can call your own snow day just about any time you want. In this section, I show you the basics: what to wear, how to buy gear, and especially, how to have fun in the snow.

Chapter 1 shows you how to survive the ski area equivalent of *Nightmare on Elm Street:* the rental shop. Perhaps I exaggerate, but it's a lot more complicated than the shoe counter at the bowling alley. I tell you how you can avoid waiting in a line that makes the DMV look like the Quickie Mart. How you can tell if your boots really fit. How you know what length your ski should be. (Yes, size matters, but not in that way.) And everything else you need to know to escape with a smile on your face.

In Chapter 2, you find out why the right pair of boots is the most important equipment purchase you'll ever make. I even discuss where you should go to buy your gear. (Does the phrase *penny wise and pound foolish* mean anything to you?)

Chapter 3 is a no-nonsense guide to the ski wall. Shaped skis, regular skis, fat skis, sort-of fat skis, racing skis—forget the jargon, I make it easy to pick the *right* ski. And I tell you once and for all how to make sense of all the advice you'll get from friends, the guy in the shop, and those magazine test reports.

Chapter 4 brings you face to face with that eternal question: What to wear? There's nothing that ruins a day on the slopes faster than having the wrong clothes. You end up cold, wet, and looking like a dork. And there's nothing worse than a cold, wet dork. But to pass muster with skiing's fashion police, you have to have an aesthetic plan, too. Skiwear is also about self expression, about making an on-snow statement. With my help, it's a snap to find the right look that matches your personality and your skiing style.

Chapter 5 covers the all-too-wide world of ski accessories, from hats and gloves to ski carriers. I clue you in on the ten things that you absolutely, positively must buy right now. I discuss the pros and cons of some useful but not absolutely necessary accessories. And I take a light-hearted look at some truly wacky ski gadgets.

Part II: Mastering the Mountain

Compared to, say, doing a half gainer or hitting a golf ball straight and true, skiing is pretty simple . . . which is a good thing, because most people get to ski only a few of times a year. In this section I show you some shortcuts on the road to becoming a better skier.

Chapter 6 takes you through your first time on skis. It's a wonderful adventure, to be sure, but there are still a few pitfalls. I tell you where to go, what to bring, and why you shouldn't under any circumstances let your husband/ father/brother-in-law teach you how to ski. I also pass along my all-time top tip for getting a great first-time lesson. (**Hint**: Set your alarm clock.)

Chapter 7 is all about ski school, the sport's bastion of higher learning. One of the easiest ways to have more fun on the slopes is to get better. You can explore more of the mountain, expend less energy, and be able to keep up with your hotshot friends. But all lessons — and all instructors — aren't created equal. Group or private? All day or one hour? Hot skier or patient teacher? This chapter contains a primer in the fine art of taking a ski lesson.

Chapter 8 outlines some ways you can improve on your own. Getting better is as much a matter of having the right mindset as spending thousands of dollars on lessons. I show you some of the games skiers play in pursuit of the perfect turn, from easy ones like follow the leader to more challenging ones like one footed turns. (I could call these drills, but they're really too much fun for that.) And I also include some mental tips that'll help you ski your very best every single day.

Chapter 9 describes alternate means of sliding. Almost every accomplished skier has a *schtick* — a membership in one of the sport's niches. I show you there's more than one way to get down a mountain, and the key is finding the right one for your personality. From recreational racing, to telemarking, to powder skiing, to those skate-like skiboards, this chapter not only discusses the gear needed for these change-ups but also gives you a peek at the cultural anthropology of skiing's subcultures.

Chapter 10 talks about ski resort geography. No, this geography lesson has nothing to do with identifying the capital of Bolivia. This is geography you can use. You discover how to get around on the mountain, how to ride a lift . . . safely, how to read a trail map, so that you don't get lost . . . or in over your head. And how to find the best snow, at any hour of the day, while beating the lift lines at the same time.

Part III: Staying Safe and Getting Fit

There's more to a great ski resort geography. A great day begins with getting around the mountain safely and efficiently. It's about taking advantage of everything the mountain — and the sport — has to offer. It's about continuing on with skiing's version of the good life even after you get off the slopes. And most of all, it's about having some money left in your wallet after you're done.

Chapter 11 is about safety and etiquette. You find out how dangerous skiing really is (not very, actually). To help keep you safe, I outline the basic rules of the road. To keep you from looking like a dork, I let you know about those unwritten rules that separate real skiers from wannabes. And as an added bonus, this chapter includes a little bit about snowboarders and how to coexist with them peacefully.

Chapter 12 talks about getting in shape for skiing, and staying in shape once you're out on the hill. Sports medicine research has shown that skiing places the kind of demands on your muscles that most athletes don't even dream about. That's why you're so sore at the end of the day. But a little bit of pre-season strengthening, combined with some pre-ski stretching, can go a long way toward making skiing the breeze it ought to be and keeping you injury free. Don't miss the tips on dealing with altitude sickness and on-snow skin care.

Chapter 13 clues you in about skiing with kids. You find out how to know whether your child is ready to ski, how to choose a ski school program, and how to outfit your kids right without going broke.

Part IV: Getting Away

What's the best thing about skiing? The fact that you have to get away from home to do it. What's the worst? Ditto. Traveling to ski can be either an adventure — or a disaster. The key is being prepared. That's where the next three chapters come in.

Chapter 14 tells you how to plan the perfect day or weekend ski trip, from deciding how long to stay to handling winter road conditions. The secret to a great weekend trip is cramming a lot of fun into a short amount of time; I show you how.

Chapter 15 gives you the basics that apply to almost any ski vacation. These basics include how to choose a destination, how to choose a place to stay, and why the best skiing bargains — and sometimes the best skiing period — can be had after the Easter Bunny's come and gone.

Chapter 16 talks about skiing through airports. Well, not literally. But remember, you're packing heavy and flying into snow country in the middle of winter. That's not exactly a recipe for stress-free flying. I reveal the secrets to making your connections, so that you spend your vacation playing in the snow instead of snowbound in some tiny airport in the middle of nowhere. And if you don't read anything else, be sure to check out the list of the ten things you absolutely, positively must carry on board with you.

Part V: The Part of Tens

This section is two parts information and two parts fun. Everyone loves a list, and I've got a bunch of them, from slang terms, to ways to ski free, to things to do when you're not skiing, to famous skiers you should know.

Part VI: Appendixes

Finally, there's a glossary to explain the skiing terms used in this book. I also provide capsule descriptions of the top ski areas in North America, and contact information for almost any resort in the United States.

Icons Used in This Book

When I want you to pay close attention to certain blocks of text, I flag them with little pictures called *icons*. Here's what the icons mean:

 This icon highlights information that pertains specifically to skiing or traveling with kids.

 I indicate information particularly useful for women with this icon.

 I use this icon when giving advice on how to save money.

 I use this icon to highlight information you need to know to protect yourself.

 Skiing terms or lingo get flagged with this icon.

 I use this icon to indicate information that can make your skiing experience that much more enjoyable.

 Look for this icon to discover ways and methods to improve your traveling experience.

Part I
Gearing Up

The 5th Wave   By Rich Tennant

"Very impressive. However, I don't think being able to tap dance in a pair of boots necessarily constitutes a proper fit."

In this part . . .

Stuff. You need lots of it for skiing. Skis, poles, boots, bindings, and all kinds of skiwear and accessories. In the following chapters, I tell you how to choose the right stuff so you can ski better, stay warmer, and save money.

Chapter 1

Surviving the Rental Shop

• •

• •

*T*he good news: Skiing is a lot like bowling. You don't have to make a big investment in equipment in order to have fun.

The bad news: While you can have fun bowling with any old lane ball and even the funkiest rental shoe — although a spritz of Lysol is a good idea — the quality of your rental skis and boots directly affects the quality of your ski experience.

The rental shop can be a pretty scary place, like a department store on December 23: long, long lines, merchandise everywhere, and the real possibility of ending up with something that just doesn't quite work. Expert skiers who think nothing of skiing the chute called Devil's Cauldron won't even go *near* the rental shop.

What you need is an expert friend to help you navigate this jungle. If you have one, I definitely recommend bringing her along. But if not, this chapter is the next best thing.

In this chapter, I give you a five-minute tour of ski gear. I tell you where to rent your equipment, what to bring to the rental shop, how to avoid waiting in lines, and how you can make sure that you leave the rental shop with the right gear. I do everything but keep score for you . . . oh, that's bowling. Never mind.

Gearing Up for Your Debut

What's going to happen at the rental shop? You go in with your street shoes and a confused look on your face. You leave looking like a skier. But what gear effects this miraculous transformation? Here's a brief tour of the main pieces of ski equipment.

Boots

Yes, they go on your feet, and they keep your toes warm, but that aside, ski boots bear only the most passing resemblance to a pair of Timberlands or ostrich skin Tony Lama cowboy boots.

The first thing you should notice about a ski boot is its plastic *shell*. You'll see that the toe is flat in the front with rounded corners, and the heel has a crescent-shaped extension in the back. These toe and heel pieces fit into the *binding* (more about bindings later on) and are the same shape on every boot so that they'll fit every binding.

Attached to the shell are a series of *buckles* that tighten the shell around your foot and hold it closed. Most buckles have some kind of adjustment, so if the buckles are so tight that they won't close or so loose that they won't tighten the boot, ask the rental shop attendant to adjust them.

The soft part inside the shell is called the *liner* or innerboot. It's generally made of foam, which keeps your feet warm and has some padding that conforms to the shape of your foot.

Bindings

These devices attach to the top of your skis and have two interrelated functions. First, they hold your boot securely onto the ski. This is important because a ski that comes off unexpectedly, especially at higher speeds, almost always causes a fall. On the other hand, sometimes skiers fall without any help from their equipment. And in certain types of falls, the ski acts as a big lever that transmits a lot of force to the skier's leg. The binding's second job is to sense this force and release the ski from the boot before it can cause an injury. The front part of the binding is called the *toe piece*. The rear is called the *heel piece*.

Skis

Knowing the basic parts of a ski is important when the time comes to choose your skis from the rental shop. (See "Finding your skis" later in this chapter.) The *tip* is the rounded, upturned part in the front of the ski. A ski is rounded at the tip to enable it to go up and over small clumps of snow instead of digging into them. The *tail* is the rear section of the ski.

Now take a look at the business end of the ski. The bottom of the ski is called the *base* of the ski. It's made of a special plastic that's both slippery and rugged and should be should be flat and smooth. *Edges* are the metal strips on the side of the ski. They perform a little like a skate blade, helping the ski slide straight more easily and not slip sideways on icy snow. The edges should be smooth and free of nicks. The *topskin* is the protective sheeting that covers the ski and includes the graphics and manufacturer's name.

Refer to Chapter 3 for more detailed information on the parts of a ski.

Poles

Poles are relatively straightforward compared to the rest of the ski ensemble. The main part of the pole is called the *shaft*. Most shafts are made of aluminum tubing, tapered so that it's wider at the grip and thinner at the tip. The *grip* is the part of the pole that you hold. It's usually made of rubber or plastic. The *strap* attaches to the grip and basically keeps you from dropping the pole. (See Chapter 8 to find out how to grip the pole correctly.) The round or snowflake-shaped disc at the end of the pole is the *basket*. In soft snow, it helps keep the pole from sinking like the *Andrea Doria*.

Where Should You Rent?

Every ski area has a rental shop. Some rental shops are better than others, but it is as much a part of a ski area as the snow.

But as you're driving to the mountain, you may pass any number of ski shops with big signs advertising rental equipment. Should you stop? If you've never skied before, don't stop. There are a number of good reasons why you should keep driving.

First, many ski areas offer packages for first-timers that include equipment, a lift ticket, and lessons. So it's much cheaper to rent at the mountain.

Second, many resorts, especially larger ones, have special beginner's equipment, and the ski school builds the lesson plans around the assumption that everyone's on the same gear. If you're on different gear, you're at a disadvantage. Also, there's always the possibility that your gear may have or develop a problem — a binding that won't stay closed or a boot buckle that breaks. If you rent your stuff at the mountain, you're just a short walk away from getting your equipment fixed or replaced. If you rent off-site, it's a short walk followed by a short drive followed by a short drive back, and before you know it a good portion of your ski day goes down the drain, glug . . . glug . . . glug.

Finally, beginners progress rapidly. You may find that over the course of a weekend, or even during a day, that you can move up to longer skis. Again, this kind of swap is easier if you rent on-site.

That said, after you have a few days of skiing under your belt, you have a better idea of how your boots should fit, how your bindings work, and whether a pair of skis is trashed. At this point, an off-site rental makes sense if it saves you a few dollars.

What to Bring to the Rental Shop

Your rental shop experience will be much better if you prepare yourself ahead of time. I don't mean Boy Scout-style preparation — a pocketknife and waterproof matches. If you forget to bring the following items, you may end up hiking back to the car or the condo all the same.

- ✔ **A pen:** You have forms to fill out, and just like a bank, sometimes those pens-on-a-string work, and sometimes they don't.

- ✔ **Your vital stats:** The technician at the rental shop asks you for your height, weight, and shoe size. (And your kids' if you're renting for them also.) Although you may be tempted, don't fudge the weight question — the shop uses that information to adjust your bindings — and safety is much more important than vanity.

- ✔ **A credit card:** This is for leaving a security deposit. You get it back after you return the skis, but they won't fork over the skis to you without one.

- ✔ **A driver's license:** This is more please-don't-walk-off-with-our-skis-insurance for the resort.

- ✔ **Socks:** You need to wear the socks that you plan to wear for skiing. A single pair of thin ski socks is the best, with a pair of synthetic fiber athletic socks a close second. Cotton or cotton blend socks tend to get wet and stay wet, and, well, argyles or panty hose just don't cut it.

▶ **Gloves:** Skis get cold quickly after you're outside, and you can't keep your hands in your pocket while you're hauling your gear.

▶ **A distraction:** Bring along a newspaper, a Walkman and a Cowboy Junkies CD, or a book in case you have to wait. I highly recommend *The Snows of Kilimanjaro,* not *Alive!.*

▶ **A friend:** A little outside assistance is invaluable to make small talk, offer reassurance, help shuttle boots back and forth between the rack and your feet, or even to hold your place in line while you go to the bathroom.

The Best Time to Visit the Rental Shop

The best time to be in the rental shop is before everyone else gets there. The lines are short, you get personal attention, and you don't have to worry about the shop running out of boots in your size. But, if you're thinking, "I have no intention of getting up at 5:00 a.m. like I'm camping out for Pearl Jam tickets," then you don't have to.

The key, if possible, is to go the night before. If you're going on a weekend or week-long trip, try to arrive early enough so that you can go to the rental shop the night before you plan to ski. At most ski areas the lifts close around 4:00 p.m., and the rental shop is open for at least another hour. Call before you show up to get the exact hours because not every area allows you to keep your skis overnight. Remember to ask about a lift ticket/lesson/rental package. You want to have the rental voucher before you show up at the shop.

Getting Your Gear

The first thing you do at the shop is fill out a bunch of paperwork. This can take a few minutes, but do it as carefully as your Form 1040. Make that *more* carefully. Leaving something blank only delays you later on.

You then need to pick out your equipment. Find a pair of boots (make sure they fit well), skis, bindings, and finally, poles.

Finding the right boots

The first piece of equipment you should get is your boots. At some ski areas, the boot section is self-serve. Racks and racks of boots adorn that part of the rental shop; enough to make Imelda Marcos' shoe closet look downright barren. What you need to do is focus on the boots that are your size and find the pair for you.

What to look for in boots

When looking for boots, look for:

- ✓ **A pair on a high shelf:** Most people are too short, or just too lazy, to reach for the pair above shoulder height. This means they probably don't get as much use as their cousins on the lower shelves.

- ✓ **Cleanliness:** The only way for a pair of ski boots to get truly filthy is by taking an unplanned excursion into the mud. Not cool. That's usually caused by pilot error, but you don't want to find out firsthand. Likewise, giant gouges in the plastic or a shredded liner are also hints that you should grab another pair. Be especially wary of boots with well-worn soles. Well-worn soles can pose a safety problem because the binding may not release properly in case of a fall.

- ✓ **A full complement of buckles:** If any of the buckles are missing, it's back to the drawing board.

- ✓ **A left and a right:** No, this isn't a joke. There are plenty of skiers who complain about the fit of their boots, only to find that they're wearing two lefts, or that one boot is a half size smaller than the other.

- ✓ **A good fit:** Your street shoe size is just a starting point. Boots often run smaller, or sometimes larger, than street shoe sizes. For more about the fit of your boots, read on.

Check for proper fit

How do you know if a boot really fits? Rental boots are, by their very nature, a bit of a compromise. Like that Abraham Lincoln saying about fooling all the people some of the time — or was it the other way around? — rental boots are designed to fit everyone pretty well but only a few lucky souls get that bunny slipper fit. Here's a checklist for finding boots you can live with, at least for the day.

- ✓ **Can you get the boot on?** If all the buckles are unbuckled and you still can't get the boot on, you ought to think about the next larger size.

- ✓ **Do your toes hit the front of the boot?** After you have the boots on, pretend that you're skiing in them. Stand with your feet flat on the floor, shoulder width apart, and flex your knees. That's pretty much a skiing stance. Do your toes hit the front of the boot — as opposed to the top — when you assume the skiing stance? If they do, the boot is too small.

In contrast, if your toes just barely touch the front, the fit might be perfect. With the boots buckled and your feet flat on the floor, bend slightly at the knee, flexing the boot cuff forward a bit. If your toes now pull away from the front of the boot, you've hit the jackpot. If they still touch, the boot's too small.

✔ **Can you wiggle your toes?** If you can't wiggle your toes, then the boot is too small.

✔ **Does your heel lift up?** If you flex forward with all the buckles buckled, and your heel comes up off the insole while the boot itself stays flat on the floor, you need to have the shop technician adjust the buckles. If that doesn't help, then the boot is just simply too big.

✔ **Do the boots hurt your feet?** No, a pair of ski boots is not going to fit like a pair of running shoes. The rigid plastic shell gives you great support, but at the expense of super-cushy comfort. On the other hand, your boots shouldn't be causing you pass-the-morphine-Sarge kind of pain, either. If that's the case, find another pair in the next size up.

✔ **Does only one foot hurt?** If one foot hurts but the other one's fine, look for two possible causes. The first cause could be that one of your feet is larger or shaped differently than the other one. Don't laugh, it happens, although you probably would know that by now. The second, and more likely scenario, is that something's wrong with one of your boots. It could be it's a different size or there could be something—an old sock, maybe—inside the boot. You can deal with these problems yourself.

The liner may not be in straight or the buckles or one of the other adjustments may be out of whack. If you suspect this is the case, take the offending boot to the guy at the counter and let him try to fix it.

Nancy Sinatra notwithstanding, these boots aren't made for walking. When you first try to walk with your boots on, you may feel like Gigantor. Stomp . . . Stomp . . . Stomp. That means you should be careful around other people's toes. In another way, you may feel like Michelle Kwan. Not graceful, but like you're sliding around on ice. So be doubly careful on stairs, in the bathroom where the floor may be wet, and for that matter, everywhere else.

Finding your skis

After you have your boots — although not necessarily on — it's time to walk down to the ski department. In most ski areas, the ski department isn't self-serve. It's more like a deli. You hand over your rental ticket that is emblazoned with your vital stats — height, weight, age, and skiing level. The rental tech hands you back a pair of skis. Hold the mayo.

Yes, this process is simpler. There are no lefts and rights, and if the two skis are different sizes, it's abundantly obvious. However, you should check over a few things before you move down the line.

✔ **The base:** As they say in the career-counseling biz, you gotta start at the bottom. Look at the plastic bases. Are they relatively flat and smooth? Big, deep gouges aren't good, nor is a level of fuzziness that makes you want to take them to Al's Poodle Parlor.

✔ **The edges:** Are they rusty? Are they nicked? Do they seem relatively sharp? (You can test for sharpness by scraping the surface of your nail with the edge. If it shaves your nail just slightly, it's sharp.)

✔ **The topskin:** Don't concern yourself with cosmetic problems — after all, you're renting the skis, not buying them. But give them a quick once-over to make sure that there are no obvious structural problems such as cracks or delaminations.

✔ **The length:** If you're a beginner, your skis, standing on end, should come somewhere between your shoulders and your nose. Don't sweat small variations, but if the skis are over your head or down around your navel, then someone couldn't read your handwriting — is that a seven or a two? — and you should ask for another pair.

Getting into your bindings

Your bindings are your best friends. If — I mean *when* — you fall in a way that could hurt your leg, the bindings release and send your ski skittering away. Pretty nice of them, huh? And all they ask for in return is to be adjusted properly. Adjusting bindings is something that even the most experienced skiers trust to trained technicians. But you can do your part in the rental shop by making sure that the information on your rental ticket is both accurate and legible, so that the tech can adjust the binding properly. You also need to make sure that your boots have clean, unworn soles.

What's the number one complaint from beginners about their gear? Well, if it doesn't have to do with hurting feet, it has to do with bindings and how they work. It's actually quite simple, if you follow these three steps:

1. **Cock 'em.**

   Your bindings are dependent on spring tension. This tension holds your boot in and also releases your boot in case you fall. To get that spring ready to do its thing, you need to make sure that you push down the big buttons on the heel piece of the bindings, if they aren't already. You can push them down with the end of a pole, or just stomp on them.

2. **Clean 'em.**

   To release properly, your bindings need to have a tight, clean connection to the bottom of your boot. As you clomp around, snow often sticks to the bottom of your boot. So before you do anything else, scrape the snow off the bottom of your boot. You can use your pole or even the toe piece (see Step 3 for the definition) of the binding itself, as long as you also remember to brush the snow off the binding before you proceed.

3. Click 'em.

Now comes the fun part. Make sure you're standing on a flat section. If you aren't, you may start sliding as soon as you get your skis on. Support yourself by using your poles and put your toe into the front of the binding — known as the *toe piece*. Then put your heel down firmly, listening for the binding to click in. Now do the same with the other foot. Congratulations, you're ready to ski.

Sizing up your poles

Your rental poles must be two things: They must be straight, and they must be the right length. I leave the straight versus bent comparison to you.

Here's how to tell if your poles are long enough. Take the pole and turn it upside down. With your elbow bent, grab the pole just below the basket. See Figure 1-1. If your forearm is parallel to the ground, the pole is the right size. If your forearm is below parallel, you need longer poles. If it's above parallel, shorter poles will do the trick.

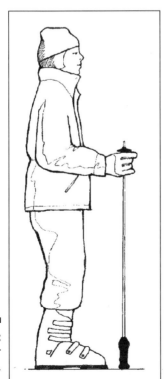

Figure 1-1:
Sizing your
ski pole.

Chapter 2

Buying the Right Boots

● ●

In This Chapter

▶ Understanding the parts of the boot

▶ Getting the best fit

▶ Buying boots: Where to shop

● ●

*Y*our ski boots are the only connection you have to your skis: Anything you do in skiing you do through your boots. Your ski boots perform more important functions than a Swiss Army Knife.

- ✔ They keep your feet warm.

- ✔ They put you in an athletic stance on your skis.

- ✔ They support your feet against the forces that build up when you ski even moderately fast.

- ✔ They allow you to flex your ankles naturally to help you balance on your skis.

- ✔ They transmit energy from your legs and feet to your skis, allowing you to steer. In skiing, your boots are a combination of a steering wheel and a transmission.

While you could send your boots a thank-you note or take them out to a nice dinner now and then, mostly what you need to do is make sure you get the right pair in the first place. Simply put, buying the right pair of ski boots is one of the most important investments you make in skiing.

If you have the wrong boots, your feet may get cold, or they may hurt worse than if a hungry weasel were gnawing on your instep, and you have to fight your skis every step of the way. There's a name for people with these kinds of boots: ex-skiers.

And while people can exist happily on rental and demo skis for years, even the most casual skier should own his or her own boots. Fortunately, it's easier than ever to get a great-fitting, great-performing pair of boots if you know how and where to shop.

In this chapter, I describe the parts of a boot and explain the different kinds of boots and their pros and cons. I also explain how to determine if a boot fits properly, describe the easy and inexpensive way to get your boots to fit like they were custom made, and tell you where you should buy your boots (and your other ski gear).

Parts of the Boot

The ski boot is essentially broken down into two parts: the shell and the liner. These parts are discussed in the following sections and labeled in Figure 2-1.

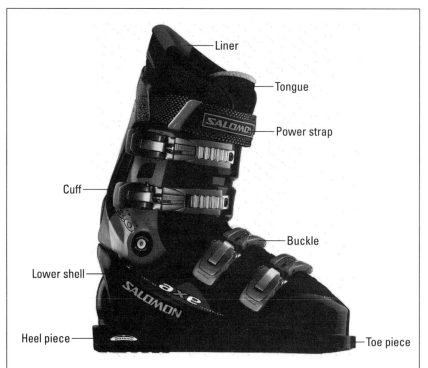

Figure 2-1:
The parts of the ski boot.

Courtesey Salomon N.A./Mavic

The shell

How is a ski boot like a turtle? They both have shells. On a ski boot, the shell helps keep your foot warm and dry. It determines how well a boot does all that energy transmission stuff I mention earlier in this chapter that is so vital to good skiing. The shell also largely determines how well a boot fits, which I discuss in depth later in this chapter. Needless to say, it's pretty important.

As befitting such an important part of the boot, the shell has a number of sub-components. Here they are.

- ✔ **The cuff:** The cuff, which extends from the ankle to the lower part of your shin and calf, is actually a component part of the shell. Its primary job is transferring energy — you move your leg, it moves the ski.

  Some skiers, especially women, have fit issues with their boot cuffs. A boot that fits fine in the foot may not close around the calf. I discuss this in the boot fitting section later in the chapter.

- ✔ **Lower shell:** The lower shell is basically the part of the boot that extends from the ankle down. It's the component that looks most like a regular shoe, and in terms of fit, it's the most important part of the shell. All boots (not just ski boots) are built on a model of a foot called a *last*. Every ski boot manufacturer uses its own lasts. If the last used to mold the lower shell on Model X conforms pretty well to your particular feet — narrow heel, low instep, wide toes, or whatever — then Model X is going to fit pretty well. If not, do yourself a favor and try some other model. (More on this later.)

- ✔ **The buckles:** One, two, buckle my *boot?* Once upon a time ski boots had laces — back when they were made of leather and Eisenhower was President — but modern ski boots close with buckles. Almost all boots have four buckles these days, two on the cuff and two on the lower shell. Most buckles are widely adjustable, and you can latch them on any of about five settings. In a boot that fits correctly, your buckles are generally in the middle of their adjustment range. Better buckles have a micro-adjustment feature that allows you to fine-tune the tension on the buckle. Screw in the bail (the moveable part of the buckle) to tighten it, unscrew it to loosen it. Depending on the model, there may be more ways to adjust it, too — for instance, by moving the whole buckle. The salesperson should know.

- ✔ **The power strap:** In politics, power corrupts. In skiing, power helps you turn. The power strap is a nylon or vinyl band that attaches to the top of the cuff and wraps around the area above the top buckle. It fastens with a hook-and-loop fastener on the front of the tongue. Its function? It's almost like a fifth buckle, securing the fit in this crucial area without the weight or complexity of an additional buckle.

✔ **The toe and heel pieces:** Notice that your boot has two little extensions at the front and the rear. They're not just there for show. The toe and heel pieces of the boot are made precisely to a standardized shape — determined by a German standards organization called DIN — that fit perfectly into the toe and heel pieces of your binding. This fit allows for a universal compatibility between every boot and binding, no matter which company makes them.

✔ **The footboard:** Also called a *zeppa*, the footboard is a hard plastic plate that looks a little like an insole and fits between the sole of the liner and the sole of the shell. This is a little-known piece of the boot — with good reason, because it doesn't do much more than take up space. Call your attention to the footboard only because in certain cases you can have it ground down to help fine-tune the fit of a boot.

The liner

Also called an *innerboot*, the liner really is just that — a boot within a boot. You can literally remove the liner from the shell, and you can even walk around the store in it. Because the liner cradles your foot, it's far cushier than the shell. Innerboots consist primarily of foam padding combined with wool, nylon, or other fabrics, and harder plastics, sculpted to fit around the bones of your ankle and hold your foot comfortably and securely within the boot. The liner, too, has a couple of sub-assemblies. Here they are.

The tongue

The tongue of your ski boot is found in about the same place as in your Air Jordans, and it serves roughly the same function. The tongue serves as a moveable barrier between your foot and the area where your boot closes. Be sure that your shin and the boot tongue are compatible — when you're skiing, they are in almost constant contact.

The insole

Think of your boot insole as one of those supermarket insoles on steroids. Actually, most stock insoles leave a lot to be desired, and one of the easiest and best ways to upgrade the performance of your boots is to replace them with a pair of custom-fitted insoles or orthotics. I discuss this later in the chapter.

Choosing the options

Boots are a little like cars in that manufacturers don't let you order options *a la carte,* but they do offer different trim packages — higher-line boots have more features. Here's a quick rundown of some of them.

✔ **Forward lean adjustment:** Bend your knees. That's common advice, and good advice, in skiing. To help you do that, the cuffs of all ski boots are angled forward slightly. On most models, you can find an adjuster that enables you to dial in this angle to suit your preferences.

✔ **Flex adjuster:** The resistance that a boot offers when you bend your ankle is called *flex*. (I discuss this in some detail later in the chapter.) Some boots incorporate a spring or other device that allows you to adjust the flex of the boot or, more accurately, to make the flex stiffer (which isn't necessarily an advantage.)

✔ **Cuff release:** Remember that forward lean? It's great for skiing, but not so hot for walking. Also called a walking adjuster, this lever allows you to unlock the forward lean of the boot cuff, allowing you to stand straight up — a real boon in the cafeteria line. Just remember to refasten it when you get back out on the slopes.

✔ **Ramp angle adjustment:** This raises or lowers the back of the footboard to help fine-tune the fit of the boot.

✔ **Cuff-angle adjuster:** This enables you to adjust the cuff of the boot later-ally — so that it conforms more accurately to the shape of your lower leg or the alignment of your stance. This is sometimes erroneously called a *canting* adjustment, but canting actually entails a much more complicated series of adjustments.

✔ **Removable sole and heel plates:** Boots with worn soles from clomping around in the parking lot can be downright unsafe because they don't allow the binding to release properly. To address this situation, many manufacturers include sole and heel plates that you can unscrew and replace when they get worn.

Boot Basics

Boots come in two basic flavors: front-entry and mid-entry (sometimes called central-entry). Front-entry boots work pretty much like a sneaker — you open the buckles in lieu of loosening the laces, you spread the tongue for-ward, and you slip your foot in. Depending on the fit of the boot and the shape of your foot, front-entry boots can sometimes be a pain to get on, but most people manage fine.

Mid-entry boots have a similar configuration in the front, but add one addi-tional wrinkle — the rear part of the cuff hinges backward, opening the boot wider and making it easier to get on. The drawbacks? A little more weight, a little more complexity, and, because most boots are front-entry, a somewhat narrower selection of models. Performance-wise, there's little to choose between the two configurations.

Bringing up the rear (entry)

There's a third kind of boot that has gone the way of the dinosaur and *Family Matters*: the rear-entry. Introduced in the early '80s, the rear-entry boot was the spiritual predecessor of the mid-entry. The rear entry did away with buckles in the front, and the rear half of the shell opened clamshell-style. You won't see any on store shelves anymore, but they're fairly common in the lift line and in rental shops.

While rear-entry boots were easy to put on and take off, they didn't conform to the shape of most feet very well. Some didn't allow you to flex your ankle at all. And with only one or two buckles in the back, it was often difficult to fine-tune the fit. In short, they didn't ski very well.

But boot manufacturers did the right thing. They took the things that people liked about rear entries — the comfort and the convenience, and incorporated them into today's better-performing front- and- mid-entry boots. Now if they could just do something about Urkel.

Picking the right type of boot

Like everyone else, boot manufacturers love labels. They love to define, categorize, and pigeonhole their models. Here's a quick guide to what those labels mean in terms of performance.

- ✔ **Beginner boots:** These are often budget models based on the boots that you find in rental shops. This should tell you something. The fit is often less than optimal — the liner is often too soft and not well-contoured. And strangely, the flex is often relatively stiff because the hinge between the cuff and the shell isn't well-designed. Even if you are a beginner, it's probably wise to invest a little more for a boot that lasts for the long haul.

- ✔ **All-mountain boots:** These are the solid citizens of the boot world. These boots used to be called intermediate boots, and next year they may be called something else. Most fit well, include most of the important fit options, and strike a good balance between comfort and performance. Most mid-entry boots fit into this category. More importantly, these boots have a flex pattern that's well suited to most casual skiers.

- ✔ **High-performance all-mountain:** This is a relatively new category. These boots have the bells and whistles of racing boots, but the fit is designed for all-day wear. The flex is better suited to skiing at fast-but-not-insane speeds over a wide variety of terrain. These are a good choice for advanced to expert skiers.

  These boots are legitimate high-performance boots. Skiers such as instructors and ski patrollers, who ten years ago wouldn't have been caught in anything but racing boots, today often choose these boots and ski better for it.

✔ **Racing boots:** Have you ever watched Picabo Street ski? Do you ski anything like her? So why do you think you should wear the same boots? Racing boots are great — if you're skiing at 40 miles an hour on a slope that's as glassy as an NHL rink. Most real racing boots — as opposed to some high-performance boots that wear a racing label — are so stiff that they perform well only at very high speeds. The fit is so tight that the first thing that racers do after crossing the finish line is unbuckle their boots. If you bash gates, go right ahead, but for most skiers, cruising in a racing boot is like trying to drive a Formula One race car to the local convenience store.

Hard or soft? Finding the right flex

The most important difference between boots — besides the way they fit — is their *forward flex*. The forward flex of the boot is the resistance the boot provides when you try to bend your ankles. The kind of plastic used to make the boot shell largely determines the flex of the boot. Soft-flexing boots make it easy to flex your ankle. Stiffer boots are a little more stubborn.

Which is best? It depends. The correct boot flex depends on you and how you ski.

✔ Lighter skiers need softer boots.

✔ Racers and experts who ski very fast need stiffer boots.

✔ Skiers who ski bumps and other uneven terrain need softer boots.

In general, most skiers, and almost all beginners and intermediate skiers, should go for a soft boot. While racers love stiff boots, don't think of buying a soft boot as a sign of weakness. I went from a moderately stiff racing boot (which was the only one that fit well) to a moderately soft all-terrain boot (again primarily because of fit considerations). In the process, I experienced a quantum leap in my skiing because I was able to make subtle adjustments with my ankle more easily and maintain an athletic stance even at low speeds, a must with today's shaped skis. And my new boots were also more comfortable. The good news is that boot companies are listening and making boots with a softer and more progressive forward flex.

The Role of the Bootfitter

A root canal. An IRS audit. A Barry Manilow CD on continuous play. Skiing with a boot that doesn't fit is worse than any of them.

The first thing you have to understand about buying ski boots is that it's not like buying a pair of sneakers or wing tips. Your foot is being held quite firmly inside a molded plastic shell. (Leather shoes eventually mold themselves to the shape of your foot, but a plastic boot shell never will.) Unless that shell and the liner of the boot follow the shape of your foot quite closely, you're going to have problems.

The job of the bootfitter is to optimize this boot/foot interface. For most of us, the bootfitter is the salesperson in the shop. Bootfitting is essentially a two-part process: finding a boot that closely matches the shape of a your foot and modifying the boot to fit your foot.

- ✔ **Matching your foot shape:** The first part is finding a boot that closely matches the shape of a skier's foot. A simple concept in theory, but given the intersection between hundreds of boot shapes and millions of possible foot shapes, it's not easy to do. This is why a good bootfitter is worth her weight in platinum. And why the most important part of the bootfitting process requires nothing more than a trained pair of eyes.

- ✔ **Modifying the boot to fit a skier's foot:** This is done by grinding it, padding it, stretching it, and otherwise making it something it wasn't before. It's fun to talk about, cool to watch, and can be a lifesaver when there's one small but persistent problem with a boot. But it costs money, and if taken to extremes, these modifications can compromise the integrity and function of the boot. I discuss the modification process in more detail later in the chapter.

Your goal should be to find a bootfitter who's really good at the first part, someone who can find you a boot that fits just right — or at least pretty darn close — right out of the box. Achieve that goal and you have less padding, grinding, and modifying to do later.

How do you find a good bootfitter? Ask an instructor. Ask a ski patroller. Ask someone who spends all day every day in their ski boots. Find someone like that and they either have a very high pain threshold or a recommendation for a really good bootfitter. Probably the latter.

Do They Fit?

That's the question that every skier asks himself or herself. A pair of ski boots is not going to feel like your broken-in boat shoes. But they shouldn't hurt. In fact, they should be comfortable enough that you can wear them all day every day and not have to unbuckle them until the lifts close.

Unfortunately, while you can run eight or ten feet in the sneaker department when you're trying on running shoes, most ski shops don't have a beautifully groomed cruising run for you to test out a new boot. But don't try to judge a pair of ski boots by clomping around the store. Do your best to simulate skiing. Stand with your feet hip width apart, keep your feet flat on the floor, bend your knees, and flex your ankles — that's skiing, or at least a reasonable facsimile. So what happens when you do that? Here are some questions to ask yourself:

> ✔ **Do my toes touch the front of the boot?** In a well-fitted boot, the tip of your big toe should just touch the front of the boot when you're standing relatively straight. And your toe should just pull away when you flex your knee.

> ✔ **Do my heels come up?** If your heels pull up off the insole when you flex your knees while the boot sole stays perfectly flat on the floor, then the boots are probably a little too big.

> ✔ **Can I wiggle my toes?** Although you're not buying sandals, you should have just enough room for some moderate toe wiggling.

> ✔ **Are there any hot spots?** Is there one place that feels like the proverbial weasel's gnawing at it? If the boot fits great otherwise, the shop may be able to fix that one little pressure point. If your shin hurts, though, that may be hard or even impossible to fix.

> ✔ **Is the boot *too* comfy?** Beware of this. A boot that feels like a bedroom slipper the moment you slip it on may either be the absolute perfect boot for your foot or a full size too big. In most cases, it's too big.

You wouldn't go to test drive a car without your driver's license, would you? When you're going boot shopping, make sure you bring a pair of ski socks with you. (See Chapter 5 for more information on socks.) I prefer relatively thin socks, but whatever you settle on, make sure you bring the same pair every time you try on boots so you can make an apples-to-apples comparison. If you don't have any ski socks yet, most shops have some try-on pairs available or at least should be able to sell you a pair of ski socks. If you buy a pair of boots that you tried on with argyles and the boots hurt, I won't say "I told you so," but I'd be tempted.

Sizing the shell

The relationship between the size and shape of your foot and the size and shape of a boot shell determines whether a boot fits. You can modify the innerboot quite easily, but if the shell is too small, the boot's going to hurt. Or, more likely, if you buy a boot with a shell that's too big, your foot is going to slop around and you won't ski as well. Then you'll tighten your buckles extra hard to compensate, creating pressure points on your instep. And once again, your feet will hurt . . . at least until they go numb.

Here's how to determine if you have the right shell size:

1. **Remove the liner from the innerboot.**

2. **Place your foot in the shell with your sock on.**

With your toes just touching the front of the boot, you should be able to reach inside the cuff and just slip your index and middle fingers between your heel and the back of the shell. See Figure 2-2. If you can't, the boot's too small. If there's more room than that, the boot's too big.

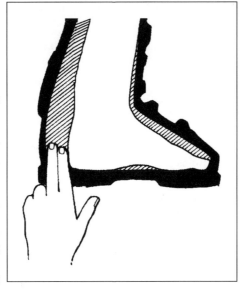

Figure 2-2:
With the liner removed, you should fit two fingers between your heel and the boot shell.

The three excuses of bad bootfitters

You spend an hour in a ski shop, a pile of boot boxes as tall as the Chrysler Building surrounds you, and a couple of the boots feel sort of okay, you think. At this point, the salesperson may try to convince you that the boots fit you better than they actually do. Here are some common explanations the salesperson may give you for boots that hurt and why you shouldn't believe him or her:

✔ **Your boots will pack out:** Yes, it's true that the liners in a pair of boots may compress a little after you wear them — in ski slang this loosening-up process is called *packing out.* But modern boots only pack out a little — far less than a pair of penny loafers may stretch — and it takes time. It takes about a minimum of ten days of hard skiing — a full season for most folks — for meaningful changes in the way a boot fits. Buying ill-fitting boots with the expectation that they may pack out is like marrying someone with the expectation that they may get smarter, funnier, and taller. Not a wise move.

The shell game

Here's a little-known fact. Because it's expensive to build different molds for boot shells, most boot manufacturers find a way to economize. They limit the number of shell sizes they build and compensate by fitting larger boot shells with thicker liners to fit smaller feet. For example, a size 9 and a size 9½ may share the same shell size. How can you tell?

On the bottom of the boot, usually under the arch, is a three-digit number. That's the sole length, which tells the shop mechanic how long the boot is so that he can adjust the binding. Look at the numbers on two adjacent-size boots, and see if they're the same. If you're in the smaller of the two sizes and the fit is a little loose, consider going down a half size to the next smaller shell size.

✔ **Your boots will feel different when you're out on the hill:** Yes, they will likely feel worse. If a boot really hurts in the store, it may hurt even more when you try to ski in it. In the cold, the shell is less pliable. When you're skiing, the forces involved in turning put stresses on your foot that you never encounter in street shoes. And when you're a third of the way down the mountain, you can't just decide to sit down because your feet hurt.

✔ **We can always fix it later:** Ski shops can and do remarkable things to a pair of boots for people with feet that belong in a freak show, for racers whose feet fit Brand A but are getting paid to endorse Brand B, and for people who bought the wrong boots in the first place. The key to smart boot shopping, as I mention earlier in the chapter, is to find the boot that requires little or no aftermarket surgery.

Fixing Boots That Don't Fit

Let's say you didn't follow the previous advice and you end up with a pair of boots that, well, just don't fit right. Or you have a pair that doesn't fit like they used to. Or you're ready to buy a pair that fits perfectly except for one little thing. This is where your friendly neighborhood bootfitter comes in. There are any number of ways that you can make your boots fit better. Here are a couple rules and some common problems and fixes:

✔ **Modify the liner first:** It's easier and cheaper to make small changes to the liner, grinding it down or padding it. In general, you should leave the shell alone until your bootfitter has modified the liner first. If you stretch the shell, it's liable to create a new problem somewhere else. And, unlike many liner tweaks, shell modifications can't be undone.

The Cinderella syndrome

Buying boots can be a discouraging process. I actually have a pair of the weirdest feet found on any upper-level primate. They're almost wider than they are long — the width is EEE for a size 12, but I'm only a size 9 — and have arches so high you could float a supertanker under them.

I didn't think I would ever find a pair of ski boots that would really fit. I took the widest pair of boots on the market, and I tinkered. I removed half the insole. I applied pads and lifts. I had the boot board ground down. I had the boots stretched — twice. After two years of on-and-off tinkering, I got the fit just about where I wanted it. At that point, the boot started leaking from all the tinkering I had done.

Then I was skiing at a demo day with my friend Jeff Rich, who is one of the world's most gifted boot fitters, the kind of guy who spends the morning modifying a pair of boots for a guy with only three toes and the afternoon making orthotics for Elle McPherson. At lunch, I casually told him about the troubles I'd been having. He took one peek at my funky feet in stockings, and without putting his turkey sandwich down, he said, "Lange Mid 5.5s or Koflach 837s." I tried on the Langes. A really nice fit out of the box, a little too roomy, but almost as good as my Frankenstein boots. Then I tried on the Koflachs. They were the glass slippers and I was Cinderella. I bought a pair, slipped out the stock insole, slipped in my orthotics, and haven't touched them since.

The moral of this story: If there's a boot on the market that's perfect for my Barney Rubble feet, there's a boot that's perfect for you.

> ✔ **Try a custom footbed:** A quality footbed is the aspirin of bootfitting. Because it supports the foot, it can cure any number of fit ills. See "Insoles insights" later in the chapter.

Solving common problems

Problem: You have hot spots in your boots. There's one little spot — near a bunion, perhaps — that feels like that weasel is gnawing at your foot.

Rx: There are any number of solutions to this, depending on the nature and severity of the problem. Solutions can range from lightly grinding the outside of the liner to modifying the footboard to blowing out the shell to adding padding to areas adjacent to the hot spot on the liner. Even seemingly unrelated modifications, like heel lifts, can resolve the problem by moving your foot slightly within the boot. Like good doctors, good bootfitters try milder solutions first, leaving major cutting jobs as last resorts.

Problem: Your boot is too loose. Sometimes a loose boot is a matter of buying it too big in the first place and sometimes it's because your boots are older and they are packing out. Whatever the cause, if a boot lets your foot flop around, it makes skiing as hard as speed chess.

Rx: You can put extra padding in the liner. A whole cottage industry has sprung up around pads to tweak the fit of a boot. X-pads wrap around your Achilles tendon. Instep pads help keep your heel from coming up, and heel lifts do any number of good things. Pads are great because they're cheap, they're easy to install, and if they make the problem worse, you can just yank them off.

Problem: The calves of your boots are too tight. This is a particular problem for women — most boots are designed for men's narrower calves — and one that forces many women to buy boots that are otherwise too big.

Rx: The wine bottle stretch. Using a wine bottle or perhaps a two-liter soda bottle as a mold, the boot fitter stretches the upper part of the cuff.

You can also improve the fit of your boot by buying a whole new custom liner. These liners used to be very expensive, but now they're merely expensive. A couple of technologies are available. Essentially, you get a liner actually molded around your foot. If the shell already fits your foot pretty well, you're nearly guaranteed a sweet, sweet fit.

Insoles insights

Even if you're as happy with the fit of your boots as Fred Flintstone at a smorgasbord, you ought to consider upgrading the insoles. The standard insoles in a boot are, of necessity, pretty generic. Custom insoles fill in the cavity under your arch more effectively, cradling and supporting your foot and keeping it stable inside the boot.

An upgraded insole should be the starting point of any bootfitting process. Why? Do this simple experiment. Take your socks off, relax your foot, hold it a couple of inches off the ground, and take a good look at it. Now put your foot down on the ground so it's supporting your weight again. Notice how your foot spreads when you put weight on it. A good insole can minimize that effect, which can cure any number of bootfitting headaches.

In "fixed-foot" sports like skiing, cycling, and even golf, your foot doesn't bend — you're not running or jumping. But in skiing you are applying unnaturally large pressure to the inner edge of the foot, and you want all that pressure to be transmitted to the ski edge rather than being lost in the process of deforming the foot. So supporting the arch from underneath will make you ski better.

Another reason to upgrade your insoles is comfort. If your foot does squish around while you ski, it'll be rubbing up against a rigid plastic shell. That'll hurt. Your foot has a tough time getting comfortable in a shell even in one position. No way is it going to be comfortable through a whole range of rolling and squishing positions.

Here are three levels of custom insoles that can help you pamper your feet:

- ✔ **Off-the-shelf insoles:** These non-customized models are generally better than what comes with your boots, with more arch support and a deeper, firmer heel pocket. If you don't ski much and you're not having serious fit problems, these can be an inexpensive upgrade, although springing for customized insoles is usually a better bet.

- ✔ **Heat-molded insoles:** These are made in the shop — they put the insole in a microwave or a small oven and then mold the still-warm insole to your foot. They represent a significant upgrade over generic insoles for not much more money. These insoles are a good choice for skiers whose boots fit pretty well and who don't ski all day every day.

- ✔ **Orthotics:** These are custom-built by a podiatrist or a pedorthist after taking a plaster cast of your foot. He or she fills the area beneath the arch and precision-grinds it — a process called *posting* — for extra support. Orthotics also help to hold your foot in alignment, which can not only improve your skiing, but also alleviate the symptoms of some knee and foot injuries. Orthotics are expensive, but if you have foot problems or ski a lot, they're an excellent investment. Because doctors prescribe them, some health insurance plans cover the cost of orthotics. You can also use them in your running or tennis shoes, providing a way to spread the cost over the other three seasons.

Where to Shop

Before you can start your search for that perfect pair of boots, you have to answer a more fundamental question: "Where should I do my shopping?" When you go into a ski shop, you're not just buying a pair of boots; you're buying the expertise of the shop's boot fitters. If they've done their job right, the guys who work in the shop have sifted through the hundreds of models on the market and narrowed the choices down to a manageable few. And more importantly, the right boot fitter understands which boots work best for which skiers. Sure, things like low prices and impressive money-back-if-you're-not-satisfied warranties are important. But the bottom line is coming home with the right pair of boots (or skis or bindings, for that matter). You stack the odds in your favor by starting off at the right shop.

Sporting goods stores

Almost every large sporting goods store has some kind of a ski department. In a lot of ways, it's less intimidating to waltz into the same place where you bought your basketball or your running shoes and start trying on boots. That is exactly why you may want to think twice about making a sporting goods superstore your only gear-shopping stop, for these reasons:

- ✔ Because a sporting goods store has so many other things it has to fit in the store, the selection of boots, both in models and in sizes, may be limited.

- ✔ Due to limited space in the store for skiing-only items, backshop facilities to make after-sale adjustments may be limited or nonexistent.

- ✔ You may find a salesperson who's an experienced and knowledgeable boot fitter, or you may find someone who was selling fly rods just yesterday and has never even worn a pair of ski boots.

If you're lucky and you have a relatively standard shaped foot, you may come back from a sporting goods store with a great-fitting boot. If not . . .

Ski chains

Picture a mid-size sporting goods store filled with nothing but ski equipment. These ski chain stores have a number of locations, and the stores tend to have very large inventories (although they tend to stick to well-known brands) with much of it on display so you can poke around on your own. They also have a backshop where they can make at least minor adjustments on a pair of boots. The prices at a ski chain are often very low, but in some cases, shops make their profits by concentrating on higher volume.

And there's the rub. Chain stores can get very busy, especially on weekends, and many of the salespeople in these chain stores work on commission, so there's an inherent tension in the process. They may want to get you a good enough fit so that you buy the boots, but without taking up too much time that he or she could devote to the next sale. On the other hand, some of the best bootfitters around work in chains. So if you choose to shop at one, make sure you come home with a boot that really fits.

Specialty shops

Look in the Yellow Pages under ski equipment, and this is the kind of place you're likely to find. The shop is usually small and has been in business since Billy Kidd was just a kid. The ambiance is generally the opposite of your local mall, whether it's a neighborly kind of place with knotty pine on the walls or a mini-boutique swanked out with antiques and a cappuccino machine.

Your foot's guardian angel, the bootfitter of your dreams, could be working anywhere. But at the specialty ski shop, it's reasonably certain that the boot fitter will be experienced and knowledgeable, and the backshop should be equipped to do major or minor surgery on your boots if necessary. You may have to pay a little extra for the expertise and ambiance. A small shop doesn't have quite the buying power of chains or sporting goods stores, so its prices may be a little higher. In terms of sheer numbers, a specialty shop may not carry as many lines as a chain store, but it may be more likely to have some smaller manufacturers which make boots that work for hard-to-fit feet.

Shop globally, buy locally

It makes sense to buy gear nearby, but nearby what? If you live in an area where there aren't many ski shops, consider buying at a shop that's near the mountain where you ski frequently. Ski town shops tend to have especially good boot fitters because the locals ski a lot and they won't stand for boots that hurt. And even occasional skiers are more likely to bring boots back for a little tweaking if they drive past the shop on the way home.

If you're taking a week-long trip somewhere, consider buying your boots slopeside on the first day. Then you can go straight from the slope to the shop for daily tweaks throughout your trip, and you can go home with great-fitting boots to match your great new outlook.

SHE SKI

For women only: Ski shop sexism

I can't tell you how many times this has happened. I go equipment shopping with my wife — who's also an instructor and a better skier than I may ever be. And the shop guy comes to *me* and says. "What kind of a skier is she?" As if Sally were invisible, a five-year-old, or a deaf mute. I say "Talk to her." And she says, "I want to try on a pair of Lange XR-9s in a six and a half, in black." Or we just walk out.

The world is a sexist place, and it's nowhere more obvious than in a ski shop. And while you can't change the world, you can at least make sure that the salesman's (and I'm using that gender-specific term advisedly) Neanderthal sensibilities don't get in the way of getting the right gear. Here are some do's and don'ts.

✔ **Do make the salesperson talk to you:** You're the one who's going to be using this stuff, not your husband, brother, or boyfriend. If the salesman insists on treating you like a non-entity, help make his perception conform to reality and walk out.

✔ **Don't get sold down:** Some salesmen operate on the mistaken assumption that "girls can't ski." So no matter how many times you tell them that you've been skiing black diamonds for a decade, they keep trucking out these cushy pink boots designed for someone who spends more time in the lodge than on the slope.

✔ **Do consider women's models:** The good news is that manufacturers are actually beginning to take women's needs seriously. Today's women's boots feature more than just pretty colors. They feature fit enhancements that work better for women's feet. The boots have flex patterns that are better suited to a woman's generally lighter weight. And most have a measure of performance comparable to men's models.

Courtesy Skis Dynastar

Chapter 3

Buying the Right Skis

· ·

In This Chapter

▶ Understanding ski terminology

▶ Selecting a ski that's right for you

▶ Understanding the different types of skis

▶ Buying the right bindings

▶ Gravitating to the appropriate poles

▶ Maintaining your equipment

· ·

*B*uying skis can be a downright daunting experience. You walk in and on one side you see a ski wall that's a quarter mile long. Different brands, colors, lengths, shapes, and prices.

You get up closer and the tags that hang from the merchandise seem to be written in a different language. Kevlar torsion box construction. Parabolic sidecut. Sintered base material. You scratch your head and wish Bill Gates were here to help because it's all geek to you.

But there's a light at the end of this tunnel. The right gear helps you ski better with less effort and, most importantly, helps you have more fun. And today's ski equipment is better than ever. Skis turn more easily. Bindings have never been safer. And even poles have improved.

But to make sure you get the right stuff, you need a ski shop survival guide. And that's exactly what this chapter gives you. In the following pages, I tell you about the different kind of skis, how to get the best deal, and how to decide whether you should rent or buy equipment.

Beyond Boards: A Guide to Ski Basics

Despite what you might think after a brief visit to a ski shop, skis all have a lot in common. They have the same parts, they share a similar construction, and even though ski shapes have changed a bit in recent years, they're more alike than they are different. In this section, I give you an outline of these common threads in ski design so you can cut through the jargon when you're ready to buy.

A guided tour of a ski

Before you start worrying about what model to buy, it helps to understand the basic architecture of the ski. (See Figure 3-1.)

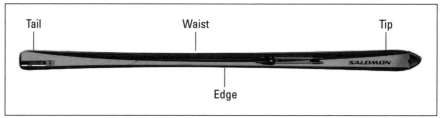

Tail   Waist   Tip

Figure 3-1:
The parts
of a ski.

Edge

Courtesy Salomon N.A./Mavic

The *tip* (sometimes called the *shovel*) is the rounded upturned part in the front of the ski. The tip is shaped that way to enable it to glide up and over small clumps of snow instead of digging into them. The *tail* is the rear section of the ski. The part underneath your foot — notice that it's narrower than the tip or tail — is the *waist*. The ski's hourglass shape enables you to turn the ski better. (I talk more about this shape — called *sidecut* — in "Shaped skis and the sidecut factor" later in the chapter.)

Inside the ski, where you can't see it, is the *core*. (See Figure 3-2.) It's a piece of fiberglass-wrapped wood or foam that is designed to flex in a specific way to make the ski stable and easy to turn. On top of the core is the visible part of the ski, which is called the *cap*. On some skis, the cap is a structural member, while on others it serves an aesthetic purpose. The protective sheeting on top of the cap that includes the ski's graphics is known as the *topskin*.

The *base* is the bottom of the ski. It's made of a special plastic that's both slippery and rugged. Ideally, the base should be flat and smooth. *Edges* are the polished metal strips on the side of the ski. They perform a little like an ice skate blade, helping the ski slide forward more easily and not slip sideways on icy snow.

What are skis made of?

When you go to a fine restaurant, do you ask whether the vegetables are cut *chiffonade* or *gratinée* style? Do you quiz the waiter on whether the *mousse au chocolat* is egg-based or cream-based? Unless you're a culinary arts student, you don't and you shouldn't. The same is true with skis. The materials and construction of a ski certainly influence the way it performs on the snow. However, just like you can't read a recipe and understand how a dish tastes, you can't just read about a ski's construction and know how it skis.

In general, skis have a core made of foam, fiberglass, or laminated wood. The core is covered with a cap, usually fiberglass and occasionally stainless steel, that may be structural or primarily cosmetic. See Figure 3-2. Ski designers use different materials in different ways to adjust the performance characteristics of a ski. Adding fiberglass or changing how it's positioned in the ski changes a ski's *flex*, or its resistance to bending or twisting. Adding other materials can improve *vibration damping*, the ski's ability to ride smoothly on rough snow.

Figure 3-2:
Most skis feature a variety of materials.

Courtesy Rossignol

You can make some generalizations about how construction affects performance. Wood-core models tend to feel a little more solid, while foam-core models are generally lighter and a little more lively. In reality, however, it's the interplay of many other variables, like sidecut, flex pattern, and even length, that determines how a ski feels. In short, it's more the chef than the ingredients.

The shaped-ski revolution

If Thomas Paine, Georges Danton, or even Leon Trotsky were around today, they would feel right at home in a ski shop. The world of ski gear, you see, has just undergone a revolution, and we're all better off because of it.

If I were writing this chapter five years ago, it would have been much shorter and much simpler. Skis were all pretty much the same shape, give or take a millimeter or two — long, relatively narrow, without many curves.

All that changed in 1993 with Kneissl's Ergo and, soon after, Elan's SCX, shown in the accompanying figure. These skis (called shaped skis, although to be technical *all* skis have shape) were funny to look at. The squashed profile and the wide tip and tail made them look almost like a Tex Avery cartoon — "Alpine Bugs" — come to life. But the skis performed. Skiers found that because of its exaggerated shape, a ski with a deep dish sidecut would make expert-style carved turns (see "Coming to terms" later in this chapter) almost effortlessly (something that only expert skiers could do) and at low speeds (something that even Alberto Tomba couldn't manage).

Courtesy Elan

This radically designed ski opened the door to a brave new world of ski design. Many other companies offered their own interpretation of these shaped skis — some more exaggerated, some more like conventional skis. The shaped-ski revolution had begun.

The result of all this out-of-the-box thinking is a generation of skis that are easier to turn, more maneuverable, and more versatile.

Shaped skis and the sidecut factor

A sidecut isn't something you can order from your butcher or something you lay down in a recording studio. *Sidecut* describes a ski's shape. Take a look at a modern shaped ski. (Refer to Figure 3-1.) Notice how the ski is shaped a little like Marilyn Monroe or some other '50s starlet. It's wide on top, gets markedly narrower in the waist, and widens out again in the tail. Skis have had sidecut since the 19th century, but this marked curviness is very different from what was seen in the "conventional" ski of five years ago, which was shaped more like Twiggy — with only the slightest of curves. Fashion trends aside, this pronounced hourglass shape helps a ski to turn more easily.

How? If you had a ski with perfectly straight sides and tilted it up on edge and pushed it forward, it would scribe a perfectly straight line in the snow. When you do the same thing with a shaped ski, its hourglass profile allows it to scribe an arc in the snow. Pretty cool.

If you look at a bunch of skis in a shop, you may notice that some skis are curvier than others are. This difference is reflected in a term called *sidecut radius,* which is a shorthand measurement that combines information about both sidecut and the length of the ski. Essentially, if you put a ski flat on a big piece of paper and traced one edge, you'd get a curved line. That curve is part of a giant circle, so you can talk about your ski's shape in relation to the radius of that circle. And it's called the sidecut radius. These days, what passes for a conventional ski has a sidecut radius of about 35 meters. A mid-1980s ski might have a sidecut radius of 50 meters. The shortest, most radical of today's shaped skis have a sidecut of only 9 meters. Most middle-of-the-road shaped skis have a sidecut of around 25 meters. In general, skis with a shorter sidecut radius make it easier to carve turns on groomed snow. Skis with a more moderate sidecut radius are more versatile and forgiving and require less of a technique adjustment if you're used to conventional skis.

When it comes to choosing a ski type, the rules have changed. Or rather, there are no rules. Better skiers used to ski with longer, stiffer skis. Now if you're the hottest skier on the hill, you might opt for a short ski with a super-deep sidecut — or a wide-waisted relatively soft ski that's ideal for crud. If you're a weekend intermediate you might opt for — surprise, surprise — a short ski with a super-deep sidecut or a wide-waisted ski ideal for crud.

Coming to terms

Before you buy a ski, you have to understand what a ski does. Here are some of the sometimes contradictory things that skiers want their skis to do and quick explanations of which design parameters affect a ski's ability to perform.

- **Glide:** *Gliding*, as I'm defining it here, is the ski's ability to slide in a straight line. It's influenced by the ski's length (longer skis tend to glide better), by its shape (less radical sidecuts glide more easily), and by its construction (materials with better damping tend to glide better).

- **Turn:** *Turning* is the ski's ability to deviate from a straight glide and trace an S-shaped path down a slope. If you're not doing it already, turning is not only a skier's primary method of directional control, it's also the primary method of speed control. (See Chapter 7 for more on this.)

- **Carve:** This is a ski's ability to turn while on its edge, much like a figure skate. *Carving* is a precise way to turn without scrubbing off too much speed. In general, skis with stiffer torsional flex (in other words, more resistance to twisting) carve better. And skis with a deeper sidecut will carve shorter turns.

- **Skid:** *Skidding* is the ski's ability to slide sideways in a turn. It's not only important for beginners, who skid their turns in an attempt to keep their speed in check, but is also important for advanced skiers in the bumps and on very steep terrain. Skis with a shallower sidecut and a somewhat softer flex skid more easily.

✔ **Float:** If you've ever stepped into a snowdrift and sunk in up to your navel, you know that snow is not a solid medium. Most ski areas groom the slopes so that they are both flat and firmly packed. There are times (such as after a snowfall or in the spring after the snow softens) that the snow becomes essentially a 3-D medium into which you and your skis can sink. *Float* is a ski's ability to do just that, to float on top of soft or powdery snow instead of sinking. Generally, the wider a ski is at its waist, the better it floats.

Just My Type: A Look at Ski Categories

Now that you understand the basics of ski design and construction, it's time to explore the different genres of skis and find the one that's best for you.

What kind of skier are you?

What kind of skis do you need? These days, it's as much a matter of attitude as ability, so take this quiz to see which boards are right for you.

1. It snowed 12 inches the night before. At 8:00 a.m. on this powder day, you're . . .

    a) Eating breakfast.

    b) In the lodge putting on your boots.

    c) In the middle of your third run — you started hiking at 6:30.

    d) Waiting for the groomers to come out.

    e) What's a powder day?

2. As far as you're concerned, a perfect run is one . . .

    a) Where you can keep up with your friends

    b) Where you mix tasty bumps with some perfectly groomed corduroy

    c) Where you blast through the powder

    d) Where you hit 30 mph — twice

    e) Where you don't fall

3. If your skis were a car, they'd be . . .

    a) a Honda Accord

    b) a BMW sedan

    c) a Range Rover

    d) a Porsche

    e) A rental car

4. You usually ski . . .

    a) Beginner trails and easy intermediate trails

    b) Intermediate and the occasional groomed expert trail

    c) Ungroomed intermediate and expert trails

    d) Groomed expert trails and the race course

    e) The beginner hill

5. If you were representing Morocco in the Olympics, how would the announcer describe your skiing?

    a) A little tentative

    b) Solid as a rock

    c) Creative

    d) Surprisingly fast

    e) You can't use those kind of words on a TV-PG broadcast

6. At the end of a great day, you're . . .

    a) Happy, tired, and ready to take your boots off

    b) Happy, tired, and wishing the lifts were open for another hour

    c) Praying that tomorrow's a powder day

    d) Bragging about the 20,000 vertical feet you racked up

    e) Ready for a beer

If most of your answers were As, then you're having fun skiing, but maybe you're looking for the breakthrough that can take you to the next level. A game-improvement ski can help you get there.

If most of your answers were Bs, you're a pretty solid skier and you're starting to develop your own style and explore more of the mountain. Try an all-mountain ski.

If most of your answers were Cs, you're the Lewis and Clark of your local ski area, always waiting for powder and ready to venture off the groomed trail at the drop of a snowflake. Take a mid-fat ski along with you.

If most of your answers were Ds, then speed is your need. A cruising ski is the perfect high-velocity tool for your Mach 5 adventures.

If most of your answers were Es, then you're still feeling your way around. Look at a beginner ski, or maybe even stick to the rental shop for a while.

Understanding ski categories

As you may guess, the aftermath of a revolution can be kind of messy. One of the casualties of the shaped-ski revolution is ski labeling. It used to be that skis were labeled according to the event their World Cup relatives were designed for: slalom skis for short turns on narrow terrain and giant slalom skis for wide open spaces. Now, the skis are better, but the labels are a little more confusing. Here's a guide to different genres of skis.

Beginner skis

Only a couple of years ago, anything labeled a beginner ski or a learning ski was about half a step up from awful. Traditionally, beginner's skis were mid-line skis mellowed out to the point of being almost non-performers and beefed up to withstand the abuse heaped upon them by rental shop customers. They were the Rent-a-Wreck of the ski world.

But over the last season or so, the rethinking that has swept the entire ski world filtered down to the beginners market. Spurred on by innovative instructors looking for a ski that would help beginners progress more rapidly, ski makers introduced a line of short skis —120 centimeters — with pronounced sidecuts. (See Figure 3-3.) Manufacturers designed these ultra-short skis to be maneuverable at low speed while still providing a stable platform that aided a beginner's still-developing balance. Manufacturers design some of these skis in short length increments. Beginners can move rapidly from a 120 to a 130 to a 140 as they gain skills and confidence in their first few days on snow.

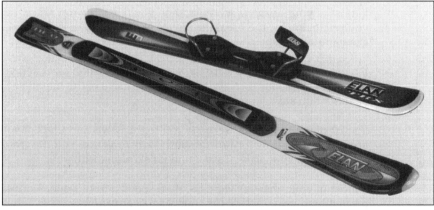

Figure 3-3:
A short beginner's ski (left) next to a skiboard (right).

Courtesy Elan

These ultra-short skis are so new that it's not clear whether they will make it out of the rental shop and onto the ski wall. Some experts are suggesting that the ultra-short skis may be an emerging market niche, the perfect ski for twice-a-year skiers, while others counter that they're primarily teaching tools, and skiers looking to invest in skis are better served with a longer, more conventional–shaped ski. Time, as they say, will tell.

Game improvement skis

Game improvement skis are the meat of the market, and compared to the mid-level skis of a decade ago, they're filet mignon. The ski's sidecut makes turning much easier, while improved *vibration damping* allows them to be stable even at much shorter lengths. And the wider *shovels* help these skis power through shallow powder and slushy or cruddy snow, although their relatively narrow waists make them less than ideal for truly bottomless powder.

There is some diversity of opinion among manufacturers. Some companies — notably Elan and Rossignol — offer deep sidecuts on their game improvement skis for better maneuverability, while others, like K2, make more skis with moderate sidecuts for enhanced stability and a more traditional feel. Demo both and see what works best for you.

All-mountain skis

All-mountain skis are kind of like game improvement skis on steroids. They're designed to go everywhere on the mountain, from cruising groomed trails to bashing the bumps to even doing some off-piste exploring. All-mountain skis are designed for aggressive intermediate to expert skiers who want versatile boards that will go anywhere on the mountain. Most all-mountain skis boast a moderate sidecut that excels in a variety of conditions and have a slightly stiffer flex for a better response at higher speeds.

Cruising skis

Cruising skis are the racing skis of yesteryear. They're designed for rapid transit on groomed snow. Cruisers hold tenaciously on hardpack — or even on an icy racecourse — and carve precise high-speed arcs on freshly groomed corduroy. Enhanced vibration damping keeps them unrattled even at seriously high speeds, although this unflappability sometimes comes at the expense of lower-speed liveliness. Cruisers are happiest, however, when you point them down the hill, and at lower speeds they can be less than responsive.

Mid-fat skis

Mid-fats are the all-terrain vehicles of the ski world and actually are a lot more versatile than a Range Rover. A mid-fat, the left ski shown in Figure 3-4, takes the sidecut of a shaped ski and combines it with a wider profile underfoot for better floatation in powder and cruddy snow. The result is a ski that performs almost as well as a conventional-shaped ski on groomed snow and even in icy conditions, but can power through crud like a bulldozer and float through powder like Garfield in the Macy's Thanksgiving Day Parade. Mid-fats are a great everyday tool for skiers who deal with soft snow and powder typical of the West or like to venture off-piste anywhere.

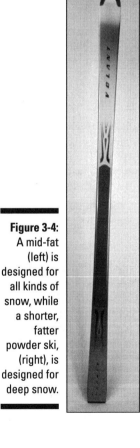
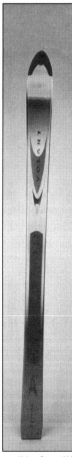

Figure 3-4:
A mid-fat (left) is designed for all kinds of snow, while a shorter, fatter powder ski, (right), is designed for deep snow.

Courtesy Volant Sports, LLC

Specialty skis

Most skis are designed to be all-purpose tools, working on almost any terrain in any kind of snow conditions. Sometimes, however, a skier's fancy or the prevailing conditions dictate using a ski that's specially designed for a particular purpose. Here are some of the most popular one-trick skis.

Racing skis

Only a few years ago, there were two kinds of skis — racing skis and lousy skis. While I may be exaggerating, it's only by a little. No, the slopes weren't dominated by a race of super skiers who slid straight from the finish line at the Olympic downhill to the cafeteria line at the local resort.

The ubiquity of racing skis was just a marketing thing, kind of like EuroDisney in reverse. In Europe, World Cup racers are as big as baseball's Mark McGwire. Ski companies have always sold a lot of skis by pushing the racing connection, even if the skis they sell in the store are about as close to the pair that Olympic champion Hermann Maier uses as Jeff Gordon's NASCAR Chevy is to the Lumina in your driveway. In the U.S., the subsidiaries of these largely European companies simply followed suit.

At the same time, the prevailing design philosophy was to design the fastest and best racing ski and then tame it for mere mortals. This logic has been turned upside down as racers initially shunned shaped skis, but recreational skiers saw them as a breakthrough. The result is that manufacturers have started designing most skis with the way that most people ski in mind. And that, as Martha Stewart might say, is a good thing.

Racing skis come in three sub-genres. _Downhill skis,_ which are made for the likes of Picabo Street and Hermann Maier, simply won't turn for most mere mortals, and you can't buy them in the average ski shop anyway. Most recreational skiers make modern giant-slalom style turns, round and largely carved, but real _GS skis_ are a handful for all but the strongest skiers. _Slalom skis_ are almost like ice skates, designed to carve abrupt turns on icy race courses. Starting in 1999, according to the people at _Skiing_ magazine, slalom skis also have deeper sidecuts, below 30 meters. (See Chapter 9 for more information about racing.)

Mogul skis

Some skiers just live for the bumps and measure their existence from mogul to mogul. Mogul skis are flexible to absorb the pounding that the bumps can dish out. They are reasonably narrow at the tip, so they don't skewer the backside of a bump, and they are relatively short for optimum maneuverability. These skis are practically the only ones on the rack these days that don't have a dramatic sidecut.

Powder skis

The first powder skis, built by Atomic, were literally made by slicing a snow-board in half on a band saw. The result was a ski that revolutionized the sport. Skiing in *powder* — deep and at times bottomless snow — has always been a nirvana for expert skiers. Less-accomplished skiers found it frustrating because they sink into the waist-deep snow, and they lack the combination of skill and strength that deep-snow skiing demands.

Powder skis — also called fat skis — changed all that. Short (usually about 160 cm) and very wide (up to twice as wide as a conventional ski), powder skis allow skiers to float just below the surface of even the deepest powder so that groomed snow technique works fine in even the deepest fluff. (Refer to Figure 3-4, the ski on the right.) Powder skis made *heli-skiing* (where you ski acres of copter-accessed powder in a day) so easy that even Christie Brinkley can do it.

Unless you're rich enough to go heli-skiing on a regular basis — flying to the top of the mountain by chopper to ski untracked powder — or you live in a ski town where overnight dumps are the rule, you probably don't need to buy a pair of powder skis. All heli-skiing and snowcat skiing operations, and most Western ski resorts, rent powder skis on a daily basis. But be forewarned: After the Weather Channel warns that a storm's a comin', they can get snapped up pretty quickly. (See Chapter 9 for more information about powder skiing.)

Hypercarving skis

What do you get when you cross a skier and a snowboarder? I'm not going to touch that one with a ten-foot pole. But I will venture a guess as to what it may have on its feet — a pair of *hypercarving skis*. These short skis have a deep-dish sidecut that allows a skier to throw away his poles and lean over at extreme angles to lay snowboard-like carves. Hypercarving skis may actually look like a pair of short beginner skis, but they're beefier and often have *booster plates* mounted between the ski and the binding for increased leverage and, hence, better carving.

Skiboards

"Hey, you, did you leave your skis in the dryer too long?" Those are the kind of taunts that skiboarders have had to endure until just recently. *Skiboards* are very short skis — under 90 centimeters, often with non-releasing bindings. See Figure 3-5. Skiboards go just about everywhere that conventional skis go, as well as a few places — like the terrain park — where long boards fear to tread.

Skiboards are one of the hottest trends in skiing, cropping up everywhere from resorts to your TV screen. How hot are they? Skiboarding even won a slot in ESPN's Winter X-Games lineup. (See Chapter 9 for more information about skiboarding.)

Figure 3-5:
Skiboarding
is one of the
hottest
trends in
snowsliding.

Courtesy Salomon N.A./Mavic

Buying Your Skis

Now that you've narrowed your choices, you're ready to plunk down your plastic and head to the slopes. But not so fast. You've still got a few things to figure out, from what length you need to when is the best time to buy.

Selecting the proper length

How much have ski lengths changed? Three years ago, I was skiing on a pair of 203-centimeter skis. Now I ski on a pair of 183-centimeter skis. Needless to say, the ski world has changed radically.

Length has also become an increasingly important performance parameter. The wife of a ski company executive I know, a petite woman and not a particularly aggressive skier, skis a mid-fat model in a 173-centimeter length. I ski the same ski in a 183-centimeter length. A former world extreme skiing champion skis the very same ski in a 193-centimeter length.

As you can deduce from the previous example, smaller and less aggressive skiers should ski on shorter skis. Heavier and more aggressive skiers need longer skis.

When you're choosing a length for a specific ski, it's important to check out manufacturer recommendations, read ski tests, and seek the advice of a salesperson. If possible, try the model out in different lengths on the hill. (You can find more information on trying out skis in "Demo daze: Testing before you buy," later in this chapter.) However, here's a simple formula that should give you an approximate idea of how long your skis should be.

1. **Start with 175 centimeters for a man or 165 centimeters for a woman.**

2. **If you're very tall and/or significantly heavier than average, add 5 cm. If you're very short or light, subtract 5 cm.**

3. **If you're an intermediate skier, add 5 cm.**

4. **If you're an expert skier, add 10 cm.**

5. **If you're buying a mid-fat, subtract 5 cm.**

6. **If you're buying cruising skis, add 3 cm.**

7. **If you ski bumps often, subtract 2 cm.**

8. **Total your points.**

   This gives you a ballpark figure for your appropriate ski length. But keep an open mind. More and more, the ski rack is a lot like the ladies' dress department — all size sixes are not created equal.

Demo daze: Testing before you buy

The good news is that buying a pair of skis is a little like buying a car. You get to try before you buy — if you ask. Many ski shops offer demonstration skis, more commonly known as *demos*, which they let you try for the day for a nominal fee. Some ski areas have on-mountain demo centers, in which you can try different models for a few runs, often for free. Additionally, many ski areas sponsor demo days in which a large number of manufacturers show up with skis that you can try for free. Pretty cool, huh?

To get the most out of a demo, you have to be a little bit organized. Here are some tips for trying out equipment successfully.

- ✔ **Have your own skis tuned:** If you already have a pair of skis, you should have them tuned — the bases flattened and waxed and the edges sharpened. This way any differences you feel will be attributable to the ski itself and not to a better tune.

- ✔ **Focus your search:** It's best to come to a demo day with some idea of the skis you want to try — you can do this by reading the test reports in the ski magazines or simply by poking around a ski shop.

- ✔ **Ski the same terrain:** When you're trying to compare two skis, it's important to compare the proverbial apple to the proverbial apple. You want to pick a route that offers as much variety as possible — both steeper terrain and gentler terrain, some bumps, perhaps, different snow conditions if possible — in short, pick a run that offers a sampler of your typical skiing day. Ski that terrain over and over, with different skis. Then use the chair ride to jot down some notes about the last ski you try. This is the way that the ski magazines compare skis. And that's the way you should compare them too.

Seasons in the snow: When to buy gear

In a world where Christmas displays go up in October and the season's swimsuits are sold out by March, is it any surprise that the new skis and boots hit the stores in August and often go on sale by December? No, it doesn't make much sense, and yes, you can take advantage of it to save big bucks.

Consider the source

"This is the best ski in the world."

"Well, _this_ is the best ski in the _history_ of the world."

"Really? _This_ ski is better than sex."

"Fine. But _this_ ski is better than a box of Peanut Butter Kandy Kakes and a quart of ice-cold milk."

That kind of hyperbole runs rampant in the ski world. Everyone, it seems, has a very definite opinion about equipment — from your next-door neighbor to the guy at the ski shop to magazine testers — and, of course, they all disagree. So how do you sort it all out?

First you have to understand that ski preference is subjective. Like the "boxers or briefs" question, there is no right answer to the question "What's the perfect ski?"

Magazines like _Skiing_ and _SKI_ that publish their gear guides in late summer have tried to address this issue by tailoring their gear recommendations to a skier's interests rather than just his or her ability level.

Often the most telling information in a capsule review of a ski is a quote from a tester:

"I've never used a ski that's more responsive or easier to turn on groomed snow. I love it more than my own mother."

To make sense of this advice, you first have to consider the source of the advice. A ski that an aggressive 210-pound, 23-year-old male ex-racer may love is likely to be a huge handful for you if you're a 40-year-old female intermediate who likes to cruise. Height, weight, skiing style, preferred terrain, and attitude all affect whether a skier's going to love or loathe a piece of equipment. So after you get a piece of advice, do a little detective work. If you're reading a test report, and find a comment that piques your interest, turn to the tester's bio page to find out about that skier's background and biases. Is she a little like you, or not? And if you're getting unsolicited advice from a real, live human being, feel free to ask a few questions about how they ski so you know whether to take it to heart or merely nod politely.

✔ **Pre-season:** If you're looking to spend as little as possible on gear, consider doing your ski shopping while most of your friends are at the beach. In late summer, most of the new gear is arriving in your dealer's stockroom. This new stock makes it imperative to get rid of last year's skis and boots. Can you say _50 percent off?_

✔ **Late season:** The other time to buy gear is at the end of the season. At some shops, end-of-season sales can begin as early as December. But most shops start to mark down the current season's gear by the beginning of February, which gives you plenty of time to use it this season. And while the discounts aren't as deep as the pre-season sales, the selection is usually better.

You do have to do your homework. Read the gear previews in the ski magazines and check each manufacturer's Web site. If the company is making a significant change next season in the construction of a ski, then you may want to wait. The other thing to realize is that a pair of skis in the wrong length or a pair of boots that doesn't fit is never a bargain, no matter what the price. (For more information on where to buy gear, see Chapter 2.)

Bindings

From a safety point of view, bindings, shown in Figure 3-6, are your most important piece of ski equipment. Bindings perform two important and very different functions. They attach your boot securely to your ski; obviously, having your ski come off unexpectedly is not a good thing. On the other hand, after you fall, having your ski attached is not such a good thing because the ski becomes a giant lever that can transmit dangerous forces to your leg. The binding's second job is to sense these forces and to cause the ski to release before the forces can cause a bad sprain or fracture in your lower leg.

Modern bindings incorporate a *ski brake*, two little spring-loaded pins under your foot that drag on the ground when you're not in the binding, to keep the ski from sliding down the mountain after it releases or before you click in. Pretty nice, huh?

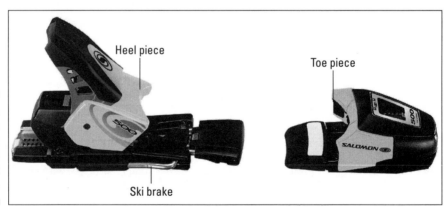

Figure 3-6:
Bindings secure your boot to and release it from the ski.

Heel piece

Toe piece

Ski brake

Courtesy Salomon N.A./Mavic

Is one binding safer than another?

That's a loaded question. Manufacturers are continually trying to make their bindings release more predictably and in ways that address a wider range of potentially injurious falls. And they all meet the same international engineering standards. In the real world, however, ski injuries involve so many variables that it's hard to isolate the binding's role in the equation.

Buying beats renting. Or does it?

Gearing up for skiing used to be simple, too. You bought a pair of skis because renting was for beginners and dorks, and, well, rental skis just sucked. Not anymore. Most shops and ski areas are offering high-performance rentals and demos that are every bit as trick as the skis you can buy in a ski shop, and they even use their computer systems to eliminate a lot of the waiting and paperwork. But is it a good deal?

Let's whip out the ol' Hewlett-Packard. I'm assuming you're an avid but not fanatical skier — you ski ten days a year spread out over one week-long trip and a few day trips. And I'm going to assume that a pair of skis may last you about four seasons. Of course, I'm assuming that you have your own boots because rental boots *are* for dorks. (See Chapter 2 for boot-buying advice.) Here's a rundown of the numbers attached to buying a pair of skis.

The cost of owning skis

Expense	Price
Rossignol Bandit ski	$589.00
Rossignol FTX 105 binding	$230.00
Binding mounting	$30.00
Ski bag	$50.00
Ski lock	$19.00
Roof rack	$100.00
Annual tune and wax, binding test (once a year @ $40)	$160.00
Airline excess baggage costs (4 @ $34 round trip)	$136.00
Total	$1,284.00
Interest charges: 15% for 1 year	$154.08
Grand total:	$1,438.08 divided by 40 (10 days for 4 seasons) = $35.95 a day

To rent that exact same pair of skis at Kenny's Double Diamond ski shop in Vail would cost you $31.95 a day plus $1.60 tax for a total of $33.55 a day. So from Milton Friedman's point of view, it would be pretty much a toss-up. If you ski a lot more than ten days a year, definitely buy. If you ski substantially less, then renting is the better deal. But if you're pretty close to our typical skier, it comes down to a lifestyle choice. Ask yourself: What bothers you more — waiting in line to rent your skis or having your skis fall out of your hall closet in the middle of August? You pay your money and you take your choice.

All modern bindings do a good job of protecting you against the kind of lower leg fractures that were commonplace 40 years ago. Those sorts of injuries have gone the way of the $10 lift ticket. On the other hand, bindings do little to protect you from knee sprains, many of which actually occur *before* the skier falls. In short, there are plenty of things you can do to be safer on the slopes — see Chapter 11 — but worrying about which binding to buy probably isn't one of them.

Can bindings have an effect on how I ski?

While bindings are important, they're not really sexy. And, lawyers being what they are, manufacturers are wary about making safety claims about their products. So in an effort to add a little glamour to this segment of the market, companies have turned their attention to making their bindings enhance a ski's performance. Almost every manufacturer includes booster plates that mount between the binding and the ski to raise the height of the binding for better leverage. Marker's SSC bindings allow the skier to adjust the flex of the binding and hence the flex of the ski. Salomon features the Propulse system, which claims to make a ski livelier by storing energy in the bottom part of the turn and releasing it at the top. Do these features work? By all accounts, they do affect the feel of a ski. Whether those changes represent an improvement is a matter of personal opinion. These enhanced bindings do come with a price tag: They're heavier than conventional bindings and, of course, more expensive.

DIN, DIN, DIN

What's your DIN setting? That's a question you hear around ski shops a lot. The *DIN setting* is a number that reflects how tight the springs in your binding are set, and consequently how much force it takes to release the boot from the binding. Your individual DIN setting is determined by your weight and your aggressiveness as a skier. (Aggressive skiers need their bindings set tighter, because hitting a bump at high speed can sometimes make a ski come off when the binding is set at a lower DIN setting.) In general, DIN settings aren't something you should worry about too much, except when you're buying bindings. All bindings have a range of DIN settings, but in some models the range is higher than others. In general, bindings function best in the middle of their DIN range. So if you're a mellow, lightweight skier, make sure you buy a binding that allows you to set the binding comfortably in the middle of its DIN range.

Don't ever mess around with any of the settings on your bindings. If you turn the wrong screw, you could change an important adjustment without even realizing it. You'll only discover the error of your ways the next time you ski, when the binding releases when it shouldn't or the next time you fall, when the binding doesn't release when it should. Leave binding installation and adjustments to qualified mechanics in your ski shop.

On the Pole

When it comes to gear, ski poles often get the short end of the stick (groan). But seriously, while poles may not be as slick as skis or as high-tech as bindings, they're every bit as important to skiing well.

Poles are also one of those places that the skiing hedonist can indulge. Poles are all about feel. If deciding on skis is a "boxers or briefs" question, then picking poles is a "chocolate chocolate chip versus Heath Bar Crunch" kind of decision. The grip, the weight, and the look should all influence your decision.

A ski pole has three parts, as shown in Figure 3-7:

- ✔ Grip
- ✔ Shaft
- ✔ Basket

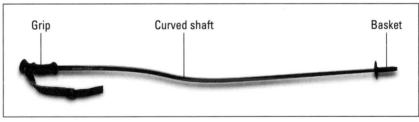

Figure 3-7:
The parts of a composite ski pole.

Grip   Curved shaft   Basket

Courtesy Smith®

Getting a grip

The grip is not only your point of interface with your pole, but it's the thing that keeps your hands amused throughout your ski day while your feet are doing all the work. So be sure to get a grip you like. Most modern grips are made of rubber or plastic, with adjustable nylon straps. It's a personal thing, but I (and most experts) prefer minimalist grips that aren't particularly bulbous at the top and taper smoothly into the shaft below. These low-profile grips are lighter in weight and just feel less restrictive.

Although they've thankfully been all but driven off the market, I'm here to warn you about _strapless poles_. These clunky plastic monstrosities wrap all the way around your wrist, a feature that may come in handy on American Gladiators but doesn't help your skiing much. And not only do they mark you as a hopeless geek, they also prevent you from making a proper pole touch. (See Chapter 8.)

The shaft: Aluminum versus composite

Most pole shafts are still made of tapered aluminum tubing. Aluminum is a good choice as a pole material. It's lightweight, it's relatively inexpensive, and it bends before it breaks. And aluminum isn't fazed by the abuse dished out by ski edges.

But not all aluminum poles are created equal. More expensive poles are made of harder aluminum alloys, which are both lighter and more resistant to bending. The best aluminum poles have a great feel. My current favorite pair of poles is a top-of-the line aluminum model, which I use while a couple pair of composite poles sit unused in my basement.

Recently, composite poles have begun to make significant inroads into the pole market. These are made of the same kinds of materials that a tennis racket is made of — different combinations of fiberglass, carbon fiber, and other exotic materials. Composite poles come in a wide variety of shapes and configurations. Some composite poles mimic the tapered-tube aesthetic of aluminum poles, while others have slinky curved shapes (refer to Figure 3-7) designed for easier pole plants that would make Brancusi proud. Still others, called pencil poles, are as thin as Kate Moss from grip to tip. To continue the supermodel analogy, other composite poles are lighter than aluminum, which is usually a good thing.

As for the disadvantages of composite poles, they are a little more fragile than aluminum poles. The "skin" of the pole can be sliced by an errant ski edge, and if a composite pole does break, it doesn't bend but instead splinters like a piece of wood (which is, after all, the original composite). Composite poles can also be significantly more expensive, with some top-of-the-line models costing well over $100 — which can make them attractive to thieves — although an increasing number of budget models are on the market.

Basket cases

That thing on the bottom of your ski pole is called a *basket*. It's there to keep your pole from piercing the snow like something out of a *Friday the 13th* movie, while you sink up to your wrist. If you stick to groomed snow, all baskets are pretty much created equal — if you like the way the basket looks and if the pole swings well (I get to *swinging* in a second.)

But if you ski in deep snow regularly or you're heading off for a heli-skiing trip, small, half-dollar-size baskets don't cut it. You need to get a pair of *powder baskets* — about the size of a demitasse saucer — that will keep your poles from sinking in soft snow.

The swing test

Speaking of proper pole touch, this is a rare opportunity for you to do a meaningful gear test in the store. Grab the pole. Adjust the wrist strap. Do a pole touch. (Don't know how? See Chapter 7.) How does it feel?

Now try doing a pole touch with a couple of different models, including some expensive ones, so you get a point of reference. With a really good pole, the combination of its overall weight and its balance point — called *swing weight* — allows it to move with just the tiniest flick of your wrist.

Tuning In, Tuning Up: The Ins and Outs of Ski Maintenance

As you may have figured out by now, good ski equipment can be expensive. So naturally you want to get the most from your money and keep your gear operating at its best. The following sections tell you about tuning your skis, having your bindings tested, and storing your gear for the winter.

Maintaining your skis

I have a friend who inherited a perfectly fine pair of hand-me-down skis from another friend. But nonetheless, my friend bought a new pair of skis for himself the next Christmas. And oh, was he a happy camper. "It's like comparing an F-16 to a Cessna," he exclaimed. After I looked at his old skis, his new skis, and his same old turns, I didn't have the heart to tell him that most of the difference he was feeling was from the freshly waxed bases and freshly sharpened edges of the new skis. Instead of spending $350 on a new pair of skis, he could have gotten the same performance boost with a $35 tune-up on his old skis. Ski maintenance is *that* important. In the following list, I review a few of the main tuning parameters and how each one affects the performance of your skis.

- **Stone grinding:** A ski base should be flat. The problem is that the plastic base material does wear, and it tends to wear more in the center than at the edges. This is what's called a *railed base* because it kind of looks like railroad tracks.

  Unfortunately, railed bases often perform that way, too, making the skis hard to turn. Less common, but even more problematic, is a convex base, which makes the ski squirrely and unstable. In either case, have your skis stone ground — flattened and textured on a large machine at a ski shop — about once a year.

✔ **Edge sharpening:** The edges on a pair of skis should be sharp, about as sharp as an ice skate. You should be able to draw the surface of your fingernail across the edge of the ski and have it scrape a thin filing from the surface of your nail. Edges get dulled by the abrasive texture of icy snow, and they can get nicked by rocks and other solid objects in the snow. Edges that aren't sharp enough won't hold on icy or hardpack snow.

However, to make it easier to start your turns, the edges should be beveled or recessed. Either way, when your ski is flat on the snow, your edge will be just slightly off the snow. You can't see the difference, but you can feel it. The edge will only start to bite when you've begun to tip the ski.

Sharpening and beveling can be done quickly and inexpensively at a ski shop whenever you feel like your edges are getting dull. That can be as frequently as every few couple of skiing or as rarely as once a season.

There is such a thing as *too* sharp. If you get your skis sharpened and they feel "hooky," as if they want to start the turn before you're ready, take the ski back to the shop and have the shop dull the edges just at the tips of the skis with some fine emery paper.

✔ **Gouge filling:** There are rocks on them thar hills, and they gouge the bases of even the most careful skier. If your ski is scarred, take it to the shop and have the gouges filled. Although small scratches don't affect performance, a deep gouge or a long gouge that runs near the edge can be a problem and can get worse in a hurry.

✔ **Hot waxing:** Don't worry. Waxed skis don't really go any faster. Waxing makes skis much easier to turn and generally a lot more fun to be around. Hot wax is actually absorbed into the pores of the base material, which helps the ski not only perform better but also last longer. Serious skiers have their skis waxed after every two days of skiing. You can get away with doing it twice a season, or maybe three times if you ski a lot. Wipe-on wax works fine between trips to the shop, but it's no substitute for regular hot waxing.

Getting your bindings tested

When you take your skis into the shop for a tune-up, it's a smart idea to have your binding's release tested. The tech makes sure that the binding is lubricated and working properly. It's a cheap procedure, and it's cheap insurance.

Storing your skis

No matter how you look at it, your skis are going to spend six months of the year in storage. If you want your skis to treat you right in the winter, store them right through the other three seasons. Basically, a cool, dry place is fine, which lets out most attics and some basements. Store your skis vertically, base to base, with the bindings uncocked. An extra-thick coat of wax — applied at the end of the season — can protect the base.

Chapter 4

Skiwear: Dressing for Success

• •

▶ Layering for warmth

▶ Protecting yourself against the elements

▶ Sweating the details

▶ Dressing with style

• •

Do clothes make the skier? Well, I never saw a pair of ski pants make a graceful giant slalom turn without a little input from the pilot. But the right ski clothes can make a skier many other things: Warm. Dry. Stylish. Happy.

Let's face it. While we all love to ski when it's 40 degrees and the sun is shining — and in six inches worth of fresh powder while we're fantasizing — most days are less than perfect, meteorologically speaking. That is why good quality skiwear performs a delicate balancing act worthy of those death-defiers at Ringling Bros. Keeping you warm, but not too warm; dry on both the inside and the outside; and well sealed, at least until you have to open a zipper or flap.

Skiing is also about being seen, about making a statement on-snow. The right jacket and pants that fit just so can make you feel like a million bucks, even if your skiing isn't quite in the seven-figure range.

In this chapter I tell you how to dress smart. I explain why layering is the best strategy for dealing with the ever changing mountain weather. I tell you what to look for in skiwear in terms of features, fit, and affordability. I show you how to take care of your new skiwear so that it stays like new season after season. And finally, I also give you some down-to-earth fashion advice, so you look as good as you feel.

Layering: Three Easy Pieces

Once upon a time, just about every skier wore a big puffy down coat and cotton long underwear — and a grimace because they were cold, wet, and could barely move.

The times, as Bob Dylan so sagely observed, they are a changin', and today's skiwear is way better than it has ever been. Shall I sum up the improvement in one word? Layering. With skiing, as with chocolate cake, there's no doubt about it, two layers are better than one. And for that matter, three layers are generally better than two — although seven layers works much better on a dessert plate than on the ski slopes. This team approach to dressing has many advantages.

- ✔ Each garment can be designed with a specific task in mind — wicking sweat, keeping you warm, or blocking the wind.
- ✔ Layers can be mixed and matched to provide just the right amount of warmth and protection.
- ✔ Layers can be added or shed during the course of the day to keep pace with the often-unpredictable mountain weather.
- ✔ Layers can be laundered individually depending on their use and proximity to the skin.
- ✔ Layers can be worn separately — many of them through all four seasons — making them much more versatile, both on and off the slopes.

A modern ski outfit generally consists of three layers: a base layer, an insulation layer, and a shell layer. Each layer serves its own function, and when combined properly, the result is a division of labor that would make Adam Smith proud.

The Base Layer

You could call these long johns — and many people still do — but that term just doesn't do justice to the technology involved. Unlike that baggy, cotton thermal underwear you wore as a kid, today's base layers, shown in Figure 4-1, use advanced fibers to keep you warm and dry. The second part — dry — is the real godsend.

Cotton long underwear does a reasonably good job of keeping you warm — as long as you're, say, standing at the bus stop. The problems begin once you start shoveling snow or having a snowball fight. You start sweating, and the cotton material absorbs the sweat like a sponge. And with the sartorial equivalent of a wet dishrag sitting next to your skin, you can't help but get chilled, or at least soggy and uncomfortable.

Figure 4-1:
A good
base layer
wicks sweat
away from
your skin.

Courtesy Smart Wool

Today's base layers combat the wet and cold problem through a process known as *wicking* — and no, this doesn't have anything to do with candle making. Wicking is the means by which fabric draws moisture — also known as sweat — away from the skin, and moves it to the outer layer of the fabric where it can evaporate.

Poke around your ski shop and you find wicking fabrics galore — with every major and minor manufacturer touting the properties of their own name brands. Most of these high-tech fibers are some sort of polyester, a few incorporate silk, and some are wool — not the itchy, uncomfortable wool of yesteryear, but the cushy, newfangled wool that really is a pleasure to wear next to your skin. Although there are real differences among base layer fabrics, the technology changes so quickly (almost invariably for the better) that it's difficult to make concrete recommendations. Try a few brands, find something that works for you, and then stick with it — at least until something better comes along.

Base-layer fabrics also come in different weights — generally light, medium, and heavy or expedition weight. I tend to stock up on lightweight base layers because they're especially versatile; the same garment works for spring skiing and all but the coldest winter days. Other less warm-blooded mammals may find that the medium-weight fabrics do the same for them. Keep in mind that your insulation layer (which I discuss later in the chapter) does most of the job keeping you warm.

Even a great fabric won't work its best if the garment's construction isn't up to snuff. Here are some features to look for in a quality base layer:

- ✔ **Flat seams:** The seams should be flat and well-finished to avoid chafing your skin, especially at the cuffs of the bottoms, which you tuck inside your ski boots.

- ✔ **Close fit:** The fit should be reasonably snug — wicking depends on close fabric-to-body contact — without restricting your movements. I often buy my base layers a size smaller than the rest of my skiwear.

- ✔ **An unobtrusive zipper:** A zippered turtleneck is a big advantage on a base layer shirt, because it helps you regulate your temperature, a real benefit on a warm day, or even when you're just ducking into the lodge for a cup of hot cocoa. Beware of zippers around the ankles of the bottoms — they can chafe if you tuck them inside your ski boots.

Remember one other thing when shopping for base layers. You need a freshly laundered set for every day of skiing. If you're going on a weeklong trip, you need at least three tops and bottoms, or even five if you can't stomach the idea of doing a quick midweek wash in the hotel room sink.

The turtleneck controversy

Turtlenecks are a source of controversy in my household. My wife, Sally, thinks that turtlenecks are a vital addition to any ski wardrobe, and she thinks I should tell you about them. I think that a skier needs a turtleneck like a fish needs a bicycle, but in the interest of free speech and domestic harmony, I shall discuss them anyway.

She said: Turtlenecks have been a tradition in my family for generations. They're soft. They feel nice. They keep your neck warm, not to mention the rest of you. And while guys — you know who you are — don't worry about modesty, we ladies have our reputations to consider. I, for one, will not walk around in public wearing nothing but a skin-tight base layer.

He said: It's not that I object to turtlenecks per se, it's that most of the turtlenecks sold for skiing cost $10 on sale, and are made of cotton. These turtlenecks are fine for wearing under a tweed jacket if you're after that Hugh Hefner look. But they get wet and stay wet. They're not performance skiwear.

As I discuss previously, introducing a cotton layer into a ski outfit sort of bogs down the whole moisture transfer process. (Not to mention throwing a monkey wrench into my neat base/insulation/shell outline.) So if you're sold on the advantages that my lovely wife outlined earlier, then do one of two things. Buy a turtleneck made of Thermastat or some other synthetic fiber *and wear it over a base layer or just by itself* as a base layer (which is, I confess, what I do). Or buy a $10 cotton turtleneck and stuff it in your bag. When you're done skiing for the day, slip it over your head. It'll be dry, you'll be happy, and all will be right with the world. As to the definitional dilemma — is a turtleneck an outer base layer or an inner insulation layer? — I'll leave that for you and William Safire to decide.

The Insulation Layer

Just like your house needs insulation, your body needs some too. But instead of pink Owens-Corning fiberglass, your ski outfit uses something a little cozier to keep you warm.

To understand the mechanics of how insulation works, read the "Full of hot air" sidebar in this chapter. But, in general, the thicker the insulation layer, the warmer the garment is.

Note also that most skiers eliminate the insulation layer on their legs, which are, of course, doing most of the work and thus tend to stay warmer than your torso. They opt for slightly heavier base layer bottoms if it's really cold, or in some cases buy a pair of ski pants with a built-in layer of thin insulation.

Insulation layers come in three basic forms — fleece, filled garments, and sweaters — each with its own pros and cons.

Fleece

Mary's little lamb notwithstanding, in skiwear fleece is a soft, thick, and downright cuddly polyester fabric that's often made into pullovers, jackets, and vests. See Figure 4-2.

Full of hot air

My dog Alison is pretty amazing. No, not because she gets to sleep 16 hours a day while the rest of us work. No, I'm really impressed by the way she can go from sitting on the couch in our 68 degree house to a tail-wagging walk outside in 7 degree weather with nary a shiver. And needless to say, no change of clothes. (She's not that kind of a dog.) What keeps her warm? Well, it has something to do with her brown fur, but mostly it's air. The air that's trapped between the hairs of her fur in her coat serves as insulation, keeping her toasty despite the 60 degree drop in temperature.

What does that have to do with skiwear? The insulating layers of your clothes work exactly the same way. The loose fibers in your insulation layer trap and hold a blanket of air — warmed by your body heat — between you and the outside world. The process is simple but very effective. And it's pretty easy to determine a garment's insulating value: for any given fabric, the thicker it is, the more air it can trap, and thus the warmer it is.

Figure 4-2:
Fleece
pieces are
warm and
versatile
insulation
layers.

Courtesy Marmot

Configurations

Fleece fabrics generally come in different weights: 100, 200, and 300.

- ✔ 100-weight fleece is very thin and is used for very lightweight insulating pieces and some heavyweight base layers.

- ✔ 200-weight fleece is the most common and, with its middle-of-the-road weight, is the most versatile. It's heavy enough to wear as a stand-alone, but not so warm that it has to be reserved for bone-chilling days as a layering piece.

- ✔ 300-weight fleece is the heaviest commonly used fleece, and it's very warm; often too warm, I found, for skiing on all but the coldest days.

However, because of its open weave, conventional fleece can get chilly on a breezy day. Some companies, such as Gore with its Windstopper fleece, have addressed this problem by making fleece with a built-in windproof lamination. Garments made of these fabrics are great for stand-alone use. However, this feature does add considerably to the price, and windproof fleeces lack the luxurious baby-blanket feel of regular fleece.

Pros

What's not to like? Fleeces are warm, easy to care for, and relatively inexpensive. Fleeces can do double duty in your wardrobe, serving as a casual pullover in the spring, fall, and even summer. That's why in only a few years they've become the most popular choice for skiwear insulation.

Cons

After you have them a while fleeces tend to get a little scruffy looking as the loosely woven fabric tends to pill, developing little balls on its surface. Most fleeces are designed as long-sleeve pullovers, which can be a bit of a pain — I much prefer a zippered jacket. And as I mentioned above, most don't protect you from the wind.

Filled garments

These garments are built a little like a sleeping bag — with an inner and outer layer of nylon and down fill or some kind of synthetic insulation such as Primaloft in between.

Configurations

You have two basic choices here, down or synthetics. Ounce for ounce, high quality goose down is the warmest insulation available. However, it's more expensive and it loses its insulating properties when it gets wet. If you're looking for a sleeping bag for winter camping, down is great. For skiing, down is probably overkill. Synthetic insulation is generally thinner, impervious to moisture, and still plenty warm.

Pros

Filled garments keep you plenty warm, and their nylon shells make them wind resistant. And the puffy, quilted look feels nice and oozes a certain retro style.

Cons

Filled garments can be bulky, and at times a little too warm. You also have to be careful not to puncture the nylon shell, or the down will leak out. Filled garments are less versatile than fleece pieces or sweaters for off-slope wear.

Sweaters

You know about sweaters, don't you? Ski sweaters are pretty much like what you have in your bureau only more so. They're warm, woolen, and cozy. After getting swamped by the fleece invasion, sweaters are beginning to make a comeback.

Pros

Sweaters are very stylish, sporting anything from sleek, Jean Claude Killy-inspired retro racing stripes to classic Norwegian snowflake designs helping you make a fashion statement. Sweaters also do double duty on a ski trip. A nice sweater makes for a very swanky apres-ski look.

Wool is also a great fiber. It's warm, natural, and it doesn't retain odors. If it's tightly woven, a sweater is also more windproof than fleece.

Cons

Like most nice things, ski sweaters require a little extra care. Wool needs to be washed carefully and stored in a mothproof environment. And just like those Shetlands in your dresser drawer, ski sweaters can be itchy.

Insulation layers are supposed to keep you warm. However, you don't want to aim just for maximum warmth. There is such a thing as *too* warm, even when you're skiing. If you overdress, you can get so warm that your sweat production overwhelms your base layer's wicking ability, and just like a basement without a sump pump, you begin to get wet inside. And the wetness invariably leads to being much colder than if you had dressed just a bit more moderately in the first place.

Vested interests

Vests aren't just for lawyers and blackjack dealers anymore. Sleeveless — or should I say sleeve-free? — garments are becoming an increasingly popular insulation option, with good reason. Vests keep your torso toasty without restricting your arm movements the way a second layer of sleeve can. They're also a great spring skiing alternative when worn with a turtleneck or even just a base layer. Most vests are made of fleece and they make great basic insulation options. I also have a nylon vest filled with Primaloft insulation, which has become one of the most versatile items in my ski wardrobe. Worn under a shell, it's the ultimate weapon on those Arctic Express days. Worn over a fleece jacket, being windproof makes it ideal for those only slightly chilly days when there's no rain on the horizon. The only thing missing? A pocket watch pocket.

Courtesy Marmot

The Shell Layer

Think of the shell layer as protection. Your shell layer — ski jackets and ski pants — keeps at bay the wind, the snow, and anything else Mother Nature can throw at you. The outer layer makes up the bulk of your fashion statement. Outer layers can also cost as much as the rest of your ski wardrobe combined, which is why it's important to make smart buying decisions.

The materials

Most basic shell jackets — jackets without insulation — are made of some sort of nylon. Figure 4-3 shows a shell jacket. In most conditions, even relatively inexpensive nylon jackets do a pretty good job. They're both windproof and waterproof. The problem, of course, is that the same qualities that seal out the rain can also seal in sweat.

Figure 4-3:
A quality shell keeps the rain and wind out.

Courtesy Marmot

Waterproof-breathable fabrics — Gore-Tex and Entrant are two of the most popular — address this very real conundrum. They act much like a turnstile. They allow water vapor from the inside to exit basically unimpeded — *bye, bye, thanks for coming.* But when rain or snow tries to sneak in from the outside, they bar the door — *Ticket please? I'm sorry, then, you have to wait out here.* How do they do this? Well each manufacturer has its own secrets that it guards just about as closely as the recipe for Coca-Cola. But basically, waterproof-breathables use either a laminate or a coating to accomplish this cool and very important trick.

Pros

Waterproof-breathables keep you much drier when it's raining or snowing, and keep you much more comfortable when you're skiing hard.

Cons

They're more expensive — usually at least twice the price of a regular nylon shell jacket.

Now that you understand the theoretical aspects of this outermost of layers, let's get down to the nitty gritty and discuss individual garments and what to look for.

Jackets

How important is a ski jacket? A few seasons ago, I bought a new blue jacket after years of skiing with a brown one. For the first couple of days, my wife literally couldn't find me on the slopes. To her, I had become a brown Obermeyer parka.

While you may not have your identity intertwined quite so completely with your jacket, realize that it's probably the most important piece of ski clothing you can buy. Take home the right one, and you can be warm and stylin' for years. Take home the wrong one, and you could be a cold, wet nerd well into the next century.

The cut

When choosing a style, practical considerations abound. *Short jackets* may be racy, but if you fall and get snow in the gap between the bottom of your jacket and the top of your pants, the only place you'll be racing is to the base lodge to change your clothes. A *three-quarter length* jacket (refer to Figure 4-3) is really the most practical alternative. It offers more protection against the snow and cold sneaking in. Its shape is very flattering to real-world figures. It can also provide an extra layer of protection for your butt when you're riding a cold chairlift.

Sizing

When you're buying a shell jacket make sure it's big enough to fit a fleece or other insulation layer underneath. (If you've got a fleece already, bring it along. If not, get one from the store of the same size and weight you think you'll be using.) Not sure if it's big enough? Raise your arms over your head, snow angel style, and see if it binds.

Two more reasons it's better to buy too big than too small: On cold days, the warm air trapped by the shell helps the insulation layer do its job better, and the bigger the jacket, the more warm air it can trap. On warm days, the air circulation afforded by a looser cut allows the base layer to do its sweat evaporation thing with greater aplomb.

The features

Just like when you go car shopping, every jacket has its own combination of features. I highlight some of the ones that I find make my skiing life happier and more fulfilling.

Pockets

Like it or not, when you're skiing, you have plenty of junk to carry with you: your keys, your wallet, your sunglasses, your sunscreen, your lip balm, your Milky Way bar, and your copy of *The Peloponnesian Wars*. Naturally, you need a place to put all this stuff.

That's why you need a jacket with good pockets. What's a good pocket? A good pocket is big — everything fits without bulging like something out of *Alien* — but not too big — your keys won't play hide-and-go-seek at the bottom of a pocket that's deeper than the La Brea Tar Pits. A good pocket is also well-sealed with a zipper and a flap that's easy to use. To make sure that your pockets hold what you want them to hold, bring along a selection of ski essentials and try loading up any jacket you're considering.

Underarm zippers

Running from the middle of your bicep to the top of your ribcage by way of your underarms, these zippered vents help to regulate temperature, by allowing excess body heat to escape, without allowing a draft (or precipitation) in.

High collar

Think of your collar like a chimney. The warmth generated by your body tends to rise like a hot air balloon. A collar that cinches close around your neck keeps every single BTU inside during cold snaps. And on balmier days, it opens wide to allow you to get rid of some of that excess warmth. At the same time, a well-designed collar also keeps the rain, snow, and just about everything else out. Still, a collar should also be comfortable — so zip it up to see if it chafes your chin — fleece lining can be a Godsend.

Drawstring hood

Yes, a hat should take care of most of your head protection needs. But mountain weather is unpredictable. When a storm comes up suddenly — or even not so suddenly — a hood that rolls up into your collar can keep you as dry as a Charles Grodin monologue. Note, however, that ski jacket hoods are primarily to keep the elements out, not to keep you warm. That's what hats are for.

Adjustable cuffs

Same deal as with the collar. Cuffs with adjustable plackets and flaps with a hook-and-loop closure keep heat in and snow out when its cold, and allow you to cool off when the weather heats up.

A drawstring waist

This serves both a functional and an aesthetic role. A drawstring at the waist on a three-quarter length jacket helps to seal in heat and seal out the elements. If you cinch it strategically, it can also take ten pounds off your appearance.

Powder skirt

No, this is not what you wear to a formal ski function. If you think of the lower part of a three-quarter length jacket as a skirt, then the *powder skirt* is really a skirt within a skirt. It hangs down about six inches from the waist on the inside of the jacket, snaps in front, and is rimmed with elastic for a snug fit. It's especially useful if you ski a lot in deep snow, or if you fall a lot in shallow snow.

Easy-opening zippers

Good zippers are the hallmark of good skiwear. You want to see bi-directional sliders — in layperson's terms that means that it slides up as well as down — and good beefy pulls that you can open and close without taking off your gloves.

Pants

Pants come in two basic varieties: shell pants and stretch pants. *Shell pants* are the spiritual cousins of a shell jacket — they're made of nylon and generally feature a looser fit.

Stretch pants, which these days are generally a women-only option, are made of an elastic material that hugs your curves like a Porsche on a mountain road. Which is right for you? Shell pants are more functional and weatherproof. Stretch pants are sexier. You make the call.

Shell pant fit

Shell pants should give you plenty of room without feeling downright baggy. Do they fit like Levi 501s? Then they're too tight. You should be able to do a deep knee bend — and for that matter a whole range of lower body stretches — without worrying about whether you're going to pop a seam.

Shell pant features

Like electricity and a politician in an election year, snow follows the line of least resistance. As you may have guessed, the area of overlap between your jacket and your pants is crucial to keeping you warm and dry. Bib shell pants, which extend up in the front and the back, provide an extra line of defense in this crucial region. See Figure 4-4.

Figure 4-4:
Many guys like bib pants. Most women do not.

Courtesy Marmot

Most ski pants also don't have belt loops, so in lieu of your belt with the Taking-Care-of-Business buckle, you need something to hold your shell pants up. (If your stretch pants are sagging, you have major fit problems.) The suspenders on a pair of bib pants perform that function admirably as well. One caveat: Most guys find bibs pretty comfortable. Many women do not. I think we can chalk this one up to basic physiology.

Selecting stretch pants

The editors of *SKI* once suggested, in all seriousness, that stretch pants were one of skiing's great inventions, right up there with the releasable binding and the detachable quad chairlift.

However, getting the right pair is hardly a no-brainer. That's why I enlisted the help of Hollis Brooks, a nationally known fashion writer and former fashion editor at *Skiing*.

Here are her tips for getting the right pair of stretch pants:

Enlist Aid: Like watching *Fried Green Tomatoes* or eating Haagen Dazs ice cream, buying stretch pants isn't something you should do alone. First, find a salesperson, preferably a woman. She should be able to take one look at your figure and point you to a particular brand, and give you a ballpark of sizes to try. A friend — a truly honest friend without a catty bone in her body — can also lend support and counsel at this crucial time.

Be Prepared: Sizing stretch pants is a little like working on the bomb squad. There's not much room for error. So what can you do to stack the odds in your favor? First, remember to bring a pair of base layer bottoms — a pair of long underwear can make the difference in a marginal fit. Bring your ski boots, too, so

you can see how they fit at the cuff. Make sure to check the fit in a three-way mirror, or better yet enlist that friend. Most faux pas occur where you can't see them.

Sweat the Cuffs: A salesperson may tell you there are two cuff options — in the boot and over the boot. Your fashion consultant will tell you there's only one. "In-the-boot stretch pants scream 'ski bunny'," says Our Ms. Brooks. The bellbottom pant that zips over the boot is a perennial classic — think Princess Grace, think Audrey Hepburn — and something you can be proud to wear for as long as you can fit into it.

Go Classic: Part of the reason that you wear stretch pants is because they make you look slimmer — the stretch fabric is like control top panty hose on steroids. But your color choice can determine whether you look as skinny as you feel. Black is the most obvious choice, according to Hollis, followed by dark shades of navy, brown, or gray. Lavender stretch pants are not only scary, they're far from flattering. Going with a neutral also helps you get extra mileage out of them, on and off the slopes. Brooks often pairs her dark stretch pants with a sweater and wears them to dinner, a feat you'd dare not attempt with a pair of shell pants, not to mention chartreuse stretchies.

Side zips

Running from hip to ankle, the full-length zippers found on many shell pants are useful for everything from adjusting a knee brace without removing your boots to, um, using the facilities. Stretch pant fans have to be content with shorter zips that run from ankle to mid calf and allow you to adjust your boot buckles and power straps.

Pockets

While your jacket should be your primary gear storage area, a pocket in your pants can come in handy for stashing keys, a credit card, or even a wallet, an important security factor if you plan to be shedding layers or changing jackets during the course of the day.

Lift ticket loops

Smart skiers hook their lift tickets on their pants, so they can shed upper layers with impunity if — I mean, when — the weather changes. A little loop for this purpose is much more elegant than clipping your ticket wicket on your zipper.

Padded knees

My favorite ski pants have removable knee pads. It's a great feature if you plan to wear your ski pants for snowboarding — riders spend a fair amount of time on their knees, and as an added bonus, the pads tend to keep those precious knee ligaments warm as well.

One-piece suits

Just ask an astronaut. One-piece suits, shown in the accompanying figure, are eminently practical. On the slopes, they're much warmer than a comparable pants and jacket outfit — I often wear mine in mid-winter with just a base layer underneath. You don't have to worry about deep snow infiltrating your outfit — that's why they're often called powder suits. One-pieces are also sleek and stylish. Find the right one, and you'll look like you lost 10 pounds.

But as with everything in life, there are trade-offs. If you have a less than perfectly proportioned body, it's sometimes hard, or certainly harder, to find a one-piece snow suit that fits. That's especially true for women. The top fits, the bottoms are too tight. The bottoms fit and the top is too loose. The tops and bottoms both fit, but the sleeves and cuffs are too long. And most ski shops don't do alterations.

You do lose some measure of dressing flexibility with a one piece. For example you have to pack an extra coat to wear when you're going to dinner. After years of doing the jacket and pants

thing, I was a bit skeptical about one-pieces. Then I found a Gore-Tex powder suit at a price I couldn't resist and I took the plunge. It took only one day of suddenly streamlined skiing, and I was a convert. You may be one, too.

Courtesy Sport Obermeyer, Ltd.

Ankle skirts

Like a powder skirt for a shell pant, these inner liners attach tightly around the cuff of your boot, keeping snow where it should be — outside.

Caring for Your Skiwear

Because it's made from some pretty high-tech fabrics, you should probably think twice about just tossing your skiwear into the wash with the dish towels and your Jockeys. The first line of defense is to read the hangtags and labels that come with your skiwear. However, here are a few rules for skiwear care, including *how often* you should wash your skiwear.

Jackets and pants

You should wash your shell as infrequently as you can get away with it. Every time you wash it, you compromise the waterproofness a little. So once a season is plenty for most skiers, and even hardcores can get away with two visits to the Maytag per season.

Use only powdered detergents. Why? Because the manufacturers say so, that's why. After you finish washing your skiwear, put the shell in the dryer on the medium setting — the heat actually tends to reactivate the water resistance. At the same time, if you have a shell that doesn't shed water like it used to, a quick post-wash pass with a warm iron often makes it work like new.

Fleeces

One of the nice things about fleece is that it's pretty much stainproof. If you spill coffee on your fleece, a quick dab with a wet napkin is all it takes to clean it up. Plan to wash your fleece a few times a season.

Just toss your fleece in the washer — warm temperature, medium cycle — and pre-soak for any stubborn stains. (Windproof fleece may need special care, such as using powdered detergent, so consult the tags.) You can throw a fleece in the dryer, but since they don't absorb water, just shaking it out and hanging it up works just as well, and bypasses the lint problem if you — horror of horrors — mixed light and dark colors.

Base layers

You should wash your base layers immediately after every wearing. Aside from the simple question of hygiene, the polyester base layers retain odors, and by the second day you can end up smelling like a judge at the Limburger Festival.

Throw your base layers into the washer. They can sometimes shrink in the dryer, so just yank them out and hang them up. Since they're designed not to absorb moisture, base layers dry very quickly, just the thing for a midweek hotel room sink wring-out.

Finding Your Style

Now you know how to buy skiwear that helps you stay warm, dry, and comfortable. But how about looking great? Any fashion designer may tell you that dressing well is dressing up — as in Halloween. Decide who you want to be, what vibe you want to project, and you're halfway there. I help you by outlining some of the basic looks that dominate the slopes these days. Keep in mind that these are extremes — fashion caricatures if you will — so feel free to mix and match, albeit with some caution. The fashion police, after all, are on patrol.

Backcountry chic

In an age where you're as likely to see an Expedition-grade down parka on the New York City Subway as on Mount Everest, it's no surprise that the mountaineering/backcountry aesthetic has taken root in ski land. See Figure 4-5. The black shoulders, the utilitarian fit, and the technical features — pit zips — are dead giveaways. But style aside, these are function-first garments designed to handle even the worst elements and afford maximum freedom of movement.

The statement: I'm capable. I'm adventurous. I'm an *Outside* subscriber.

The accessories: Duct tape and an avalanche transceiver.

The companies: Marmot, The North Face, and Mountain Hardware.

Figure 4-5:
The back-country look turns high function into high fashion.

Racer chic

Tight and bright, that's what passes for chic on the racecourse. They don't call it the Alpine Circus for nothing. Of course there's a practical reason for this — bright colors show up better on television cameras, and form-fitting clothes are more aerodynamic, and thus marginally faster. But if you're not wearing a number, race-inspired clothes are the on-snow equivalent of driving a Dodge Viper with a racing stripe down the middle. They call attention to you — and by extension your skiing. If you ski like Alberto Tomba, that's great. If not . . . well . . . maybe you should consider another look.

> **The statement:** I have experienced the thrill of victory . . . and the agony of defeat.
>
> **The accessories:** A stopwatch and a vial of Cera F ski wax.
>
> **The companies:** Spyder, Phoenix, and Descente.

Neo-Retro

There was a time when skiers set the fashion trends — about the time that Robert Redford starred in *Downhill Racer*. The look was sleek, with racy striped sweaters and form-fitting silhouettes. This style was nothing if not sexy. Ironically, it took snowboarders, no doubt rummaging through their parents' attics, to rediscover the rightness of this look. Soon skiwear manufacturers jumped on the bandwagon and began adopting their old patterns and making old-is-new-again garments. See Figure 4-6.

> **The statement:** I appreciate the classics. Is that your copy of *Seasons in the Sun?*

> **The accessories:** A pair of white sunglasses and an MIA bracelet.

> **The companies:** Sessions, Bombshell, and Sport Obermeyer.

Figure 4-6:
Blocky stripes make a retro fashion statement.

Courtesy Sport Obermeyer, Ltd.

Post grunge

Skiers have traditionally stayed on the perky side of the color palette. Any deviation from primaries is toward the occasional pastel and the unfortunate neon. But in the early '90s, snowboarders brought subdued hues to the slopes, and they've earned a permanent place in the color pantheon. Browns, blacks, and muted plaids linked to an oversized silhouette are typical of this style.

Getting the most for your money

Good ski clothes aren't cheap. A quality waterproof-breathable jacket can retail for over $400 and a pair of good shell pants for maybe two-thirds of that. It's definitely not pocket change.

Here are some guidelines for getting the most for your money and avoiding buyer's regret:

✔ **Choose colors carefully:** The idea here is to focus on colors that will look good four years down the road and blend easily with the things you have or may add somewhere down the line. Think mix-and-match colors, like black, which should be your first choice for pants. For jackets, primaries — like red and royal blue — are perennial good bets as are jewel tones like emerald green. Deep tones don't show dirt or stains as readily, which can also contribute to a garment's longevity. Still feel the itch to brighten things up? Save your experimentation for your accessories (see Chapter 5 for more about add-ons).

✔ **Go for enduring silhouettes:** Go for garments that won't look out of style by next season. Three-quarter length jackets, with a flattering, moderately fitted shape are likely to look as fresh in three years as they do today. They're the little black dress of the ski world.

✔ **Look for dual duty:** No matter how many days a year you ski, if you stick to one hemisphere, you spend more days off the snow than on. So when you're picking out a jacket, consider how it may work the rest of the year. Could you wear this to work? Would you wear it for a run to the grocery story on a stormy day? The same is true with fleece pieces, which make perfect three-season pull-ons, and base layers, which are ideal for running or cycling in cold weather.

✔ **Buy quality:** Getting a garment that really works — one that's going to keep you warm and dry, and makes you look like you stepped out of a fashion shoot — is worth whatever you pay for it. Expensive garments are expensive for a reason; they use better fabrics, which not only feel better and look nicer but also perform better. They use better *findings* — snaps, zippers, and hooks — little things that may not mean much now, but can send an otherwise perfectly good jacket to the clothing drive when they break. And good design, which contributes to a garment working well in addition to looking great, costs money, too.

The statement: You can take the skier out of the city, but you can't take the city out of the skier.

The accessories: A Morphine CD and a copy of *Raygun*.

The companies: Napapijri Geographic, Nike ACG, and Kaotic.

High style

For some, it's only a short step from the runway to the slope. Skiing has its own haute coture, but for the most part the vibe is conservative — think Georgio Armani, not Jean-Paul Gaultier. These garments exude a luxury-car feel, with rich materials and findings — and prices to match.

The statement: Daddy's an oilman.

The accessories: A cell phone, a Cartier tank watch, and a platinum card.

The companies: Bogner, Prada, and Polo Sport.

Don't Be a Fashion Victim

Does the phrase "What *was* I thinking?" mean anything to you? You need only look at a ski magazine that's a couple of seasons old to figure out that certain things just don't age well. Well, I'm here to help you avoid these fashion faux pas.

- ✔ **Neons:** If a color isn't found in nature — not even on a tropical bird — then leave it to the road crew.

- ✔ **Fur trim:** Forget what your friends at PETA may say. Fur makes you look like Ivana Trump.

- ✔ **Leather:** It looks great, yes. But while cows are waterproof, leather isn't, and on the slopes distressed leather is simply distressing.

- ✔ **Skin-tight fit:** Can you absolutely positively guarantee that you won't be four pounds heavier next winter? I didn't think so.

Rent-a-parka

Now that you know everything you need to know about buying ski clothes, I have to tell you one more thing: You don't have to. An emerging trend in the ski business is, believe it or not, rental skiwear. Rentals come in two different varieties.

Basic rentals are simple, straightforward garments aimed at folks who live in Florida and never need a jacket off the slopes or someone who's in the area on business and wants to spend a day skiing on the spur of the moment.

The other option is more intriguing. In Aspen, one enterprising soul is pioneering rentals for the style-conscious. A van parked right by the mountain sets you up with very cool vintage skiwear in mint condition — shag haircut, optional.

Chapter 5

Accessorizing, Alpine Style

• •

In This Chapter

▶ Pursuing the perfect glove

▶ Eyeing the right glasses and goggles

▶ Staying warm with the right hat

▶ Carrying it all with bags and racks

• •

$\mathbf{1}$n the fashion world, accessories make the outfit. The Hermes scarf. The Persol sunglasses. The freeze-dried piranha necklace. Accessories make the outfit on the slopes, as well. They might not make your friends ooh and ahh, but they can make your day better all the same. For years, the Thomas Edisons of the alpine world have been trying to find better ways. And unlike skis, boots, or parkas, they don't need a three-figure price tag to keep you warm and dry, keep your vision clear, and help you haul all the stuff you need.

In this chapter I tell you why all accessories are not created equal. I cover finding the right hat, gloves, and even socks. I give you the big-picture view of goggles and sunglasses, clue you in about a few indispensable items that you may never have thought of, and discuss bags and racks to hold it all. I end the chapter with a rundown of a few things you *don't* need — besides the piranha necklace.

Living a Glove Story

I'm very particular about my ski gloves, and you should be, too. A good pair of ski gloves is just about the most important accessory you can buy. It isn't hard to find a pair of gloves that keep you warm. A $10 pair from a department store does just fine, and if they have a nylon shell, they do a reasonable job of keeping you dry as well.

A well-designed, well-constructed pair of gloves, however, is a special joy. The insulation is soft and the leather or grippy rubber on the palm is pliable. The shell moves *with* your hands instead of against them, making everything from pole plants to buckling your boots easier. And they fit like, well, a glove. Here are some different kinds of gloves and what they are best for:

✔ **Insulated nylon gloves:** These workhorse gloves work pretty much like the filled garments I discuss in Chapter 4. These gloves have a nylon or polyester shell, a layer of insulation, and a plush liner next to your skin.

As to the exact construction, people have different preferences. I prefer soft, loosely filled gloves with down-like fill such as Primaloft. These gloves are a little like a down comforter for your hands. Others prefer the less cushy but more precise feel of a thinner insulation such as Outlast. Take special note of the leather or faux leather on the palms. If it's stiff, it can ruin the feel of an otherwise fine glove.

✔ **Component style gloves:** One of the hotter trends in gloves is the component glove. The glove within a glove concept — a fleece inner glove zips into an insulated outer shell, either of which can be worn separately — is an extension of the layering concept. While some skiers swear by these, I'm a little more skeptical.

My problem with component gloves is fit. To fit together properly, the outer glove needs to be slightly oversized so that the inner liner fits inside. Although you may get the theoretical equivalent of three gloves, it's likely that at least two of them aren't going to fit very well. A better alternative for especially cold hands is a pair of paper-thin synthetic or silk glove liners under regular gloves. As for versatility, I prefer to go skiing equipped with an arsenal of gloves.

✔ **Mountaineering style gloves:** The guys who climb Mt. Everest have learned a few things about how gloves work. Manufacturers are taking that knowledge and incorporating it into ski gloves. Gauntlet-style gloves, with skirts that cinch around your jacket cuffs, can help to keep the snow out of your sleeves. *Idiot cords*, not dissimilar to the ones attached to your mittens when you were four, wrap around your wrists and allow you to dangle your gloves off your wrists while you're zipping up your jacket or re-buckling your boots. Why the name? Because dropping a glove off a 2,000-foot ridge — or even a chairlift — can make you feel like an idiot.

✔ **Mittens:** If you're especially prone to cold hands, you may consider a pair of finger-free gloves. You give up a little dexterity, but you more than make up for it in added warmth. And because snowboarders, who don't have to worry about holding poles, have given mittens a little new-school cachet, you don't have to sacrifice looking cool for staying warm.

✔ **Spring gloves:** Sometimes winter gloves are just too warm. Those are the times when you need a pair of spring gloves. Spring gloves are mostly leather with fleece or stretch nylon on the back, and no insulation. Think of them as golf gloves weatherprooofed and ruggedized for on-snow use. A recent variation in spring gloves is the all-fleece glove. Often made of wind-resistant fleece, they're soft and cozy, if not particularly waterproof.

A good pair of spring gloves is also very comfortable. How comfortable? For a while, my favorite pair of gloves was a pair of fleece-backed spring gloves, and for a couple of seasons I wore them all day, every day, through even the coldest days.

SKI TIP

I always pack at least three pair of gloves on any ski trip, and I suggest that you do likewise. I carry:

✔ A good pair of insulated gloves or mittens as my primary handwear.

✔ A pair of spring gloves in case the weather gets warm.

✔ A not-so-good pair. This beat-up pair is your scrape-the-windshield/throw-a-snowball/carry-firewood-into-the-condo pair. The beat-up pair is also your change-into pair, in case that first pair gets wet. They may get dirty, they may get ripped, and losing them is a distinct possibility, but you should throw them into your ski bag, just in case.

Treating Your Feet

Find me a pair of happy feet, and I'll show you a happy skier. If your feet are warm, dry, and unblistered, your odds of having a great day increase exponentially. Even the most epic day can be ruined by a pair of dogs that are yapping back at you. In this section, I discuss some of the ways you can be nice to your feet so they'll do likewise to you.

The myth of the waterproof glove

Check out the hangtags in the glove section of a ski shop, and you may read lots of claims about waterproofness, water resistance, and breathability. I suggest that you take those claims with a grain of salt. Some of the fabrics and inserts in these gloves are indeed waterproof and breathable. The problem is in the seams. Unlike a jacket, a glove is full of seams. It's just about impossible to waterproof all these seams thoroughly and still allow for any dexterity in the glove.

If you want truly waterproof gloves, you have to do what my friend Mary did during a particularly rainy winter of teaching in the Poconos. She went to an outdoor store and bought a pair of big, florescent orange, rubber deer-gutting gloves. She took a lot of ribbing about air traffic control and downed power lines that season, but she was the only one with dry hands after an hour-long beginner lesson in a downpour.

Sock it to yourself

If gloves are the most important skiing accessory, then socks are a close second. Good socks mean warm, dry feet and good-fitting boots. Putting on a pair of argyles or your Kobe Bryant sweat socks just won't cut it. Nearly all ski socks (shown in Figure 5-1) are made of synthetics or wool, or some combination. These two materials, like any good base layer (see Chapter 4 for info on layers), wick moisture away from your feet.

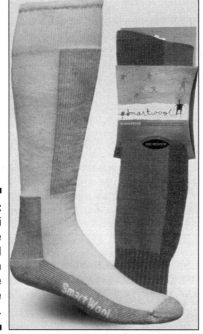

Figure 5-1:
Good ski socks have a contoured fit and thin pads at the pressure points.

Courtesy of SmartWool

A more subjective criteria is thickness. I believe in thin socks — very thin. Thinner than a supermodel. Thinner than a Patsy D'Angelo's pizza. When someone invents paint-on socks, I may be the first in line to try them. Why do I like thin socks? Because thin socks help me to get a better boot fit. I find that wearing cushy socks in ski boots is like trying to wear penny loafers with sweat socks — it makes them tight and uncomfortable.

Other folks, who don't have the same kind of boot-fitting problems that I have, actually like somewhat thicker socks, and that's fine. But you should understand one thing: Thicker socks don't keep you warmer. Warmth is mostly a function of the insulation in the boot liner.

No matter what you decide, remember that it's one sock per foot, please. If anyone suggests wearing two pair of socks, politely ignore them. Wearing two pair of socks is an old-husband's tale from back in the days when boots were made of leather and had no insulation at all. If you try to wear two pair with a modern boot, you only end up with a sloppy fit, cold feet due to reduced circulation, and maybe even a couple of blisters.

Here's what you should look for in a good pair of socks:

- ✔ **A contoured fit:** Tube socks don't work inside ski boots. You want a pair of socks shaped like your foot. Ski socks do come in different sizes, so make sure you get a pair that fits. A pair that's too big will only bunch up inside your boot and cause irritation.

- ✔ **Flat seams:** Bulky seams and ski boots just don't mix. If the seams aren't flat, they could rub against your foot inside your boot and cause blisters.

- ✔ **Great height:** Ski socks have to extend at least beyond the top of your boots. I find that the over-the-calf styles are the most comfortable and less likely to slide down.

- ✔ **Reinforced pressure points:** My favorite socks have a series of thin pads — areas of extra-thick fabric — at some strategic points: the toe, the heel, and the shin.

Remember, you need a clean pair of socks for every day you ski, so plan to take at least five pairs for a week-long trip.

Throwing heat: Boot heaters

In my experience, the number one complaint in skiing — more than long lift lines, more than mystery chili in the cafeteria — is cold feet. It's hard to be happy when your feet feel like icicles. Reduced circulation, usually resulting from bad bootfitting, is the number one cause of cold feet. If you have chronic cold feet, your first stop should be the bootfitter. (See Chapter 2.)

If seeing the bootfitter doesn't solve the problem completely, you may need a pair of boot heaters. Boot heaters are after-market items that consist of a heating element that a ski shop installs in your insole. A rechargeable battery that attaches to your boot cuff powers the heater. You can turn on the heaters when you need a blast of warmth — on the chairlift for example — and then turn them off to conserve battery power. Newer models with improved batteries last up to eight hours, and some models can even regulate temperature automatically. Boot warmers are not exactly cheap — $100 and up — but if your feet are perpetually frozen, they're worth it.

If your hands and feet get cold only sometimes, here's a budget alternative for frigid days: a disposable heat pack. It's a small plastic pouch containing two chemicals. When you squeeze the pouch, the chemicals combine and start to heat up. You can put heat packs in your gloves or in your boots to warm up your toes. Disposable heat packs are cheap, easy to carry, available at any ski shop, and do the job.

Boot dryers

Back at the ski house I used to rent, there was one thing that was even better than eating the last of the guacamole. It was even better than getting the room with the door on it. It was even better than seizing the remote control. And that was having the boot dryer — which meant warm, dry boots first thing in the morning.

While six grown-ups used to fight, cajole, and barter over a device that looked like a good hair dryer gone bad, things have changed. Now you can get a boot dryer of your own. Better yet, it's cheap, and it fits into your own boot bag. The one I use has two electrically heated wands, each about five inches long, attached to an AC cord. Just slip the dryers into your boots when you're done for the day, and by morning your boots are not only dry, they're toasty warm.

Using Your Head

Want to be a smart skier? Then pay attention to your head. Keep it warm and dry with a good hat. Protect it with a helmet. And get some goggles and glasses to help you see better. Do this and you'll go straight to the head of the class.

Capping it off: Finding the right ski hats

Your mother was right. Most of your body heat does escape from your head, so buying some good hats is the best investment you can make in toasty skiing.

Notice the plural in the previous sentence. Owning a ski hat is kind of a no-brainer. But having just the right hat for the right occasion can make or break your day. What makes a good hat? Certain common threads run through all truly worthy headgear.

✔ A good hat doesn't itch.

✔ A good hat is neither too tight nor too loose.

✔ A good hat doesn't make you feel like a dork when you're wearing it.

Here are the categories you should consider as you fill your hat quiver.

✔ **Cold-weather hats:** On a really cold day, your noggin needs all the help you can give it. Look for tightly woven wool — preferably with a fleece liner — and maybe even earflaps. Tassels and pom poms are optional.

✔ **Warm-weather hats:** I feel this way a lot. The day is moderately warm and sunny — too warm to bring out a really heavy, warm hat. But it's too chilly to go bareheaded or even to wear a baseball cap, which is why I carry a selection of lightweight hats. Two of my favorites are a thin, knit cap with a light fleece band that's pretty similar to what cross-country ski racers wear, and a plain, lightweight fleece hat that takes advantage of the wind-porous properties of fleece for impromptu ventilation.

✔ **Foul-weather hats:** My wife, Sally, has a bright blue hat with a brim and earflaps that tie at the top when they're not in use. Picture Elmer Fudd on skis and you get the basic idea ("Get offa that chairwift you scwewy wabbit!"). I affectionately call it "The Stupid Hat." When it's raining or snowing, it becomes "The Smart Hat" — and I wish I had one, too.

✔ Baseball caps: These hats are perfect for spring skiing and indispensable for the rain or snow (provided that you get a hat leash; see the following sidebar). Because baseball caps have become the bumper stickers of the '90s, what should your baseball cap say? Wearing a *Skiing* magazine cap is fine. Wearing a cap from your brand of skis is okay. Wearing, say, a Japanese league baseball cap — the Hiroshima Carp — is beyond cool. Wearing a cap from the last ski area you visited — or the one you're visiting now — is definitely not cool.

✔ **Headbands:** Their moms notwithstanding, some folks just won't wear a hat. For them, a fleece or woolen headband is the cold day alternative. While the look is a little, well, '80s, a headband does provide an absolute defense against hat head.

Keep your hat on

The laws of aerodynamics being what they are, if you try to wear a baseball cap while you're skiing, the wind will eventually blow it off. Then you have to stop and hike back up the hill, while everyone on the chairlift is staring at you. Not fun. That is why you should get a hat leash — a short piece of nylon cord with two clips, one that attaches to your hat, the other that attaches to your collar. It's well worth the three bucks.

Bundling up: Neck warmers

On those really cold days, there's nothing better than a neck warmer — a soft, stand-alone fleece collar that you wear around your neck as sort of a turtleneck on steroids. It keeps your neck toasty, and can be pulled up over your cheeks on particularly frigid chairlift rides. A must-have accessory.

Women should be especially vigilant about keeping a neck warmer, because it can not only keep you warm, it'll save you money. My friend, ski fashion writer Hollis Brooks, explains: "How do you keep makeup off the collar of your jacket? Wear a neck warmer." And when it gets dirty? Turn it inside out and no one will be the wiser. All things considered, it's a lot easier than tossing your jacket in the washer because of a couple of lipstick smudges. Or buying a new one because the smudges won't come out.

Protecting yourself with a helmet

Are you a racer? Are you under the age of six? If you answered no to both questions, then only a couple of years ago wearing a ski helmet wouldn't have even been an issue. The few helmets on the market were for kids or racers. But over the past few seasons, growing awareness about head injuries — fueled with the high-profile deaths of Michael Kennedy and Sonny Bono — coupled with improved products have made ski helmets a viable option for skiers of all ages.

The question of whether skiing is a helmet sport is a tricky one — one I explore in more detail in Chapter 10. Some experts claim that helmet use would prevent many serious head injuries. Other experts claim that helmets would only help in a small percentage of accidents. Ultimately the risk analysis is up to you.

But if you decide to go the helmet route, today's helmets are better than ever. As demand has increased, helmets have gotten lighter, sleeker, and more comfortable. And unlike, say bicycling, where ventilation is a problem in warm weather, most skiers welcome the additional warmth that a helmet provides. In terms of protection, ski helmets aren't yet tested the way that bicycle helmets are, but a new standard by the American Society for Testing and Materials (ASTM) is bound to change that.

Goggles

For a long time I resisted wearing goggles. I was a sunglasses guy, and no matter what the weather or where I was skiing, I just whipped out shades. Until one day, my editors at *Skiing* enlisted me to test some goggles. I grumped a little at first, but after that initial adjustment period, I came back with a renewed appreciation for goggles and what they can do.

Goggles offer a wide field of vision and much better visibility in flat light conditions. Figure 5-2 shows a typical pair of goggles. Goggles protect your eyes from the air rushing past, an important bonus at higher speeds, and keep your face warm when it's cold. They also look kind of cool. Now I guess I'm a goggle guy. Here are some things to remember when buying goggles.

Seeing clearly

A goggle that makes your vision worse is no bargain. Optical quality is the most important feature of a goggle. The lens should be as distortion free as a good pair of sunglasses, both when you hold it up and when you try it on. While your main focus should be on the center of the lens, pay some attention to the edges, too.

Talking tints

In the sunglass world, darker is better — but goggles aren't sunglasses. Your primary pair of goggles should have a relatively lightly tinted lens — one designed to bring out the terrain in flat or low light. A yellow, amber, or rose lens is best.

The lens is the most expensive part of the goggle and much more easily scratched than sunglasses are. To keep from damaging your lens, store it in the cloth slipcase that it came with, or, if you're so inclined, use one of those little velvet bags from Crown Royal.

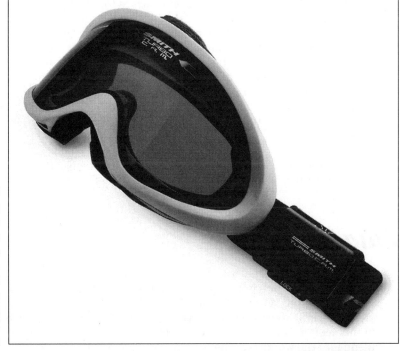

Figure 5-2: Some goggles feature battery-powered fans to prevent fogging.

Courtesy Smith Sport Optics, Inc.

Fighting fog

The biggest problem with goggles is fogging. Given the fact that it's below freezing outside, and your face is (hopefully) far above freezing, this is not an easy battle to win. Manufacturers have fought it on many different fronts. Double-layer lenses — the Alpine equivalent of thermo-pane windows — can help, but they can introduce distortions that their single lens counterparts do not. Some goggle makers employ coatings to keep the fog at bay. Still others take a cue from your car, and defog the lens as if it were a windshield — with a stream of air. This can be done passively by enlarging the vents on the frame, or actively with (no, this is not a joke) a small battery-powered fan. Then again, you could just wipe them with a tissue.

Fitting right

Faces come in all different sizes and shapes. But unlike ski pants, goggles don't come in S-M-L and XL. So if you want a goggle that won't smush your nose or pinch your ears, try it before you buy it. And if you wear prescription glasses or a helmet, remember to try your goggles on with them before you plunk down your plastic.

Sunglasses

Sunglasses are another place where form and function sometimes run at cross purposes. In reality, a pair of sunglasses for skiing is really just a goggle substitute. Those cool low-profile shades that are great for strolling down the street sometimes don't cut it when you're cruising at 20 mph down the slope. When picking a style, ask yourself this question: Would I wear this riding a bike? If the answer is yes, then it should be fine for skiing too. Tint-wise, a moderately dark neutral lens makes a great sunny-day complement to your goggles. While you're at it, buy a sunglass cord. It not only keeps you from having to search for your glasses if they come off in a fall, you're less likely to leave them on a cafeteria tray if you can just drape them around your neck instead.

Remember to look for a lens with UV protection. The combination of high altitude and sun reflecting off the snow make the slopes a harsh environment for your eyes.

Hauling Your Stuff

A ski bag is a little like a baseball umpire. Whether it's a ski bag for transporting your boards, or a boot bag that carries the rest of your miscellany, you only notice a bag when it doesn't do its job. When a zipper breaks. When a strap digs into your shoulder. When your wet clothes soak your dry clothes. In this section you find a few tips for buying boot bags and ski bags that will blend into the woodwork the way they're supposed to.

You also need a way to transport your skis to the slopes when driving. Sure, you can stuff them inside your car, but by doing so you expose yourself to a whole host of potential problems. Your best bet is to buy some sort of rack. Later in this section I explain why you need a rack and how to buy one.

Boot bags

What's an accessory? Everything that fits in your boot bag. What, you don't have a boot bag? Read on.

At its most basic level, your boot bag is — you guessed it — a bag to carry your boots in. On the other hand, it's really the on-snow equivalent of your favorite purse or your best briefcase. It's the place where you put all your, well, *stuff.*

When you're looking for a boot bag, you have to strike a balance between finding one that can hold everything you need and one small enough to carry without giving yourself a slipped disc. Traveling by plane complicates matters even more, because you absolutely, positively want to carry your boots on board with you. Why? Because airlines sometimes lose checked baggage. Which means the bag has to fit in the overhead luggage compartment or under the seat in front of you. (For more about flying, see Chapter 16.)

Here are a few other features that every good bag should have:

- ✔ A comfortable shoulder strap
- ✔ A separate compartment for wet clothes
- ✔ At least one small, zippered pocket for small items
- ✔ Bi-directional zippers for easy closing

Boot bags take more abuse than a troop of mimes, so look for rugged construction. Inspect a boot bag the way you would for a backpack: Look for durable, heavyweight fabric; sturdy zippers; and overbuilt seams. Strong seams are not only nice but also necessary. A cheap boot bag that splits a seam while you're in the airport is no bargain.

Ski bags

Ever plan to carry your skis on an airplane? Well, you can't. You have to hand them over to the baggage handlers, which is why you need a ski bag. A ski bag doesn't have to be fancy — it's essentially just a big nylon sleeve with a zipper.

Murphy's Law of Accessories

Skiers say about accessories what frat boys say about beer: You don't really buy them, you just rent them for a while. It's hard to lose a pair of skis or a jacket, but if you don't believe that holding onto a pair of gloves is like trying to hold onto water with your fingers, you should go to the lost and found of a large ski area. Dozens of goggles, glasses, and gloves wait patiently alongside the odd prosthetic limb. (Yes, someone lost one of those, too.) While there are a few measures you can take to prevent losing your stuff — sunglass cords and glove leashes, for example — mostly I'm just trying to increase your awareness. When your favorite glasses go the way of Judge Crater, adopt a little Zen-like detachment. And if you're going on a trip, tossing an extra pair of gloves or glasses into your bag is cheap insurance.

If you and your significant other both ski, it might make sense to buy a double ski bag, which — you guessed it — can carry two pairs of skis. Ski bags are an utterly annoying piece of luggage, and it's often easier to struggle with only one instead of two, even if that one is twice as heavy.

Make sure the bag doesn't fit too tight because it's smart to pack some clothes around your skis for additional protection. Make sure your ski bag has a comfortable strap for easy hauling.

Racking 'em up

You don't have to be a rocket scientist to understand that most folks don't schlep their skis to the mountain on the subway. Virtually every skier gets to the mountain in one of two ways: using either their car or someone else's car. While many folks try and cram skis inside the car, there are a couple of reasons why this isn't a good idea.

- ✔ A ski edge can do bad things to your rich Corinthian leather upholstery.
- ✔ More importantly, the skis that lie there so blithely while you're cruising down the highway can become a dangerous, and even deadly, projectile in the event of an accident. So get 'em outta there.

If you can't transport your skis in your car, where should you put them? The roof, of course. Roof racks come in two basic varieties: dedicated and component.

Dedicated ski racks

Dedicated racks do one thing and one thing only: carry skis. The rack clips onto the rain gutters or around the door frame of your car and has either vertical ski carriers (which tilt your skis up on edge as they're being transported) or scissors ski carriers (which hold the skis — or a snowboard — flat). Dedicated racks have their advantages. They're relatively cheap, usually pre-assembled, and usually can be taken on and off the car in a hurry.

Component racks

Made by companies like Thule and Yakima, component racks up the ante. Consisting of towers, clips, and crossbars designed especially for your car, component racks can also, with some additional accessories, carry any number of your other toys along with, or instead of, your skis. You can carry bikes, kayaks, a sailboat, sofa, Christmas tree, or a couple of sheets of plywood. These racks are a little more expensive, and you may have to invest an hour initially attaching it to your car, but in the long run they're more versatile. (See Figure 5-3.)

Figure 5-3:
Component racks can carry your skis and a whole lot more.

Courtesy of Yakima

Rack locks

The good news: It's easy to lock your skis to your rack and your rack to your car. The bad news: It's necessary, too. Most dedicated racks have built-in locks, while component racks allow you to add on a set of matched lock cores for each of the towers and the racks, so you can use a single key for all your carriers. Smart skiers use those locks. It's not uncommon for thieves to steal unlocked skis off a car in the parking lot of a ski country rest stop or restaurant. Unfortunately, a lock won't always stop a determined thief. A few years ago, I had my ski-less, but locked, component rack stolen right off the roof of my car, in broad daylight, in a ski shop parking lot only a few yards from a major highway.

Locking 'em down at the lodge

In general the slopes are populated by honest, law-abiding citizens. That's why most skiers leave their skis unlocked on racks outside the lodge while they go in for lunch or hot cocoa, and come back to find the skis right where they left them. But just as in every barrel there are a few bad apples, every resort has a few snowsliders with larceny in their hearts, perhaps even one looking for a five-finger discount on a pair of skis . . . just like *yours*.

Fortunately, most ski thieves aren't very organized — you don't see too many bolt cutters stuffed under ski jackets — and act mostly on impulse.

A small, retractable combination lock that loops around your ski brake and the ski rack is enough to deter most thieves, maybe because most other skis on the rack are unlocked.

When racking skis, always point the tips to the rear. Putting the tips in front

✔ Increases aerodynamic drag, reducing fuel mileage slightly

✔ Creates a lot more wind noise

✔ Actually wears your skis out — the wind vibrates the tips, and one long highway trip can be the equivalent of hundreds of runs.

So despite your instincts to the contrary, keep your *tails* pointed in the direction you're traveling. At least while you're driving.

Things You Don't Need

Maybe it's a product of summertime ski withdrawal, but there are more silly ski inventions than for any other sport. Take the Ski Stander — a magnetic clip that sticks to your fender, allowing you to lean your skis against the car without fear of scratching the paint. Corvette owners need not apply. My favorite is the See-ski. It's two small mirrors that attach to the tips of your skis and address the immortal question: What do I look like when I'm skiing? The answer: A dork staring at the tips of his skis.

Here are a few other gadgets that aren't quite as ridiculous but that you can still safely pass up:

✔ **Ski protection tape:** Yes, your skis will get scratched, scraped, and otherwise cosmetically damaged. That's life. But ski protection tape will dull the finish on your skis almost immediately. Ski protection tape can also start fraying at the ends, causing a different kind of cosmetic disaster. My philosophy: If you're skiing fast enough, no one can see what your skis look like.

✔ **Ski carriers:** Your poles clip on one side. Your skis clip on the other. Then you've got a handle for carrying and a lock for, well, locking. While carrying skis can be a bit of a burden, it's easier to learn how to carry your skis properly — I address that in Chapter 8 — than to just add one more piece of gear to the jumble.

✔ **Boot treads:** These are treaded rubber soles that attach to the bottom of your boots. They do make walking easier and protect the bottom of your boots from wear, but I found them too much of a pain to put on and too easy to lose. On the other hand, I have seen members of the U.S. Ski Team wearing them, so I'm not dismissing them entirely.

✔ **The POV helmet:** This helmet has a mount for a digital video camera, giving you a point-of-view shot of your skiing. It can also give you a point-of-view shot of you falling. But you may have to let the second unit director film the dramatic climax: a trip to the repair shop for an estimate on a snow-filled camcorder.

✔ **A baseball cap airfoil:** The goal of this brim-mounted device is to increase downforce so that your favorite cap doesn't blow off. Or you could just turn it backwards.

Part II
Mastering the Mountain

The 5th Wave   By Rich Tennant

@RICHTENNANT

"This is the 5th time down the slope you've claimed a sudden urge to make a snow angel. Why don't you just <u>admit</u> you're falling?"

In this part . . .

Want to ski better? Of course you do. Whether you're a first-timer or a full-fledged expert, dive into these chapters and find out how to take a lesson and how to improve on your own. I also share some time-tested secrets for getting around the mountain — so you spend more time skiing and less time schlepping.

Chapter 6

Your First Time on Skis

. . . .

In This Chapter

▶ Deciding who and what to bring and where and when to go

▶ Understanding why you need a qualified instructor

▶ Taking a ski lesson

▶ Getting up when you fall

▶ Riding a lift for the first time

. . . .

*E*veryone remembers their first time. The anticipation. The trepidation. The exhilaration. I'm talking, of course, about their first day on skis. Your first day on the slopes is really a doorway. If it's open and friendly with a welcome mat in front and a festive wreath a - hangin', it's a doorway to a long, happy life of snow sliding. If it slams in your face, well, it's back to the couch.

I'm not going to sugarcoat it. Your first day on skis will contain some moments of frustration, uncertainty, and even a little bit of fear. But you also experience moments of joy, accomplishment, and the kind of pure, unadulterated fun usually reserved for recess. The key to minimizing the former and maximizing the latter is, as any good Boy Scout can tell you, preparation.

And that's where this chapter comes in. In the pages that follow, I sweat the details for you. I help you avoid the hassles and help you just go out and play in the snow. First off, I run through the planning phase — addressing important questions like where you should go and whom you should take with you. Then I tell you a little about ski school — why you should enroll, what a typical first lesson involves, what you can expect, and how to get the best lesson.

My first time

I suggest that I'm uniquely qualified to be your guide through this chapter. Why? Because I've been on both sides of the fence during a first-time-on-skis lesson. First let me tell you that I'm a member of the Professional Ski Instructors of America and that I've taught hundreds of beginner lessons. Beginner lessons are my specialty, and I don't think there's anything more fun or rewarding in ski teaching than watching someone go from an anxious never-ever to a confident fledgling skier.

On the other hand, unlike most instructors, I didn't learn to ski when I was three, or seven, or ten. I was 25 years old the first time I clicked into a pair of skis. I drove myself to the resort in my own car (a beige Dodge Diplomat that looked like an unmarked police car), paid for my lift tickets with my own credit card, and schlepped my own skis. I remember that day as vividly as yesterday. The details aren't important — your first day may make a better story than mine — but what is important is that I remember what it was like. I remember negotiating the rental shop, trying on boots, waiting around at the lesson area, making my first wedge, riding my first lift, and turning my first turn. I remember the first time I fell, the first time I got up, and the first time I showed my future wife that I knew how to stop. I remember being alternately excited, anxious, confused, enlightened, bored, stimulated, and thrilled. And while those other emotions have come and gone, thrilled has been an almost constant companion, season after season, day after day, run after run throughout my skiing life. And if you're willing to ride out a few rough patches, the thrill can be your companion, too.

Planning Your Debut

In journalism school, Bob Woodwards–in-training are taught the five Ws and an H — who, what, when, where, why and how — so that a story doesn't go to press with a vital piece of information missing (So *where* did this murder take place?). This little mnemonic is a cornerstone of the newsroom, right up there with black coffee and unnamed sources. In an attempt to cover all the bases, you need to do the same kind of digging in planning your first day on skis.

Who to go with

How is skiing like swimming? You shouldn't go alone. No, you don't have to worry about stomach cramps or riptides. Skiing is a social sport, and if you go solo, you probably won't have as much fun.

Who should you recruit to come along? I leave that to you and your social secretary. But let's say you come up with two possibilities: two friends who you get along with equally well, one who's never been on skis and the other who's spent almost as much time on snow as Picabo Street. Which one should you choose? Here's a quick analysis of the situation.

A non-skiing friend

There's nothing like the excitement of shared exploration. Lewis had Clark. Alexander Graham Bell had Watson. The Skipper had Gilligan. I'm here to tell you that you can only truly share the first-time-on-skis experience with a friend who's also going through it for the first time. You can swap stories. You can commiserate. You can share high fives. More to the point, you can wade through the rental line together. You can take a lesson together. You can take hot chocolate breaks together ("You get in line and I'll find a table.")

On the flip side, have you ever heard the phrase "the blind leading the blind"? The biggest downside to bringing another beginner is that she's just as clueless as you are. So just make sure you've brought along someone who can laugh at having to wander around looking for the bathroom. As Tom Hanks might have said in *A Slope of Their Own:* "There's no kvetching in skiing."

An expert friend

Your expert friend may be a little less like a fellow explorer and a little more like a tour guide. Having skied at most of the mountains in the area, your friend can help you plan the trip. And after you get there, your expert friend will have figured out a lot of the little things — from where to park the car to how to carry a pair of skis — and thus you won't have to figure it out by trial and error.

The disadvantage of taking an expert friend is that the beginner hill isn't very exciting, so your expert friend won't be spending a lot of time skiing with you. It may be a little like your first day at kindergarten — you get dropped off with the teacher and then you're on your own. However, you shouldn't under any circumstances try to follow him and just wing it (more about that later in this chapter).

What to bring

For your first time on skis, you usually rent your skis, boots, and poles. I cover renting in detail in Chapter 1. To stay comfortable, you do need to dress for success. Here's a checklist of wardrobe items and other incidentals that you need to bring along, most of which you can find in your closet. (For more detailed information on buying ski clothes, see Chapter 4, and see Chapter 5 for more about accessories.)

- ✔ **Two pairs of waterproof gloves:** They don't have to be expensive, but they do have to be made of nylon. Woolen mittens take on water quicker than the Titanic.

Having a second pair to change into after that first pair gets wet — and they will, even if they're nylon — helps you keep your hands toasty all day long.

✔ **A knitted hat:** You don't need anything fancy, but bring a hat that's made out of wool and covers your ears.

✔ **Sunglasses:** Would you go to the beach without your shades? Well the sun reflects off the snow the same way it does off the sand. Goggles are optional, but can keep your face warm on a cold day.

✔ **A pair of ski socks:** Buy at least one pair of thin acrylic ski socks. Your boots will fit better and your feet will stay drier.

✔ **A not-too-warm jacket:** Many beginning skiers have a tendency to dress as if they were getting ready for the Iditarod sled dog race. Big mistake. Remember that skiing is an active sport, especially for a novice, and if you overdress, you'll start sweating. Sweating leaves you cold, damp, and cranky. So dress as you would for shoveling snow, not as you would for waiting at the bus stop.

✔ **Long underwear:** Buying one set of base layers (see Chapter 4) that wicks the sweat away from your skin is a smart investment in comfort.

✔ **Ski pants:** Ski pants are important, but a good pair can be little expensive. So try borrowing a pair from a friend. Can't grub a pair? Improvise. While some folks do go skiing in jeans, they're generally a little too tight, and way too absorbent to make good skiwear. A better alternative is the bottoms from a nylon jogging suit or even a pair of sweatpants.

✔ **Sunscreen:** Even on a cloudy day, you can get badly sunburned from the UV rays that increase in intensity with altitude. And those damaging rays reflect off the snow surface almost as well as off a mirror. So pack a sunscreen with an SPF of at least 25, and remember to reapply.

✔ **A credit card:** You need this for collateral at the rental shop. You won't be able to go skiing without it.

✔ **A driver's license:** Ditto.

When to go

There's a saying in the ski business: The early bird catches the turn. Well, maybe not. But if there were such a saying, it'd definitely apply to planning a first day on skis. Going early in the season, like before Christmas, is smart. Here's why:

✔ **It's warmer:** All things being equal, it's more fun to ski if it's 30 degrees than if it's 10 degrees. And at most resorts, it's more likely to be 30 degrees in early December than in mid-January.

✔ **The instructors are psyched:** After teaching 217 beginner lessons in a season, a ski teacher can get a little burned out. If you're in the 17th lesson of the season, you're more likely to get a teacher who's happy, upbeat, and ready to go the extra mile.

✔ **It's not too crowded:** Before the holidays, most folks are worrying about buying gifts and trimming trees. That means they're not skiing. It also means shorter lines at the rental shop, the cafeteria, and the chairlift as well as emptier slopes.

✔ **There's plenty of terrain:** One of the good reasons why experienced skiers wait until later in the season to ski is that ski areas, especially those that depend on snowmaking, open trails a few at a time. That means there's only a limited selection of terrain available in the first few weeks of the season. However, that's not an issue for a beginner because the beginner hill is the first thing every ski area opens.

✔ **You get a head start:** If you do your first day on skis early in the season, you have the whole rest of the season to polish your newfound skills, explore more of the mountain, or even plan a ski vacation.

✔ **It's cheaper:** Most ski areas offer discounted or even free lesson and rental packages periodically, and the best time to snag these discounts is early in the season. Call your local resort to find out the details about these learn-to-ski promotions — when, how, and what important restrictions apply.

Where to go

Think globally, ski locally. That's the advice I give beginners. What mainly separates big, glitsy destination resorts from the smaller local hills is the breadth and variety of their advanced and expert terrain. You don't need much help from Mother Nature to build a good beginner hill.

If you head off to a local area within a couple hours' drive of your doorstep, you're spending less — moneywise and timewise — than if you flew halfway across the country. (Of course, if you live in a part of the country with no ski areas nearby, it may be cheaper and easier to take a four-hour flight than a 12-hour drive.)

How long to stay

But how long should your first ski trip be? There are two schools of thought on this subject. One school of thought suggests that you should go for a day so that if you don't like it, you haven't made much of an investment. However, while day trips are great, you have to be organized. You have to pack efficiently, get an early start, and cram as much skiing as you can into a few hours. That can be a little stressful for a beginner.

The other school of thought suggests that you should just go for it — sign up for a week-long vacation which helps you get over that initial hurdle and turn you into a poor man's Alberto Tomba by the time you're ready to return home. The problem is that as you first figure out how to ski, you're using some muscles you've never used before, and you can get tired in a hurry. By the third or fourth day, you may be ready for a massage instead of another run.

I suggest splitting it right down the middle. A weekend seems like just the right length to me. If you're going for a weekend, you can adopt a more leisurely pace, taking your time at figuring out the layout of the resort and just getting used to the wide world of skiing. You can usually keep your rental equipment overnight, so you only have to brave the rental shop once. Also, a two- or three-day trip gives you a chance to rest your sore muscles at home instead of a $100 a night hotel room. (For more info on planning a weekend trip, see Chapter 14.)

Why go skiing?

Because skiing is fun. Skiing lets you thumb your nose at winter. Because it's healthier than watching the Cleveland Browns play the Jacksonville Jaguars or popping in the tape of *Waiting to Exhale* . . . again. Because speed thrills. Because Kevin Costner and Jennifer Aniston ski. Because you get to play in the snow. Because skiers are sexy. Because . . . well, why don't you just go and report back with your own reason?

First Things First

Okay, the big day is here. You manage to find the resort and park the car. What do you do now?

1. **Go to the ticket window and buy a lesson/rental package.**

2. **Put the ticket on a wire wicket on the zipper of your jacket (or your pants if it's a warm day; you may want to change your jacket later.)**

3. **Stash the lesson and rental tickets in a pocket so you can find them later.**

4. **Head to the base lodge and stake out a place to dump your stuff.**

   You can simply leave your bag under a table or place it in a cubbyhole along the wall. However, you should take your valuables — like your wallet and car keys — with you. Most areas offer coin-operated lockers, but unlocked bags are usually safe enough.

5. **Go to the ski school desk and find out where and when first-time-on-skis lessons meet.**

   Armed with that information, you should now head to the rental shop. If you haven't read Chapter 1 already, go back and read about what you can expect at the rental shop.

Enrolling in Ski School

Skiing is a lesson sport. It's as simple as that. It's true that people have taught themselves to ski. People have also taught themselves to arc weld and do differential equations, but that doesn't mean it wouldn't have been quicker and easier with a good teacher.

Why you should take a lesson

Taking a lesson your first time on skis maximizes your chances of learning quickly, safely, and enjoyably.

- ✔ **It's safer:** An instructor's first priority is to keep you safe so you won't end up on terrain that's too difficult before you learn to stop and turn.

- ✔ **It's easier:** Ski schools teach thousands of beginner lessons every year, so they have it pretty much down to a science. Which means that you'll get past the drudgery and onto the fun in shorter order.

- ✔ **It's fun:** And a good instructor makes a lesson fun. If I'm teaching a lesson and my students don't laugh, chuckle, or groan at a bad pun at least half a dozen times, I'm not doing my job. And with any luck, your fellow students will be at least as amusing as your teachers.

- ✔ **It's a shortcut:** Taking a lesson will also help you down the road because you'll learn the basics the right way and you won't have any bad habits to unlearn before you can improve.

- ✔ **It's inexpensive:** Finally, ski lessons are also cheap, and in many cases, almost free. At most ski areas, the price of a lesson/lift/rental package is only a few dollars more — and sometimes even less — than the cost of the lift ticket and the rental if you purchase them separately.

And remember, the tips in this chapter and throughout the book should be considered a supplement to, not a substitute for, a lesson (or better yet, a series of lessons) from a professional instructor.

The boyfriend factor

Let me tell you about the scariest thing I've ever seen at a ski area. I was at Ski Windham in upstate New York, and I got to the edge of a semi-steep pitch at the top of an intermediate trail. Standing at the top of the trail was a young woman with her boyfriend. They were having a conversation I'd heard a hundred times before.

She: "No, I can't. I'm too scared."

He: "Don't worry about it. It's not that steep. A piece of cake."

But she was giggling as she protested, and the guy wasn't being overly pushy, so I figured that this would end like most of these conversations do. She'd ski down slowly, making beautiful controlled wedge turns. And he'd ski fast and out of control, checking his speed with messy skids straight from a *Dukes of Hazzard* film festival.

I didn't anticipate what happened next. The young woman pointed her skis over the lip, and she just went straight down. Literally.

Skis pointed straight down the hill. Arms waving. And a faint shriek wafting back up the hill. But she didn't fall. No, she kept picking up more and more speed, and she accelerated the whole way down the trail until she reached Mach 5. Then she went down the *next* trail, still no turns, still no fall, just more uncontrolled acceleration.

What happened? I'm not exactly sure. She disappeared out of sight before she fell or hit anything. I didn't hear a Medivac helicopter, so I'm assuming she was basically all right. But it was the kind of situation that doesn't always have a happy ending. People can and do get very seriously hurt this way.

This is why you shouldn't allow your friend, your sister, your uncle, or even your father try to teach you to ski. Even well-meaning amateur ski instructors don't understand the concept of a learning progression — starting out slowly — and pull something like this, the on-snow equivalent of doing a driving lesson on the Long Island Expressway. Even if no one ends up getting hurt, the pressure of trying to figure out a new sport is enough to put a strain on even the happiest relationship. Let's put it this way — if Mike Brady had tried to teach Carol to ski, there's a good chance he would have ended up like Carol's first husband. So smile at your significant other and say, "I'll meet you after my lesson."

Off to school

You're out of the rental shop; now what do you do? If it's getting close to time for your lesson, gather up your gear and head over to the ski school meeting place. Make sure you have the following:

- ✔ **Your boots:** You should be wearing them and they should be loosely buckled.

- ✔ **Your skis:** You should be carrying them; don't put them on until the instructor tells you to.

✔ **Your poles:** Just hold them; don't put the straps around your wrist.

✔ **Your lesson ticket:** The instructor asks for it at the beginning of the lesson.

Previewing Your First Lesson

After you and your instructor exchange pleasantries, it's time to go about the business of learning to ski. Every ski school and every instructor, for that matter, has his or her own method for teaching a beginner lesson — emphasizing some drills, eliminating some others — but this is a fairly typical lesson progression. As I tell my classes right after taking their lesson tickets, "They call it ski school, but it's not much like school at all. You're going to have fun and you're going to learn something."

✔ **Boot drills:** This may be a ski lesson, but it's usually a few minutes before you put your skis on. First, you spend a couple of minutes clomping around in your boots. There are a couple of good reasons for this. The first, and most obvious, is to get the class moving and warmed up. The second is that skiing requires a few subtle movements of the feet and lower leg — actions you don't encounter while shooting hoops or doing aerobics. Boot drills give you a chance to practice these moves without the added baggage of a pair of skis. So while it may not seem like "skiing," these early drills give you a head start after you put on your skis, so pay attention and try to do them as carefully as possible.

✔ **One-ski drills:** After you complete ski school boot camp, the instructor may ask you to put on *one* ski. (If you don't know how to do this, see Chapter 1 or just ask the instructor.) One-ski drills — in which you push with one foot, scooter style — help you get the sensation of sliding and steering with one foot still on the ground.

✔ **Straight runs:** After you put on the other ski, you're ready to start sliding. You start at the top of a gentle slope, point your skis straight down, and slide. (See Figure 6-1.) Don't worry about stopping. The instructor has chosen a slope with a natural runout where the terrain stops you naturally.

✔ **Making a wedge:** This is your first step toward speed and directional control. Essentially, you point your toes in so that your skis look like a triangle or, as I tell my kids' groups, a slice of pizza (Neopolitan, not Sicilian) or a wedge. (Once upon a time, the wedge used to be called a *snowplow*, but that name led beginners to think they should be digging in their edges hard and pushing around a lot of snow.)

Because the wedge puts the skis slightly on edge, you slide a little more slowly than you did with the skis flat on the ground. Later, you make the wedge bigger, which helps you stop. You may change the size of the wedge as you're moving to help you figure out how to control your speed more subtly.

Figure 6-1:
The key to
a straight
run is a
balanced,
athletic
stance.

The secret to getting a great lesson

Wanna know the one secret to a great ski lesson? Get there early. There's a simple irrefutable logic to this. First-timers who are able to make their way through the rental shop quickly and gracefully and get to the meeting area early are generally organized and motivated, and maybe even had a little help from their friends. Ski school groups are generally sent out on a first-come, first-served basis. An experienced instructor generally volunteers for one of those early groups. Why? Because he knows that he's not going to have to worry about the guy with two left boots, the teenage girl who's going to sulk through whole hour, and the woman who forgot her gloves. He's maneuvered himself into teaching the honors class. And on slow days, lessons (and the income attached to them) are doled out in order of seniority, with the top instructors getting first dibs and the new guy walking away empty-handed.

An instructor who is smart enough to have figured this out — and is motivated enough to volunteer for a lesson — is the kind of ski teacher you want. If you land in one of these overachievers' groups, you spend more time skiing and practicing and less time fixing equipment and picking people up off the ground. So set your alarm clock. You'll be glad you did.

✔ **One turn:** After you can glide in a wedge, turning is pretty easy. Turning is largely a matter of pointing the wedge where you want to go. It doesn't require large movements, just a subtle move of your feet. This is easier to see than to describe, so watch your instructor carefully.

✔ **Two turns:** After you can make one turn, your next milestone is to link two turns. Essentially, you're taking one turn — shaped like a C — and joining it to another turn, to form something shaped like an S. After you can do this, congratulations; you can call yourself a skier. Your next challenge is to be able to do this on steeper terrain and at higher speeds.

Posture, posture: Standing up and looking ahead

Skiing isn't actually that hard. You go from clicking into your skis for the first time to making turns in a couple of hours. Here are a couple of tips that make your first day on skis better and serve you well throughout your snow-sliding career.

✔ **Adopt an athletic stance:** Skiing is a sport. And the same ready position that serves Pete Sampras or Sheryl Swoopes on the court serves you well on the snow. Spread your feet shoulder width apart. Bend your knees. (The first and last time you get that advice from me.) Flex your ankles. Put your hands out in front of you. That good athletic position helps you keep your balance and react to changes in terrain or snow.

✔ **Look where you're going:** You have these novel, unpredictable, and perhaps even somewhat uncomfortable things on your feet. So it's only natural to want to look at them. So while you're standing still, go right ahead and stare at your skis. Study every line of the topskin. Analyze every font and fillip. Memorize every mark and blemish. Now when you're ready to start moving, look where you're going.

I can assure you that your skis aren't going to do anything without input from your feet, any more than your Ferragamo loafers take on a life of their own. You don't look down at your feet when you're walking, do you?

There are plenty of good reasons for keeping your eyes up. Most obviously, you can't see where you're going — as in avoiding obstacles and other skiers — if you're mulling your ski tips. Keeping your head up puts you in the good athletic stance I mention earlier. And finally, your feet have had a lot of practice following the lead of your eyes. Fix your eyes on an object or a destination, and your feet instinctively plot a course there. You can take advantage of this built-in programming while you're on skis, too, but not if you're gawking at your feet.

I've fallen and I can't get up

If you stick with skiing for more than an hour, you are going to fall. It's inevitable. Look at a child who's starting to walk. Falling is just a part of the process, the result of exploring — and finding the limits of your balance.

However, once you do fall, you have to get up, which can be a vexing problem for a beginning skier. Getting up actually takes as much, if not more, balance, strength, and skill than skiing itself. There are three basic ways to get up, which I outline in the following sections. However, before you attempt the first two methods, ask your ski instructor for a demonstration.

The on-your-tummy method

This method seems to work especially well for kids and female skiers, who tend to be more flexible but lack upper body strength. See Figure 6-2.

1. **Orient your skis so that they're pointing down the hill (Step 1).**

2. **Roll over on your stomach.**

3. **Position your skis so that the tails of your skis are together and the tips of your skis are pointing up the hill.**

   If you have trouble doing this — your knee feels like it just won't roll any farther — don't force it. Ask for help from your instructor.

4. **When you're in this prone position, you're like a baby taking its first steps. Push yourself up with your hands (Step 2) while taking small steps up the hill with your feet until you're standing (Step 3).**

Falling isn't failing

A true story. A famous resort got a new ski school director. He asked around to find out who was the best skier in the ski school. Everyone told him, "Oh, that's Bob — he hasn't fallen in ten years." So the new director went to Bob and asked him "Everyone tells me you're the best skier in the ski school. Is that right?"

"Well, yes."

"Is it true you haven't fallen in ten years?"

"Yeah, I think Gerald Ford was president the last time I fell."

"Then you're fired."

"What do you mean?"

"If you never fall, that means you're not trying to improve, and I won't have someone like that teaching in my ski school."

The moral of this story: Falling is okay. It's even necessary if you want to improve as a skier. And fortunately, falls generally hurt your pride more than your body.

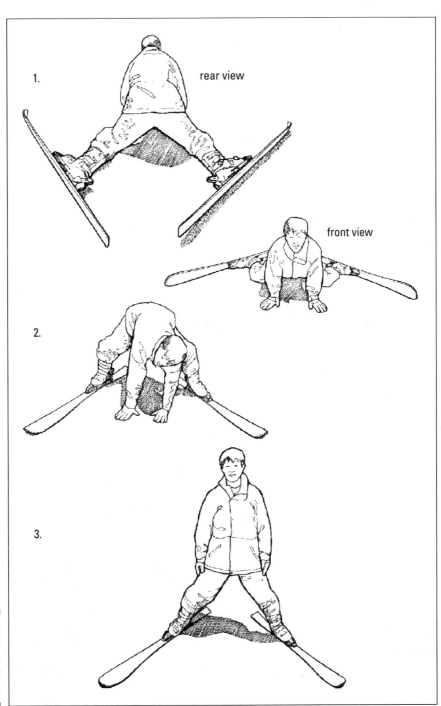

1.

rear view

front view

2.

3.

Figure 6-2:
Getting up:
The on-
your-tummy
method.

From the side method

This method takes a good bit of upper body strength, so male skiers tend to favor it. This is the way most accomplished skiers, both male or female, get up because this move is much easier if the terrain is a little steeper. See Figure 6-3.

Figure 6-3:
Getting up:
The on-
your-side
method.

1. Turn your skis so that they're perpendicular to the pitch of the slope.

2. Roll over so that you're sitting on your right hip (Step 1).

3. Plant your pole right at your hip with your right hand.

4. Take your left hand and move it up to the top of the pole grip (Step 2).

5. Push down with your right hand and gradually move your left hand up the pole as you rise (Step 3).

The take-off-a-ski method

No, this isn't a joke. If you've been struggling with the other methods and you're concerned that you're going to injure yourself or you're just simply too tired, it's the easiest way to get back up. It's also the smart thing to do if you're on a place where you're in the line of traffic and in danger of getting hit by another skier. Take off only one ski when you get up, because it's quicker and easier to put only one back on.

I can't stop

Arresting your motion is a big issue for beginning skiers. Fortunately, it's not hard if you do it right. You can stop in any one of three ways.

- ✔ **Making your wedge bigger:** As you discover, if you increase the size of your wedge, you slow down and eventually stop. This works fine at low speeds, but at higher speeds it's not as effective because the length of your legs and skis limits how big you can make your wedge.

- ✔ **Turning your skis:** Turns are not only for directional control. They're also your best speed control option. Follow this logic: When you're standing with your skis perpendicular to the pitch of the slope, you're stopped, right? So if you're heading down the hill and you keep turning your skis until they point across the slope, you slow down and, if you continue turning until the skis are pointed slightly up the hill, you'll eventually stop. This is the way all experienced skiers stop and slow down.

- ✔ **Falling:** Again, I'm not joking. A controlled — or at least intentional — fall, is generally preferable to a collision with a solid object or another skier. So if you feel yourself heading toward disaster and you can't turn or slow down enough, arrest your speed with a controlled slide, a little like a baseball player sliding feet-first into second base.

Pole Positioning: Using Your Poles

What are ski poles for? I go into the more arcane aspects of pole use — things that intermediate and advanced skiers need to understand — in Chapter 8.

But for your purposes, as a beginner, pole usage is simple. Here's what they're for:

- ✔ **Helping you maneuver:** Touching your poles to the ground while you're just standing helps keep you from sliding forward. Your poles have an even more important role when you're moving from your standing-around position to your ready-to-ski position. You have to move from a skis-pointing-across-the-hill attitude to a skis-pointing-down-the-hill attitude, and by supporting yourself with your poles, you can make this tricky maneuver without sliding forward before you're ready. Your instructor should demonstrate this for you.

- ✔ **Giving your hands something to do:** When you're not skiing, your hands are plenty busy most of the time. That's why they need something to do when you're skiing. Holding poles helps keep them from flailing around and disrupting your balance.

What ski poles are *not* for:

- ✔ **Stopping:** As your instructor should tell you, and I outline earlier in this chapter, you stop with your feet. Any attempt to use your poles to stop after you're already moving is likely to result in a wrist or arm injury. So don't do it.

- ✔ **Slowing down:** See stopping.

- ✔ **Impaling your fellow students:** While they're not exactly shish kebab skewers, the tip of a pole is pointy enough to do some damage if it's wielded with any force. Be sure to keep the baskets and tips of your poles near your ankles, with the tips pointed behind you as shown in Figure 6-1.

The Learning Curve

You may not believe this the first time you click into your skis, but skiing is actually a very natural act. It's a variation on some of your most basic human movement patterns — standing and walking. What's the proof? Most people can make turns on the beginner hill by the end of the first day and can cruise green terrain confidently by the end of a weekend. That's less than ten hours of actual skiing time. After their second day, most golfers are apologizing to the grass that they dig up while they were aiming for the ball. And even experienced skiers might ski only five days a year, which over a decade adds up to about 50 days. That's maybe two good seasons for a serious golfer. So if you feel you're progressing slowly, don't be frustrated by what you *can't* do yet — be proud of what you *can* do.

SKI TIP

Help! I lost my skis!

You left your skis outside on the rack while you stopped for a bathroom break. And now you can't find them. The good news is that no one really wants to steal a pair of rental skis. The bad news is that all rental skis look alike, so it's a little like conducting a manhunt at a family reunion. There is one difference: Each ski has a number on it — usually in permanent marker on the tip — that is how the rental shop guys know which credit card slip to give you after you return the skis. In a perfect world, you would have memorized this number while you still had the skis in your possession. But it's not a perfect world, is it? The number isn't lost forever, though. Find your rental agreement — the slip of paper the rental shop guy gave you. It should have the number of the skis written on it somewhere. Now all you have to do is match up the number to a pair of skis and you're in business.

Don't, however, under any circumstances, use someone else's skis, rental or otherwise. The bindings won't be adjusted properly, and you could suffer a serious injury if you fall.

By the end of your first one-hour or 90-minute lesson, you should be able to

- ✔ Do a straight run
- ✔ Control your speed with a wedge
- ✔ Make at least a tentative turn in one direction

By the end of your second lesson, you should be able to

- ✔ Make more decisive turns
- ✔ Link at least two turns
- ✔ Ride a lift

Upward Mobility: Tackling the Rope Tow and Chairlift

One of the biggest challenges for the beginning skier is getting back up the hill. It either involves significant physical exertion or at least as much coordination as the downhill section of the run. I'm going to walk you through the three major ways to gain vertical and how to deal with them.

Walking

Because you don't need very much vertical after you first start skiing, you start off by ascending the mountain under your own power. You can do this using one of two techniques: the sidestep or the herringbone.

- ✔ **Sidestep:** Turn so that your feet are pointing across the slope. Roll your ankles slightly up the hill so that the edges of your skis bite into the snow. Take a small step up with your uphill ski, keeping it parallel with the stationary downhill ski. Then take a step up with the downhill ski. That's really it. The only trick is to keep the ski on edge so you don't start sliding back down the hill.

  If you reverse the sequence, sidestepping is also useful for maneuvering down the hill. In fact, it's the safest way to proceed if you accidentally find yourself on a piece of terrain that's much too difficult for you to ski.

- ✔ **Herringbone:** Face up the hill and spread your feet so that the tips of your skis are wide apart and the tails are close together. (This position is similar to the end of the on-your-tummy method of getting up, which I outline earlier in this chapter and depict in Figure 6-2.) You should feel roughly like a duck. Now just walk straight up the hill, taking small steps so that you don't cross your tails.

Rope tow

Picture a clothesline with a motor attached. The rope moves, you grab onto it, and it pulls you up the hill with your skis still on the snow. That's a rope tow. While rope tows are not as common as they used to be, they can sometimes be found on beginner hills. The key to getting started on a rope tow is to tighten your grip gradually. This way there won't be a sudden jerk as you go from a stationary position to moving forward. At the top, you just let go of the rope and step away. Rope tows are practical for beginner areas because they're inexpensive and they actually teach you sliding skills as you ride.

Chairlift

While the ride up the hill is as simple as sitting on your couch, loading and unloading on a chairlift can be tricky for the novice skier. Watch a few more-experienced skiers try to load before you try it, and if it's your first time, tell the lift attendant so she can be ready to stop or slow the chair if you have trouble getting on. Here's the drill to get on the lift:

1. **Remove your pole straps and hold both poles in your inside hand.**

   If you're going to sit on the left side of the chair lift, hold your poles in your right hand, and vice versa. Make sure that you don't have a loose scarf, a hood cinch cord, or anything else that can catch on the chair.

2. **When it's your turn, shuffle up to the waiting area.**

   As the person ahead of you gets on the chair, move up right behind the chair. Look over your outside shoulder to see the chair coming.

3. **Grab the bar on the outside of the chair with your outside hand and then sit down. See Figure 6-4.**

4. **Lower the safety bar as soon as you're securely in the seat.**

   The chairlift may stop occasionally, but don't worry. The lift attendant may stop the lift, usually because someone else is having a little trouble getting on or off.

To get off the chairlift at the top of the hill, follow these steps:

1. **As the lift approaches the top of the slope, raise the safety bar.**

2. **Transfer your poles to your outside hand and grab the front edge of the seat with your inside hand.**

Figure 6-4:
A skier grabbing the chair with his outside hand.

Courtesy NSSA and Studio 404 Photography

3. **When you get to the flat part of the unloading ramp, put your skis on the ground, stand up, and push yourself forward with your inside hand.**

4. **Slide down the ramp with your skis straight — if you wedge, you may step on the skis of the person next to you — and move out of the way to allow other skiers to unload.**

If you fall on a rope tow or while unloading off of a chairlift, move as quickly as possible out of the path of oncoming skiers.

Pacing Yourself

If you were taking up running, you wouldn't start by hitting the road for six hours straight, now, would you? Well, you should be just as smart about your skiing. Learning to ski takes even more energy than actually skiing, so pace yourself. After completing your lesson, take a break. Have a hot chocolate by the fire or a cheeseburger out on the deck. Check out the score in the football game. In other words, relax. And when you go back out, plan on skiing for an hour or maybe even less, and then come in for another break. And don't forget to drink plenty of water. It's easy to get dehydrated in the high, dry air of most ski resorts.

Chapter 7

Getting the Most from Your Ski Lesson

*I*mproving your skiing skills by taking a lesson pays immediate and tangible benefits. If you ski better, you have more fun, expend less energy, get more bang for your lift ticket buck, and look better while you're doing it.

As if that isn't enough, ski lessons themselves can actually be more fun than recess if you're in the right group, if you have the right instructor, and if you have the right attitude.

In this chapter, I discuss how you can assess yourself as a skier and tell you what kind of goals that a skier of your level can achieve. I make the argument that the money you plunk down for a lesson is one of the best investments in all of skiing. I discuss how to find the right instructor and how to get the most out of a lesson. I also discuss other learning options outside of a traditional ski school setting. The best part is that you won't have to take the SATs or take out any student loans.

Assessing Yourself as a Skier

Before you can start off on the road to better skiing, you have to figure out where you are and where you want to go. Not coincidentally, that's what you're going to do right now.

First, I start by outlining some broad ability categories — in other words, a brief summary of what you can do on skis — that's where you are. And within each category, I toss out some practical and readily achievable goals for a skier at that level — that's where you want to go.

First time on skis

See Chapter 6 for a complete rundown of the beginner lesson experience.

Beginner

You're still just starting out as a skier, but you're past the bunny hill. You can link turns in both directions, you can stop confidently, and you can get on and off the lift without a problem. But you still fall quite often, and steeper terrain, crowded slopes, and hardpacked conditions intimidate you. Skiing is a lot of fun for you, but sometimes it's a little too much like work. Your goals may be:

✔ **Keeping up with your friends:** This translates into skiing a little faster or stopping less frequently to keep your speed under control and regain your balance. Either way, your instructor can show you any number of skill drills and terrain-reading tips that can keep you from bringing up the rear.

✔ **Skiing more efficiently:** Do you feel like you just ran the Boston Marathon at the end of your ski day? Then you're probably expending more effort than you really need to. Refining your technique allows you to ski more runs during the day and more days during a ski week and still have the energy to get up off the hotel room bed and go to dinner.

✔ **Skiing more of the mountain:** It's like the magicians say: if you're going to a bigger party, you need to have a bigger bag of tricks. In relation to skiing, that means having a solid base of skills and improving your ability to adapt your skiing to the conditions, whether it's steeper terrain, narrower trails, hardpacked or chopped-up snow, or even poor lighting conditions. Even when things get a little funky, you find you have another rabbit you can pull out of your hat.

✔ **Skiing parallel:** While you're still using a wedge to make your turns, you notice that many other skiers do not. This is called skiing parallel, which allows you to ski faster, more easily, and on a wider variety of terrain.

Intermediate

You're a solid and experienced skier. You can ski reasonably fast and under control on most moderately steep, groomed slopes. But tough conditions — ice, bumps, crud, or chopped-up powder — can sometimes throw you off your game. When the trail gets steep, you tend to back off, resorting to "survival turns." Your goals may be:

- **Acing the ice:** Do you turn into Mr. Freeze every time the slope gets a little icy? Figuring out how to be a little more subtle — and supple — on your skis can make hard snow almost easy.

- **Skiing the steeps:** Try this conundrum on for size — to go slow, you have to ski fast. Huh? That's the paradox of skiing on steep slopes: Any time not spent turning is time spent accelerating. A lesson can help you figure out how to make quick, decisive moves.

- **Exploring the bumps:** You see other skiers bouncing through the bumps, and you say to yourself, "That looks like fun." But when you try it yourself, you start flailing. To master the moguls, you have to be able to absorb the bumps, make quick turns, and maintain your balance all at the same time.

Advanced

You're a very accomplished skier. You can ski just about any in-bounds terrain at any resort — maybe not always elegantly or efficiently, but you always get down the slope. Your goal is to go from being an advanced skier to a "good" skier, one of those Alpine athletes who can ski any trail, any time, and make it look easy. Your goals are:

- **Dealing with adverse snow conditions:** The world is not all groomed corduroy. Hardpack demands subtle edging skills, while blasting through powder and crud demands a few subtle changes in technique as well as the pure power that stems from rock-solid balance.

- **Ripping the steeps:** Tackling ultra-steep terrain takes a combination of quick feet and total commitment, both physically and mentally, to moving your body down the hill.

- **Tackling monster bumps:** Staying on track in big, steep, icy bumps demands not only physical skills — quick feet, fast hands, and knees of rubber — but the ability to see the right line through a maze of maxi-moguls.

The PSIA

The PSIA stands for the Professional Ski Instructors of America. The PSIA is a national organization that oversees ski instruction in the United States. Virtually all ski schools and most ski instructors are members of the PSIA. One of the most important roles of the PSIA is to establish both the basic movement patterns that constitute good ski technique and the general methods to teach them. This standardization is important because it allows you to take a first-time lesson in New York and a second lesson in Colorado and have one lesson build on the other. The PSIA has also established an education and certification system for ski instructors, sponsoring clinics and exams which help teachers enhance their skiing, technical knowledge, and teaching ability. In short, PSIA helps ensure that your instructor gives you the best lesson possible.

Why Lessons Are a Bargain

Want some investment advice? The money you spend on a ski lesson gives you unmatched returns when it comes to having more fun on the slopes.

Skiers often think that new equipment may help them ski better. And in many cases they're right. But at the same time, new and better skis pop up at a rate reserved for rabbit reproduction and Internet IPOs. You can end up like I have — with a basement full of skis that are perfectly good intrinsically, but have just been superceded by something better. You can take an awful lot of lessons for the price of a pair of skis.

An investment in learning to ski better, on the other hand, doesn't get rusty, can't get stolen, and never goes out of style. After you add something to your bag of tricks, it's there for good.

Improving your skills allows you to get more out of your lift ticket. Better skiing means skiing more efficiently, so you can ski for more hours in the day and more days out of a ski week. Better skiing also means skiing more of the mountain, having the opportunity to explore terrain that at one time you could only dream about skiing. So if you're looking to get as much bang for your lift ticket buck as possible, lessons are the ticket.

Which Lesson Is Right for You?

Just like you can find any number of ways to advance yourself professionally — from a correspondence course in TV repair to a Harvard MBA program — the road to better skiing can be found in any number of places. In this section, I provide a quick rundown of some of the basic options, with the pros and cons of each.

Group lessons

Picture a small gym class where the teachers weren't moonlighting from history class and the students actually wanted to be there. That's what you get with a group lesson, shown in Figure 7-1. A group lesson is a small cluster of pupils and an instructor. The format generally runs something like this: First, there is a brief lecture — what exercise we're doing and why. Second, the instructor gives a demonstration. Third, each student takes a turn at the exercise being discussed. And last, the class repeats the process as necessary.

Figure 7-1:
Watching your fellow students is a big part of a group lesson.

Courtesy Booth Creek Resorts

The pros

Unlike a gym class — can you say atomic wedgie? — a ski lesson usually provides a supportive atmosphere. You can laugh at your mistakes, share encouragement, and celebrate your breakthroughs with someone who's in the same boat. From a practical point of view, you get to watch other students and see what they're doing right and what's still giving them fits, which can make it easier to measure your own progress. And in a beginner-level lesson, a group provides a natural sense of pacing — you ski a little and then watch a little — so you don't tire yourself out.

The cons

Group lessons are by nature democratic — and sometimes individual needs get pushed aside in the process. Upper-level skiers — intermediate and above — often have different weaknesses and improvement priorities. So the pole touch drill that's aimed at one of the other students may not be addressing your biggest need.

Group lessons are best for first timers on skis, beginners, and lower intermediates.

Private lessons

A private lesson is a little like hiring a tutor. You hire the instructor, and he's yours for an hour. The lesson plan can be whatever you want it to be. Do you want to work on making your turns smoother? Fine. Do you want to work on skiing ice? Great. Or do you just want to have the instructor show you around the mountain while you both cut the lift lines? That's cool, too.

Private lessons are best for intermediates and advanced skiers. Beginners who either have plateaued or want to focus on a specific weakness may also benefit from private lessons.

The pros

With an instructor to call your own, you can get a lot done in a short period of time. You can focus on exactly what you need to work on and learn the way that's easiest for you. And there's no time spent on "group management" waiting for the other skiers to catch up to the group.

If you're taking a private lesson, you can have the instructor of your choice, usually at no additional charge. So if you had a good time and learned a lot with a particular pro, whether it was in a group or a private, you can request him or her again for your next lesson. Or if you just have some vague criteria for the ideal instructor — a man or a woman, a rah-rah guy or someone quieter — tell the person at the ski school desk, and he'll do his best to hook you up with someone who fits your needs.

The half-price private

If you're an upper-level skier willing to roll the dice, sometimes a group lesson can be the best bargain in skiing: a private lesson at half the price. Most ski areas don't do a tremendous number of upper-level lessons. At any given lineup, only half a dozen students may show up. If there's no one else at your level, the supervisor may put you in a group of one, and voila, you have a de facto private. The gamble, of course, is that they may be short of instructors, and instead of getting an instructor all to yourself, you could get stuck in a group with a couple of other skiers who are below your level. You still may have fun and figure out some things, but you won't have the lesson all to yourself.

Learning styles

It's a fact of life. Different people learn differently. Some people need detailed verbal explanations. Some people need to see it. And some people just have to experiment on their own. In reality, most skiers require some combination of these, but for most people, there's one particular method that really clicks. Obviously, identifying your optimal learning method can give you a big head start on the road to better skiing.

How do you do this? Think about breakthroughs you've had in learning other physical activities. What did it take to iron out that hitch in your golf swing or improve your movement on the tennis court?

Don't be surprised if the answer isn't what you expect. In most things, I'm a pretty "talky" person, and given the opportunity, I discuss a problem to death. But when it comes to learning a new movement pattern, I discovered, much to my surprise, that a visual demonstration is what I need. I've made most of my biggest breakthroughs simply by watching someone hit a topspin backhand and doing likewise or by following a better skier and imitating her. So if you find that an instructor is talking too much, or not talking enough, or whatever, let her know politely. She can change her tactics. After all, her goal is the same as yours: to get you skiing better.

The cons

Sometimes a private lesson can get a little too, well, private. You don't have other members of the group to talk with and you don't have their mistakes to watch. The focus is solely on you and your skiing, and if you don't make the progress you want, it can get a little frustrating.

Clinics

Do you have some burning goal in skiing? Do you dream of racing? Are bumps your passion? Or do you yearn to explore ungroomed snow? Well, you're not alone, and most ski schools have specialized one-day clinics to help you feed your particular skiing passion. (See Figure 7-2.) Ski schools have even expanded the concept to offer general skiing clinics aimed at a particular demographic group — such as senior citizens. Women's clinics are especially popular.

Ski clinics are best for the advanced beginners and up. However, you need to explain your ability level before signing up so you don't get put into a group that's over your head.

Figure 7-2:
If you want
to improve
your bump
skiing, try
a clinic.

Courtesy Booth Creek Resorts

The pros

Good, good, good . . . good vibrations abound at most clinics, and because everyone shares at least one common interest, it's easier to strike up friendships than anywhere this side of the line at the DMV. The instructors are also hand-picked based on their skills and enthusiasm. And the curriculum is usually well thought out, packed with with battle-tested tips and drills.

The cons

Unfortunately, there are no shortcuts in skiing: it's all about making turns. So don't be frustrated if you spend the first couple hours of a bump clinic on the groomed or you don't head straight for the gates in a race clinic. While you can master a lot in a single day, it's often not enough to make a real breakthrough, so you're going to need the discipline to practice on your own.

Camps

Think of a camp as a clinic on steroids: you simply get more of everything. Whereas a clinic is confined to a day or an afternoon, a camp is spread out over several days or even a week.

Some camps have a specific focus — racing, moguls, or skiing on ungroomed terrain — while general improvement is the design of others. So if you're not skiing better when you leave, you have no one to blame but yourself.

Camps are best for intermediates and up.

The pros

Time is on your side. Since you have at least a couple of days or as much as a whole week, you can accomplish a lot. By the end of the camp, you should not only have a better understanding of how you can improve your skiing, but you should have enough time and mileage to actually implement your coach's advice. In many camps, the coaches rotate so you can take a little from each coach's bag of tricks. A camp can also be a social event — you can eat lunch, eat dinner, and hang out, formally or informally, with your fellow happy campers. It's an especially cool situation for singles.

The cons

A camp represents a big commitment of time and money. If you get along with the coaches and your fellow campers, it's likely to be one of your best on-snow experiences. If you don't, it can be a very long week. So do some homework before you sign on the dotted line.

Go to the videotape

Whenever someone says "A picture is worth a thousand words," I wonder for a moment whether I should have become a photographer. But out on the ski slopes, the ratio may go even higher. There's really no substitute for seeing what you're doing. And that's where video comes in.

In many camps and clinics, part of the day is spent taking video of your skiing. When you watch the video later on in the lodge, you can not only see exactly what you're doing, in living color with the benefit of ultra slow motion and freeze frame — you get to see the instructor's demo as well. And because there are usually several video sessions during the course of the camp, you can get the full effect of before-and-after footage.

While video is great for your skiing, it's not always the best thing for your self-esteem. Seeing yourself on skis for the first time can be a little bit of a shock. You think you're ripping it up like Alberto Tomba, while the reality is a little closer to Alan Thicke in a pro-celebrity race. But if you check your ego at the door and focus on analyzing what you're doing rather than fixating on how you look, those nasty bad habits are as good as gone.

Of course, you can also try do-it-yourself video — just bring a camcorder and a friend. Remember to bring an extra battery — cold is to batteries as kryptonite is to Superman. And understand that if you fall while you're carrying your camcorder, your next stop is the repair shop.

Getting the Most from a Lesson

In case you haven't figured it out, the road to better skiing is a two-way street. Having a smart, motivated instructor is a big help. But so is having the right attitude. In this section you can find some time-tested tips for getting the most out of a lesson.

Have a goal

I was in an instructor's clinic once. The examiner gave us this exercise. He would ski down with a specific task in mind, but he wouldn't tell us what it was. We were each to watch him very carefully and decide what his task was. He skied, and we all watched with rapt attention. One skier said, "I think you were working on your balance." Someone else suggested, "You were focusing on keeping your turn shape consistent." A third said, "The rhythm of your pole touch."

Then came the punchline. What was his focus? "I was trying to keep the tassel on my hat flying straight back," he joked. In short, he was just skiing. And each of us had inadvertently revealed what we were thinking about in our own skiing. But if he had asked us what we wanted to work on, we would have mumbled, "Oh, making better turns."

So goals are good. Everyone has them, whether they realize it or not. You're much more likely to achieve your goals if you think about them in advance and tell your teacher what they are. If there's something you want to do on skis, then say so. Whether it's technical ("I want to improve my hip angulation") or situation-oriented ("I want to ski that expert trail on the other side of the mountain"), let your instructor know. If your instructor knows what you want to accomplish, she can design drills and exercises that help to do just that.

Be flexible

In skiing, as in life, you have to walk before you can run. You may want to ski that gnarly bump trail. But before you can ski that trail, you're going to have to improve your balance and your short turns. It's best to work on those skills on the groomed. So give your pro the benefit of the doubt. Mastering the basics isn't always sexy, but they pay big rewards down the road.

Really listen

Those breaks between drills aren't just for catching your breath. Your instructor may not talk much, but when he does speak up, it's usually to offer an important explanation or a helpful tip. And even if you can't use it right away, a tip often clicks after the lesson is over and you're off skiing on your own.

Watch actively

When the instructor's doing a demo, don't just observe, *empathize*. Try to imagine yourself doing exactly the same thing, your skis behaving in the same way. Pay attention to the details — watch the instructor's feet or key in on the subtle movements of the hips and the knees.

Don't be afraid to imitate

Monkey see, monkey do. That's how you figured things out when you were a kid. And that's how you can figure them out now. As the instructor is doing a demo, try to imitate her posture and her movements while you're standing still. And when it's your turn, don't try to put your own spin on the move; just duplicate her move as exactly as you can.

Ask questions

In the immortal words of that great philosopher Anonymous, there are no stupid questions, only stupid mistakes. Don't be afraid to say that you don't understand something. A ski instructor has a tough job trying to explain complex and often subtle series of movements through words and demonstrations. A good instructor won't be offended if you say "I don't understand." Also try to get at least one chairlift ride with the instructor. This is the best time to ask questions and otherwise pick his brain in a one-on-one situation.

Do your homework

Homework? Ick! Actually, it's not only necessary — it can actually be fun. At the end of the lesson, if the instructor hasn't pointed out a couple of things for you to work on in your skiing — rather than for the group in general — ask her outright for a couple of suggestions.

After the lesson, sit down and review the instructor's main points in your mind as well as her specific comments on your skiing. Then make a list of the exercises or drills you did during the lesson. Writing it down in a notebook is actually useful.

Go out and do the drills that you listed in your notebook. You don't have to spend the whole afternoon or even a whole hour doing them. Just plan to take a small section of appropriate terrain every run or every other run and do a drill or focus on one of the instructor's points. It's also a great way to make use of some of that non-descript terrain — easy, flat, and featureless — that you may otherwise ski on autopilot. A balance between short but well-executed drills and lots of plain skiing is the best way to get better.

Put in the mileage

Unlike the world of used cars, high mileage is a good thing in skiing. Mileage is simply time spent and distance covered on skis. And it's a good thing because your muscles, just like your brain, have memory. It takes a certain amount of time or, more accurately, a certain number of repetitions for a movement pattern to become ingrained in your muscle memory. But after it is, it becomes second nature. So the best way to change your skiing for the better is to do drills until you understand the move. Then just do a lot of skiing with that change in the back of your mind, experimenting with the move on different kinds of terrain at different speeds and in different snow conditions. Before long, the changes you make will be as much of a habit as chewing your nails.

Mileage also enhances your ability to make adjustments to different snow conditions and terrain. So mix it up, skiing different kinds of trails in any and all kinds of weather. It's another way to expand your bag of tricks.

Chapter 8

Improving Your Skiing

· ·

In This Chapter

▶ Understanding the basic skills of skiing

▶ Mastering the ten keys to better skiing

▶ Exploring the mental side of the sport

▶ Facing your on-slope fears

· ·

*W*hile skiing lessons are great, there's one cold, hard truth in this sport: No one can teach you how to ski. Ultimately, you have to figure it out yourself. You can absorb an instructor's explanations like a court reporter and watch his turns the way a cat watches a bird, but in the end, it's *your* feet that turn your skis.

But self-help is a wonderful thing, and it's liberating to understand that your on-slope improvement doesn't need to be confined to the few hours each season that you're taking a lesson. What it takes is an understanding of how a ski turns and the willingness to do it better. The overviews in this chapter, as well as the specific drills, aren't substitutes for ski lessons but rather a supplement, the alpine equivalent of a trip to the library.

This chapter is about becoming a better skier, no matter what your skill level is. First, I explain some of the basic skills that make a ski turn, and then I give you ten drills — no, they're too much fun for that, let's call them *games* — that can make your skiing better, easier, and more fun. At times, your feet know what to do, but your mind won't let them go about their business, so I give you a few mental exercises to help you ski your best. I also discuss fear and how to ski your best in less than ideal snow conditions. Wanna ski better? As Sally Struthers would say, we all do.

The Four Basic Skiing Skills

While sometimes it seems only slightly less complex than nuclear physics or your tax return, skiing requires only four basic skills — steering, edging, pressuring, and balancing. Everyone from the rankest beginner to Alberto Tomba turns his or her skis using some combination of these skills. By improving, and ultimately mastering, these skills, you'll be able to ski effectively in more kinds of snow, on more kinds of terrain, and at a wider variety of speeds. I use some of these terms throughout this chapter, so consider this a brief primer.

Steering your skis

Forget about your car. Steering is simply swiveling the ski in a lateral plane — in other words, from side to side.

Off-snow example: Pick your foot up. Move your leg so that your foot turns from side to side, with your toes moving in one direction and your heel moving to the opposite. Congratulations, you're steering.

How you use it: When you try this on snow, you quickly discover that this kind of steering is easy when your ski is truly flat on the ground, and difficult, if not impossible, when your ski is up on edge. For this reason, most of your steering is done at the top of the turn, as you're beginning to point your skis down the hill.

Getting on edge

Edging is tipping your ski so that it's on — you guessed it — its edge.

Off-snow example: Stand with both feet on the ground. Lift the little toes of one foot off the ground, along with that whole side of your foot. You should now be standing on the big-toe edge of your foot. Pat yourself on the back — you're edging.

How you use it: It's simple really. When your skis are flat on the snow, they tend to slide sideways. When they're on edge, they tend to move forward along the length of the ski. This allows you to control your direction, especially at the bottom part of the turn.

Applying pressure

Pressure is simply actively transferring your weight to a ski.

Off-snow example: Stand up and lift your left foot. Guess what? You're pressuring you right foot. Now put your left foot down and pick up your right foot. Go to the head of the class — you're now pressuring your left foot.

How you use it: I get into a more detailed explanation of pressure in a minute, but for now take my word for it: A pressured ski turns more sharply than a ski that's not pressured, if it's up on edge

Keeping your balance

If you blend the other three skills — steering, edging, and pressuring — at various points in the turn, balance is the umbrella under which they all operate. When you're in balance, it's easy, or at least easier, to edge, steer, and pressure the ski. When you're out of balance, it's difficult, if not impossible, to perform these other basic skills effectively.

Off-snow example: Pick up a ball and throw it — pretty easy, huh? Now put on a pair of skates and try to do the same thing. Not quite as simple, is it?

How you use it: By constantly adjusting your balance as the terrain and snow conditions vary, you build a solid platform from which to steer, edge, and pressure the ski.

Ten Keys to Better Skiing

Good skiers ski differently than the rest of us. They make better turns. Actually, there's a grain of truth in that joke. Really good skiers aren't doing a different sport than the rest of us, they're just using the basic skills I discussed earlier in a more refined way. This section is about the practical application of those skills.

The good news is that these keys to better skiing are easy to understand and, with the games that follow each skill in this section, easy to incorporate into your own skiing, so you can get better fast.

Finding your balance point

"Skiing," World Cup great Marc Girardelli once said, "is the ability to balance perfectly on the inside edge of the outside ski." Focus for a moment on the phrase: *balance perfectly*. Straightforward, yes, but also easier said than done. The hallmark of a great skier is the ability to maintain perfect balance no matter what the terrain or snow condition may be. But what exactly is perfect balance? Try the following exercise, known as the *Leaning Tower of Pisa*, to find out. This exercise helps all levels of skiers, regardless of ability.

The Leaning Tower of Pisa

Standing still on a flat section of the slope, lean as far forward as you can, without tipping over. (See Figure 8-1, Step 1.) Then lean as far back as you can (Step 2). Thanks to the support provided by your boots and your skis, you can go pretty far in either direction, can't you? Now lean forward again, but this time not quite so far. Lean back again, only not as far. Keep rocking from front to back, each time narrowing your range of motion. Before too long, your oscillation slows and ultimately stops at a point between the two extremes.

Feel how solid you are on your feet, like you're almost rooted to the ground? That's your balance point. Now your goal is to take that balanced posture and that feeling of being connected to the snow and incorporate it into your turns.

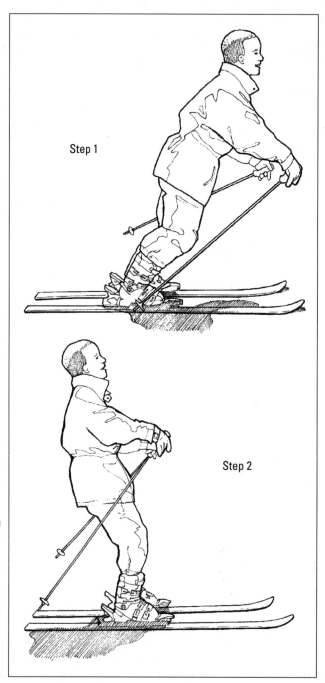

Step 1

Step 2

Figure 8-1:
The Leaning
Tower
of Pisa
exercise
helps you
fine tune
your
balance.

Skiing with your feet

Well, duh. This may sound almost ridiculously obvious, but it's not. Skiers discuss upper body position and hand position a lot. So much discussion takes place that you could forget that all the action takes place at ground level. In fact, all that discussion is about how to quiet your upper body, essentially to keep it from messing up your balance. Great skiers, however, ski with their feet. Or more accurately, they ski from their feet *up*. This means the skier focuses on movements that make the ski *do* something. Is that what you do? If not, then practice the *feet-up game* to refocus your priorities, which is appropriate for all levels of skiers.

The feet-up game

Find a gentle, groomed slope and try to ski it as quietly as possible. I don't mean that you shouldn't talk. I mean that you should calm down your turns and free them from added muscle tension and extraneous movements. Keep your hands still in front of you and relax your shoulders and lower back. Now, try to make your skis turn with as little effort as possible. Steer your feet gently at the top of the turn just enough to get the skis pointed down the hill and ride the skis around the turn. In fact, don't even think about turning. Just look where you want to go and let your skis follow your eyes. Nice, huh? Try it again, skiing just a little faster. Cue in on what your feet are doing. You may need to roll your knee in and move your hips just a little to get the ski to hold, but don't overdo it. Now go ski a whole run, and keep your focus on your feet, trying to feel the snow beneath your skis and using only those movements that contribute to making the ski turn.

Edging effectively

Want to dance over icy spots like Tara Lapinski? Then hone your edging skills, which make the difference between slicing and sliding on icy snow. Practice the *sideslipping away* exercise to zero in on this crucial skill. (This exercise is for advanced beginners and up.)

Sideslipping away

Stand perpendicular to the slope of a moderate trail and relax your ankles. Notice that you begin to slide sideways. Roll your ankles into the slope again, and your edges bite and stop you from sliding. As you refine this skill, you should be able to do these kinds of sideslips by just lightly relaxing and tensing the muscles in your feet. After you have that down, shift your weight subtly so that you drift slightly forward or backward, and your path down the hill looks like a falling leaf. Practice sideslipping at varying speeds — it's harder than you'd think to simply sideslip fast, straight down the fall line.

Skiing on one foot

Experts ski with one foot at a time. This may not be self-evident, but it's undeniably true. When a good skier is turning on a groomed slope, virtually all her weight is on the outside ski, and the inside ski should be as light as a feather and basically just along for the ride. You're probably already skiing this way, at least somewhat, without even realizing it, but you may never make the move to expert skiing unless you make a complete, conscious commitment to that outside ski.

The flamingo turn

Practicing this exercise, helpful to intermediate skiers and up, can help you commit to the outside ski. Find a moderately groomed slope. First, shift your weight to your outside ski and start a turn. Then try to pick up the whole inside ski a few inches off the ground. If your balance isn't quite perfect, you may need to put the ski back down. If you're having trouble, you may need to wait until the bottom half of the turn to lift your ski.

This drill takes plenty of practice before you completely master it. But just thinking about this commitment to the outside ski and attempting to lighten the inside ski, even if you can't pick it up all the way, makes your turns more solid. After you get the hang of it, try a variation on the theme. Try picking up the ski but leaving the outside tip of the inside ski on the snow. (See Figure 8-2.) This gives you a head start on edging the ski, and helps keep your body facing down the hill.

Turning continuously

Look at a great skier's tracks, and you see nothing but a long series of Ss. It's hard to determine where one turn ends and the other begins. See Figure 8-3. By contrast, many beginning skiers make tracks that look like Zs: long straight traverses that are connected by abrupt changes of direction. Not only does the expert's way look cooler, it's also much more efficient because the end of one turn flows seamlessly into the top of the next.

SSSSnaking down the slope

To improve your turns, practice this exercise, which is suitable for all levels of skiers. Find a gentle, freshly groomed slope. Then start making turns and actively concentrate on the transition from turn to turn. Try to roll smoothly from one set of edges to another without pausing to traverse across the hill. After you're into the new turn, just ride the ski in a smooth round arc, trusting that it will come around, because it will.

How do you know if the exercise is working? Look back up the hill at your tracks. If your turns are curvy, congratulations are in order. If they're still a little ragged, try it again, this time making the turns a little bigger.

Figure 8-2:
A variation
on the
flamingo
turn, which
helps hone
one-footed
balance.

Controlling your speed by completing your turns

Ever notice that good skiers seem to make every turn at the same speed? They don't end up going a little faster with each turn until they reach Mach 7 and then have to slam on the brakes. So how do good skiers manage their speed so effectively? They don't wedge, and they don't skid their skis sideways to scrub off speed. They control their speed by adjusting the shape of their turns. To do likewise, practice the following exercise, which is helpful for all levels of skiers.

The C-what I mean? exercise

Start by making one turn, but instead of heading into another turn, keep riding the ski and continue on up the hill until you stop. Notice the shape of the turn. It's more like a "C" than like a question mark, right? Now make one of those C turns, but don't come quite to a full stop. See Figure 8-3. When your speed is under control, begin the next turn. Experiment with this method of speed control, striking a balance between controlling your speed and moving seamlessly from turn to turn (as in the previous SSSSnake drill).

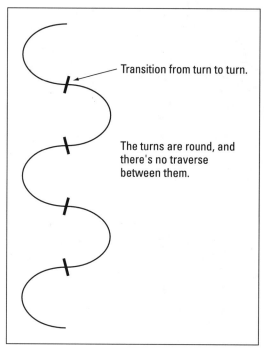

Transition from turn to turn.

The turns are round, and there's no traverse between them.

Figure 8-3:
The C-what
I mean?
exercise.

Keeping your hands in front

Good skiers leave their hands out in front where they can see them. Is it a symptom or is it a cause? I don't know; that question is a little too similar to the chicken-and-egg conundrum for me. But I do know this: Dropping your hand back can throw off your balance. I think of a tight-rope walker here. Practice keeping your hands out in front by using the following exercise, suitable for all levels of skiers.

The waiter turn

On an easy-to-moderate slope, remove your poles and rest them across your wrists, a little bit like you're carrying a cafeteria tray. See Figure 8-4. Don't cheat by trying to hold the poles with your hands. Now make some turns. To keep the poles from falling or sliding you have to keep your hands up and your poles level throughout the turn. After you have the hang of that, put your poles back on and try to maintain that hand position. If you can glance down and see both of your hands, you're doing it.

Figure 8-4:
The waiter turn keeps your hands where you can see them.

Developing a pole touch

Many intermediate skiers take the term *pole plant* too literally. They hold the pole with a death grip and augur the snow as if they're trying to dig for potatoes. A good skier uses a *pole touch,* using his pole like an orchestra conductor uses his baton. That pole touch is a signal, the trigger to start the turn and maintain rhythm. Practice the following exercise, which is appropriate for intermediate and advanced skiers.

The conductor drill

First put the pole on correctly. (See the sidebar "Gripping a pole properly.") Standing still, hold the grip with just your thumb and forefinger. Swing the pole gently forward, keeping your arms stationary and using only your wrist. See Figure 8-5. The tip of the pole should swing back and forth like a pendulum. When you can do this effectively with both hands, moving one up and the other back with synchronization that would make the Temptations jealous, it's time to move on. Touch the pole to the snow ever so gently, with the tip coming down just shy of and outside the tip of your ski. Take this new kinder, gentler pole touch, and apply it to actual turns, adjusting the rhythm of the pole movements to the radius of your turns — faster for shorter turns, slower for longer turns.

Gripping a pole properly

Gripping a pole seems like the simplest thing in skiing, but even many experienced skiers hold their poles wrong. Holding a pole incorrectly not only makes it impossible to make a proper pole touch, but it can actually lead to injury if you fall on your wrist the wrong way. To hold your pole correctly, follow these steps, demonstrated in the accompanying figure:

1. **Start with your hand under the strap.**

2. **Put your hand through the strap from underneath.**

3. **Grab the grip of the pole, letting the strap fall between your thumb and index finger.**

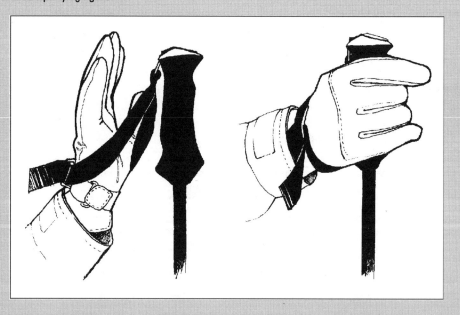

Figure 8-5: The conductor exercise sharpens your pole touch.

SKI TIP

The road to good

Kristen Ulmer, extreme skier _par excellence_, once told me this story about the road to becoming a good skier.

"A friend of mine came up to me and said he wanted to be an expert skier. 'What do I need to do,' he asked me. So I told him, 'You need to keep your hands up, look down the hill, and keep your shins always touching the tongues of your boots.' He came back a couple of weeks later and said, 'Hey, Kristen, I've been doing what you said. Now what?'

'Just keep on doing it.'

And for theatrical effect, Kristen just skied off into the fog as she recited the punchline.

The moral of this story? As I stood alone in a whiteout, I realized that good skiing is both easy and hard. It's easy because it's about maintaining a few basic body positions. It's hard, because you have to maintain that position at all kinds of speeds, on all kinds of snow, and on all kinds of terrain.

Using the ski's shape to help you turn

Effective skiers use the shape of the ski to help them turn. Tip a ski on edge, weight it, and slide it forward. It won't go straight because of its sidecut (see Chapter 3); instead, it makes a gradual arc in the snow. To tighten that arc, you need to do these two things: Tip the ski up on edge while putting more of your weight on it. The following drill (for intermediate skiers and up) gives you the feeling of doing both those things.

The power wedge drill

Put your skis into a wide, slightly exaggerated wedge, with your ski tips pointing towards each other. Bring your knees together until you feel like you're knock-kneed. That should put both your skis on edge. Now make some turns with that exaggerated stance, shifting your weight to your outside ski so that it slices through the snow. Now, try and take that slicing feel into parallel turns.

Pointing the ski down the hill

Pete Palmer, a great ski teacher, once gave me this great tip. He pointed to the tip of my ski and said, "What's that, and what's it for?" I was about to launch into a long, rambling, highly technical explanation about how the upturned tip serves to deflect snow and help engage the edge during the initiation phase of the turn, when Pete cut me off. "I think it looks like an arrow," he said. "And what are arrows for? They indicate direction." And, he added, "There aren't any arrows pointing backward or to the side."

The arrow drill

The arrow drill, for intermediate skiers and up, teaches you the feeling of carving a turn. While you're just standing, take your ski and slide it forward and back, on its edge, following the direction of the "arrow" on the tip. Feel how effortlessly it slides? Then take your ski and try to push it, from side to side, across the snow. A lot harder, huh? Now try and make some long turns, on an easy trail, concentrating on moving the ski down the hill and sliding the ski along its edge, rather than skidding sideways.

The Mental Side of Skiing

If Yogi Berra were born in Switzerland, he may have said something like "100 percent of skiing is half mental." And he would have been right, sort of. Most of us ski best when our brains are turned off. Or at least if we turn off our conscious brains — the part that makes judgements — that second guesses us, that dredges up our fears at the most inopportune times. What gets in the way of skiing instinctively is that little voice that says, "Hey, where are you going? . . . Come on, bend your knees more . . . No, not THAT much . . . Man, those turns stink . . . and by the way . . . watch out for that *bump*."

Drills to free your mind

Here are some drills that should help your skiing. These drills give your conscious mind something to do besides second-guessing your turns.

The Mr. Tree drill

On a slightly challenging trail, pick out a tree some distance down the hill. See Figure 8-6. Bond with the tree. Think of a question to ask it. ("If you were a news show host, which news show host would you be?") Then make it your priority to get from here to there. The key is to look at the tree and ignore the terrain between you and the tree, reacting to the variations instinctively. (Do, however, pay attention to any snow sliders between you and the tree.)

Figure 8-6:
Find a tree and ignore the terrain between you and it.

Courtesy NSAA and Studio 404 Photography

The "Fur Elise" drill

Find a favorite trail — something just a little easier than what you're used to and then pick your favorite song. Start singing to yourself. Out loud? Sure if you want to. The goal is to shift your conscious focus to the music and forget about your skiing a little. In fact, make your skiing follow the flow of the music. If you're channeling Beethoven's *Fur Elise,* make your turns flowing and lyrical. If the Ramones' *Blitzkreig Bop* is rattling around in your brain, turn up the volume in your skiing.

As you're skiing, hit shuffle play on your mental CD player. Go from loud to quiet. Fast to slow. From a ballad to a dance tune. Just let your feet and your skis move to your internal soundtrack. It's fun and a great remedy for thinking too much about your skiing.

The be-like-Picabo drill

This one's simple, but surprisingly effective. Decide who you want to ski like, and just pretend you're him or her. Do you want to ski with power and aggression like gold medal downhiller Picabo Street?

Do you want to be agile and nimble like Olympic mogul champion Donna Weinbrecht?

Do you want to be smooth and graceful like the instructor you took your last lesson from?

Then, as they say in the sneaker ads, just do it.

Follow me

Find someone who skis better than you, and follow her. Really follow her, though. Keep your visual focus on the back of her jacket, and follow about two turns behind. It's possible that your partner may have to slow down a little, but you should also have to push a little, too, to keep up. There are some variations on this theme. You can follow in your partner's tracks, as shown in Figure 8-7, or you can figure eight your partner's turns, turning not *where* they turn but *when.* And while it's good to start out with constant radius turns, you can spice up the exercise by having the leader change the turn radius periodically, forcing you to adapt.

Figure 8-7:
Follow a
better skier,
and you'll
begin to ski
like her.

Courtesy Booth Creek Resorts

Fighting fear

Unlike bowling, where your only fear is that your boss may see you wearing a silly shirt, skiing does inspire legitimate fears. Skiing can bring out fears such as: the fear of speed, the fear of heights, the fear of getting injured, or the fear of looking silly when you screw up. Any skier who tells you they've never been afraid is either stupid or lying — most likely the latter. Here are some ways to overcome your on-snow jitters:

- ✔ **Do a reality check:** What are you really afraid of? Try to step back and analyze the situation. Are you afraid of falling? Are you afraid of getting injured? Are you afraid of looking silly? Most of the time you may realize that you're making a mountain out of the proverbial molehill.

- ✔ **De-stress yourself:** The physical manifestations of fear can often make failure inevitable. Your muscles get tense. Your breathing gets rapid and shallow and your focus narrows.

  When this happens, you need to consciously try to relax yourself. Loosen the grip on your poles. Shake your arms out. Bounce up and down. Take a few slow deep breaths. And look not at where you are, but where you're going. (For more information, see Chapter 6.)

✔ **See yourself succeeding:** Take your mental VCR, and pop in a tape of you skiing at your best, then fast forward to a new scene of you mastering this particular situation. Try to make it as detailed as possible — a virtual reality game in which you feel the breeze on your face, the snow beneath your feet. Does this really work? You bet it does. Most racers and extreme skiers perform this ritual before every run.

✔ **Start out strong:** For many skiers, making their first turn is like an indecisive swimmer dipping his little toe into a pool. You should dive in instead. Make your first turn as solid and aggressive as you can. If you commit to one solid turn, the one after that, and the one after that become a piece of cake.

Overcoming Difficult Snow Conditions

While most of the tips I share in this chapter apply almost anywhere on the mountain in any kind of snow, certain kinds of terrain and conditions demand some special techniques, as I outline below.

✔ **Absorb the bumps:** In bumps, you have to be able to suck it up. Literally. One of the most important keys to bump skiing is the ability to absorb the bumps instead of letting the bumps bounce you around. To practice this skill, traverse *across* a field of small to medium moguls, not making any turns, but instead concentrating on using your knees and hips like shock absorbers, and keeping your skis in contact with the snow.

✔ **Finesse the ice:** Can't turn on ice? Join the club. Most skiers who aren't on the World Cup can't turn very effectively on ice. The first key to skiing well on ice is accepting that you're going to slide a little during each turn. After you stop fighting that, it's much easier. You need to be supple on your edges. Listen to the sound of your skis. If your turn is quiet, you're doing something right. If it sounds like a cat with its tail caught in a door, then you need to edge more gently.

✔ **Slice through the crud:** On groomed slopes, you're skiing *on* the snow. But when you're skiing through crud or heavy powder, you're skiing *in* the snow. And because your skis are virtually buried, it's not as easy to move them.

Unlike on the groomed slopes, you need to turn with both skis equally weighted. If you don't, your inside ski floats, your outside ski sinks, and you end up with crossed tips or worse. The other key is patience. You have to make big turns, and really let the ski take its time moving down the hill. Don't worry about picking up too much speed because the friction of the snow will slow you down. Instead of pushing the heavy snow sideways, concentrate on moving the ski forward. The motion is really like slicing a tomato with a Ginzu knife. If you try to press down without moving forward, the result is a squashed tomato — or a ski that gets bogged down. Follow this advice, though, and soon you may find heavy snow as tasty as a BLT.

Chapter 9

Different Strokes: Alternative Means of Sliding

*W*hat is skiing? That's a little like asking what is eating? What is reading? What is doing the Macarena? The correct answer, slightly metaphysical though it may be, is that skiing is something different for everyone. For some, it's the thrill of speed. For others, skiing is all about getting back to nature. For still others, it's a chance to simply play in the snow.

As you get more experience on snow, you may discover just what it is that floats your proverbial boat. And when you do, you discover that there are ways to float it that you hadn't even imagined and lots of similarly minded snow sliders who are happy to play Gilligan to your Skipper. ("Aww, shucks, Little Buddy.")

The best part is that the world of snow sliding has never been quite so open to new ideas as it is now. Resorts are doing more than ever to find new ways for skiers of all levels to have new and different kinds of fun on the snow. It's all-you-can-eat time at the great gravity buffet.

In this chapter, I take you on a brief tour of some of skiing's little niches. I explain the full-bore world of racing. I take you on a backcountry tour of the retro-chic world of telemarking. I tell you about the straight-from-the-X-Games excitement of skiboarding. For the open-minded among you, there's even snowboarding for skiers.

Finding Your Niche

How do you go about figuring out which skiing spin-off is right for you? It's more like falling in love than looking for a job. If you simply keep your eyes and your mind open, you may see something going on out on the hill that's almost irresistibly interesting. Then it's just a matter of, as they may say in some touchier-feelier book, following your bliss.

Just like asking for a first date, getting started in a new activity is sometimes easier said than done. To make the transition a little less traumatic, I'm not only giving you the skinny on each sub-genre, but also telling you how to break in. Ready? Set? Slide.

Ski Racing

The concept is pretty simple: Get down the mountain faster than the other guy. But within that basic go-fast directive, there are plenty of sub-genres. Here's a brief rundown of the events that come to your television in a Winter Olympics year:

- **Slalom** is run over a course of tightly spaced gates that require skiers to make quick, sharp turns. In modern slalom, however, the gates are spring-loaded, so skiers ski over them as much as around them, pushing the gates out of the way with their forearms and shins, and wear body armor to keep them from getting black and blue while they do so. Slaloms are generally contested with one racer on the course at a time, against the clock, and the racer with the best cumulative time over two runs wins. Missing a gate on either run, however, disqualifies the racer.

- **A Giant slalom** race — often abbreviated as GS — is run over a course featuring fimly planted gates spaced more widely than slalom. The result is that racers make turns that look a lot like regular skiing, only faster.

- **In Super-G**, skiers make some turns around giant slalom-style gates but mostly head down a fairly twisty trail, turning only where the trail turns. Racers spend a fair amount of time in a *tuck* — an aerodynamic crouch designed for maximum speed.

- **In downhill**, the fastest and most glamorous event, skiers head down a long, fast course punctuated with the fewest number of gates of any event and rolls in the terrain that serve as mini-ski jumps. Downhillers spend almost the entire run in a tuck, and reach truly breathtaking speeds — more than 70 miles an hour on some stretches.

Why ski racing is fun

Speed thrills. It's fun to ski fast, and even more fun when you only have to worry about stationary gates on a race course instead of oblivious skiers on an open slope. And, of course, there's the human drama of athletic competition — the thrill of victory and the agony of defeat.

Why ski racing is good for you

Have you ever seen a skier who skis so beautifully it makes your jaw drop? Chances are, if you do, you're looking at a racer or a former racer. Virtually all the best skiers on the planet have spent a significant amount of time running gates. Why? Because racing is the single best way to improve your free skiing. Skiing fast, and turning whenever you come to a gate, instead of when you feel like it, builds the kind of discipline and technique that most non-racers never achieve.

Getting started

You don't have to join the World Cup to get a taste of racing. Most resorts offer *NASTAR* racing, in which you can compete against a national standard, courtesy of a local pacesetter. NASTAR *is* really a painless endeavor. The courses are relatively easy — the turns are giant slalom radius, but the speeds are much lower. The entry fee is cheap and the wait is usually minimal, and it's relatively easy to win a medal. If you want to get a little more serious without quitting your day job, many resorts have adult racing leagues, often on weekday evenings. That way you can pretend you're Alberto Tomba after you turn off your computer for the day.

Gear check

Racers use the same kind of equipment as you do — only more so. Their skis are more responsive and waxed and sharpened to a fine edge. Their boots are often sized a few sizes too small, all the better to transmit every tiny movement directly to the ski. (That's why racers bend down to unbuckle their boots almost before they stop moving.) Racers wear Lycra skinsuits that are plenty aerodynamic, but not very warm. Of course, you can start recreational racing with the equipment you own. As you get a little more serious, you may find that a few moderate tweaks — such as a trip to the bootfitter or a little pre-race waxing could save you a couple tenths of a second.

Rutbusters

How do you make an old mountain new again? No, this isn't a how-to question from *Geology Today*, it's my personal pitch for finding new ways to slide.

There are a lot of good reasons why you may ski the same mountain week after week and year after year. It's the best resort in your area. It's the *only* resort in the area. Your kids are in a lesson program there. You got a great deal on a season pass. Or you're just a creature of habit.

But no matter how much you like an area, skiing the same trails again and again can get a little boring. Especially if the terrain isn't especially challenging. That's why the alternative modes of sliding I discuss in this chapter are so valuable. They can make an old mountain seem new again. Most alternative sliding modes don't require a huge investment in equipment, and mastering a new technique can be fun, and help your skiing as a whole.

How do I know? Because I've taken my own advice. After a couple of seasons teaching at the same small, local area I found that I was skiing the mountain on auto pilot. So instead of moving to the Bahamas and becoming a snorkeling instructor, I took a more moderate approach. I bought a pair of skiboards and soon I was looping 360s down the resort's steepest trail.

Then a couple of seasons later when ennui struck again, I took up snowboarding. Every week, I could feel myself getting better and better, and the wide, gentle slopes that presented little challenge on skis, were now perfect for laying carves — or trying to — on my board.

Telemarking

SKI SPEAK

Telemarking is essentially downhill skiing on modified cross-country ski gear — beefier boots, skis with metal edges, but bindings that don't lock your heel down (hence the backcountry battle cry "Free your heel, free your mind.") The distinctive-looking telemark turn — the skier vaguely looks like he's genuflecting— is actually one of the earliest skiing techniques, pioneered by the Norwegians more than a century ago. Telemarking was all but forgotten until a renaissance in the mid 1970s. Today, however, many skiers make conventional parallel turns on telemark gear.

Why telemarking is fun

While many telemarkers ski primarily on groomed trails within resort boundaries, the biggest appeal of telemarking is that it's one of the best ways to explore the backcountry. Telemark gear is lighter when you have to carry it, and when snow conditions allow, you can slide uphill as well as down, with the aid of *climbing skins*, strips of uni-directional fabric that attach to the bottom of the ski, and make it possible to ski uphill without sliding backwards.

Why telemarking is good for you

If you want to know why it's valuable to spend time in the woods, I refer you to Henry David Thoreau. If you want to know what telemarking can do for your skiing skills, here goes. Making turns on skinny skis helps your balance. Venturing off the groomed terrain of a ski area teaches you how to deal with natural snow conditions, both heavenly (fresh powder) and hellish (refrozen crud). And in a way that Thoreau would have understood, making only three or four runs in a day, and paying for every foot of descending with a corresponding foot of climbing, teaches you to live in the moment.

Getting started

The best way to start telemarking is at your friendly neighborhood ski area. Most ski schools offer telemark lessons (but probably not telemark rentals), but it's a bit of a specialty so you should try to book the lesson in advance. After you build up the skills to venture into the backcountry, be sure to hook up with a guide or an experienced partner who can show you the ropes, including avalanche safety. (For more information on avalanches, albeit not a substitute for formal training, see Chapter 11.)

Gear check

Contemporary telemark skis are still lighter than their alpine brethren, but with their wider widths and deep dish sidecuts, they're moving further and further from their Nordic roots. Telemark boots — many of them now with plastic shells — are getting more and more alpine-like. A few free-heel bindings are even releasable. Many backcountry skiers, especially in Europe, use easy-skiing alpine touring gear, which is sort of a hybrid of telemark and alpine gear. Like telemark gear, it's lighter and designed for uphill transport as well as downhill turns. Like alpine gear, both the heel and toe are locked into the binding.

Skiboards

One of the hottest trends in snow sliding, *skiboards,* shown in Figure 9-1, are tiny skis that are only slightly longer than your boot. Sometimes called snowskates, skiboards turn on a dime, and can go places that longer skis fear to tread. The short-ski craze traces its roots back to Alpine mountain guides who would hacksaw a pair of conventional skis, remount the bindings, and then carry these *figls* in their packs to slide down snow-covered avalanche chutes in the late spring and early summer.

Figure 9-1:
Skiboards
encourage
all manner
of poles-
free fun.

Today's skiboards, which are used with conventional ski boots, can be found in halfpipes and terrain garden frequented by snowboarders as well as just about anywhere on the mountain. Many skiboard converts are former in-line skaters who've adapted eight-wheel tricks and moves to the snow in much the same way that early snowboarders borrowed from skateboarding and surfing. Skiboards are surprisingly versatile for just plain cruising — they hold an edge well in hardpack, and with their wider platform, skiboards float surprisingly well in crud and less-than-bottomless powder.

Why skiboarding is fun

One of the early names for this genre — and perhaps the most apt — was *snow toy.* Skiboards encourage you to just get out and have fun. Spins, jumps, and even ski dancing are easier when there's less ski to worry about.

Skiboarding is such a new spin-off of skiing that the rules haven't been written yet. Tricks are being invented faster than the skiers can name them. It's your opportunity to be a pioneer. One small step, one giant leap, and all that. And if you get really good, who knows? You could earn a slot at the next Winter X-Games.

Why skiboarding is good for you

Skiboards are fantastic teaching tools. The basic technique is very similar to skiing (although most skiboarders shed their poles). Skiboards have significant sidecuts, so they turn like regular-shaped skis only more so. Because of their short length, skiboards are very demanding of fore-and-aft balance, so they teach you to stay centered on your conventional skis. That's why World Cup racers train on them, and many resorts have begun using skiboards in their ski school classes, teaching students from rank beginner to full-blown experts.

Getting started

You can find skiboards in many rental shops and on-hill demo centers. If you're an accomplished skier, you probably don't have to take a lesson — although many resorts are now offering skiboard instruction — but you should stick to moderate terrain until you get the hang of skiboarding. However, if you're looking to figure out tricks or master the halfpipe, and you don't want to try the trial-and-error method with its associated bumps and bruises, a lesson or clinic should help speed your progress.

Gear check

Skiboards are one of the fastest growing segments of the winter sports market, with virtually every major equipment manufacturer jumping on the bandwagon within the last couple of seasons. The result of this growth is a wide variety of products, some that are very ski-like and are designed for making turns, and others that have a wider platform for landing jumps. Most skiboards have user-adjustable, non-releasing bindings, although some kind of releasable binding may soon be available.

Snowboarding

If you've ever seen a Mountain Dew commercial, you know about snow boarding. If you've been on the mountain, you've seen how much fun snow-boarders have. And if you've ever been out in chopped up powder or mashed-potato crud, you realize that sometimes a snowboard is just the right tool for the job.

Why snowboarding is fun

Snowboarding provides a whole different way of seeing the mountain. If you're an accomplished skier but a novice snowboarder, you get to experience the thrill of learning all over again. And certain snow, that's too sloppy to ski— like soft, springtime mashed potatoes or corn snow — is still great fun on a snowboard.

Why snowboarding is good for you

Snowboarding enhances your balance and your ability to read terrain. And snowboarders carve in a way that most skiers only do in their dreams. See Figure 9-2.

Figure 9-2: Snowboards are especially suited for carving.

Courtesy Skis Dynastar

Getting started

Snowboarding, like skiing, it definitely a lesson sport. The learning curve is very steep, but the first day or two is full of hard work and more than a few falls, so prepare yourself. Take your first snowboarding lesson on a day when the snow is soft. You may get a little wetter, but you may appreciate the impact protection. Also, wearing a pair of in-line skate wrist guards is good insurance against injury during one of those frequent, early falls.

Gear check

Most snowboarders use soft, freestyle boots that resemble *aprés ski* boots. In fact, comfy boots are one of the things that attract some skiers to snowboarding. However, some crossover skiers — myself included — mount racing-style plate bindings on their snowboards and ride with their ski boots. The advantage? Some crossover skiers find that Alpine equipment makes learning easier, and it's one less pair of boots to carry, and it allows you to switch from skiing to snowboarding without changing boots.

Powder Skiing

Imagine acres of snow that's been untouched by groomers, and there's not so much as a single ski track in sight. That's what powder skiing is all about. While you do get powder days at resorts, the fresh snow is tracked up within a couple hours of the lift opening. But when you're pursuing backcountry powder, you ski virgin snow all day long. The three basic means of getting to this epic snow are helicopter, which is fast but expensive, and can be grounded by bad weather, and the kind of snowcat used for grooming at resorts — which is slower, but much cheaper. The third option is human power, which I discuss in the telemarking section earlier in this chapter.

Why powder skiing is fun

People have compared powder skiing to sex, drugs, and other out-of-body experiences — and they're not exaggerating. It's hard to describe, but I'm going to try. Because you rarely hit bottom on the snow — you're skiing *in* it as much as *on* it — you feel like you're floating. See Figure 9-3. Unlike on groomed snow, the powder slows you down enough that you're often looking for more speed instead of devising ways to control it. Because there are no lifts, few other skiers, and nothing for your edges to scrape against, it's strangely quiet. Some — at least one hang gliding operation — have even compared powder skiing to flying. Aww, forget it. Just go try it yourself.

Why powder skiing is good for you

Powder skiing is good for your soul. Face it, it's the best on-snow feeling there is, a peak experience in every way. Powder skiing gives you an appreciation of what skiing can be. It also teaches you tactics that work well in deep snow in a resort.

Courtesy Elan

Figure 9-3:
You ski "in"
powder, not
"on" it.

Getting started

Many Western resorts offer powder-cat skiing. You climb the hill in a snowcat instead of on a lift, and you pay only $200 for a day instead of several thousand for a week. You need to be at least a strong intermediate skier to enjoy powder skiing, and make sure you discuss your ability level with your tour operator before you sign up.

Gear check

All but the hardest of the die-hards — and most of them, too — make their powder turns on short, fat powder skis. Powder skis make skiing in deep, fluffy powder much easier and much less work, and make skiing in cruddy or heavy powder pretty fun too. Many skiers use *powder cords* — leashes that tie around the binding and your ankle, to keep you from having to search for your ski if the binding releases in deep snow. A one-piece suit, or a jacket with a powder skirt and tight closures around the cuffs and collar are important too. Tour operators distribute avalanche *transceivers* — small radio devices that help locate an avalanche-buried victim — and show you how to use them.

SKI SAFE

Attack of the killer evergreens

While avalanches are a possibility, most commercial powder skiing operations do everything they can to minimize that danger. For more information about avalanches, see Chapter 11. There is another hidden danger in powder (or backcountry) skiing: tree wells. Evergreen trees give off a certain amount of heat even in the winter, which, coupled with the natural umbrella effect that the tree's branches provide, keeps the snow from packing tightly around the base of the tree. This creates a deep bowl around the perimeter of the tree called a tree well. If you ski too close to a tree well, you can fall in upside down, unable to extricate yourself, and you can actually suffocate. That's why powder skiers adopt the buddy system and take the obligation to their partner seriously.

Chapter 10

Getting Around the Mountain

• •

▶ Reading maps, slopes, and grooming reports
▶ Negotiating the mountain
▶ Beating the crowds
▶ Handling the weather

• •

*Y*ou ride up. You ski down. Repeat as necessary. What could be simpler? Actually, there's plenty to know about the fine art of getting around a mountain wearing skis.

Mountains, despite Muhammad's experience, are generally quite immovable. On one hand, the guys who design ski areas do their best to make things as logical and user-friendly as they can. But on the other hand, even the smartest resort architects have to work within the confines of what a mountain allows them to do. And then you have another wild card — the unpredictable mountain weather, which can sometimes make getting around even a well-designed resort difficult.

So by taking a crash course (not literally, of course) in mountain geography — knowing a few things about Alpine climates and the way ski areas tend to be laid out — you can get the most out of your ski day. You can find the best snow on the mountain, avoid waiting in lines, be prepared for adverse weather conditions, and put more of your energy into skiing and less into schlepping across the flats. In this chapter, I show you how to gather the intelligence and use the techniques that may help make your ski day fun and easy. I discuss planning your day, reading a trail map, and having fun even on those days when Mother Nature doesn't cooperate.

Finding Your Way around the Mountain

What's the difference between Lewis and Clark and you? They didn't have a map, and you do. Cartography is the thing that separates vacationers from explorers. That is why the first order of business after you get to a ski area is to get a trail map for yourself as well as one for everyone else in your party. They're free, and you can find them at any ticket counter and at other convenient places throughout the ski area.

After you have a map, what do you do with it? First, you want to take it with you wherever you go. Few things are more frustrating than making a wrong turn or missing a trail cutoff and not knowing which way to go, and not having a map to help you out your quandary.

Reading a map

Before a map can help you plan your day, you have to be able to read it. Like the rest of society, trail maps are full of symbols, and like an amateur anthropologist, you can be way ahead of the game if you understand what they mean. Here's a primer:

Trail designations

Each ski area generally has four trail designations based on relative difficulty, compared to other trails at the resort.

- ✔ A green circle designates the easiest trails.
- ✔ A blue square designates more difficult trails.
- ✔ A black diamond designates the most difficult trails.
- ✔ Multiple black diamonds, if they're present, designate extremely difficult terrain suitable for expert skiers only.

On your map, each trail has a name, a number that corresponds to a key at the bottom, and a difficulty designation. You should find a similar sign at the beginning of each trail, usually hung on a tree or post. See Figure 10-1.

Figure 10-1: Trail signs can help you get oriented and stay safe.

Courtesy NSAA and Studio 404 Photography

The best way to plan your day is to squint a little at the map. What kind of trails do you usually ski? Green circle and blue square? Then locate the area on the map where you find the most blue and green. Most resorts have an area where there's a concentration of greens, another area where there's a concentration of blues, and another area where there's a concentration of blacks.

As for those sometimes chameleon-like blue squares — sometimes practically green, other times almost black — understand that as a rule, the blue square in a cluster of blacks is likely to be more difficult than the blue square surrounded on the map by greens. It's smart to begin your ski day, especially if you're at a new resort, on a trail that's one notch below your comfort zone. If you're happy skiing blues, warm up on a couple of greens first.

Now it's time to zero in on specific trails. While trail maps aren't done completely to scale, you can get a pretty good idea of a trail's general characteristics. Is it short or long? Is it wide or is it narrow? Is it straight or is it curvy? Does it end at a mid-mountain cafeteria where you can buy a soda and curly fries? Or at some out-of-the-way parking lot two hours from lunch?

Beware of those trails that meander too much from side to side, going as much across the mountain as down it. These trails often have long flat sections, and if they cross other trails frequently, they may actually be narrow catwalks, designed more for getting around the mountain than for real, live skiing. However, some ski areas do have one meandering trail that's nice for beginners because it lets you take a long scenic run from the top.

Remember that trails were often named in the days before trail designations. So a trail may sometimes change designation as it goes from top to bottom — say from blue to black. Be especially careful if the mountain sees fit to add an addendum to a trail's name, like Upper Tomahawk and Lower Tomahawk.

Getting a lift

After you know where you're going, you need to find out how to get there. That's where the lifts come in. The map shows you each lift, its name, how many people it seats, where it starts, and where it goes.

Understand that some lifts only access more challenging terrain. So if you only can or want to ski green trails, make sure you're riding a lift that doesn't access only blues and blacks. While you should check the trail map for intermediate and up lifts, most areas also post a sign to that effect at the bottom of the lift. Note also that at most areas some lifts go part way up the mountain, while others go all the way to the top. If you're a beginner or lower intermediate, you might want to ski these mid-mountain chairs, because they offer a nice balance between a shortish run followed by a shortish ride.

SKI TIP

Schlepping your skis

One of the real pains in skiing is schlepping your skis and gear around — unless you bring your own valet, its unavoidable. But if you're smart, it doesn't have to be a real pain.

If you're driving to the resort, be smart. All ski areas have an unloading zone near the lodge. Pull your car up, dump off your stuff, and then go find a parking place.

And how do you carry your skis? Just about any way that you can avoid dropping them is fine. But the preferred way is to rest them on your shoulder, with the tips pointed forward, and casually drape your hand over them. Use your other hand to carry your poles and your ski bag. One caution. If you turn around quickly with your skis perched this way, you could literally hit someone in the face.

You've probably figured this out, but you can't bring them into the lodge with you. So leave them on a rack outside, with your pole straps looped over the top, propped up so they don't fall over. Of course, you want to make a mental note of where you left them so you can find them when you're done with lunch. And when you're heading to the slopes, you don't necessarily want to put your skis on right away. If the lift is uphill from the lodge, you'll probably want to carry your skis and put them on when you get closer to the lift.

And finally, remember that while you should bring your skis into a condo, most hotels have a ski storage room or a set of lockers, and would prefer that you don't mess up the nice wallpaper in your room with sharp ski edges.

Finding a home base

After you decide what lifts you need to ride, you need to find a home base. At a small area, finding a home base is a no-brainer — most lifts start and end at the same place. But a big mountain can have a half-dozen or more widely spaced base lodges, where you can find a cafeteria, restrooms, and a place to just sit down for a few minutes. If you're at a mega-resort, make sure that anyone you're meeting in the morning or for lunch knows which base lodge you're talking about. If you're not sure exactly where you're heading or how to get there, look at your map or ask directions before you board a lift. Taking the wrong lift can send you on a half-hour detour.

KIDS SKI

If you're skiing with kids, you not only should tell them which lodge you're meeting at, but you should write it down, along with the phone number of the place where you're staying. Then the kids can call you if they get really lost.

Reading the Grooming Report

When you're driving, a good map is the cornerstone of getting where you're going. But you supplement that map with listening to the traffic report on the radio, right? Well, do the same when you're skiing.

Every morning, the ski area issues a grooming report. It's usually posted at the base lodge, the ski school desk, and, if you're staying at an on-mountain hotel, in the lobby or the elevators a few hours before the lifts open. The grooming report is chock-full of useful information. Here's what you're likely to find, and how you can use it:

- ✔ **Weather conditions:** The grooming report tells you what the early and overnight temperatures were on the mountain, and what the temperatures should be during the day. On its most basic level, the grooming report tells you how you should dress for the day. It can also tell you something about the snow conditions. If it was cold yesterday and cold overnight, that's great. But if the temperatures the day before were well above freezing, and the mercury dropped to well below freezing overnight (a condition typical of early or late season skiing), the snow probably refroze. Despite the groomers' best efforts, the snow is likely to be a little crunchy, so this could be a good morning for a leisurely breakfast.

- ✔ **Snow conditions:** Another part of the grooming report tells you if it snowed overnight. If it did, then skip breakfast — or wolf down a banana on the chairlift — and plan on getting out early. Even if it didn't snow, you may be able to find some freshies on the mountain. The report tells you where the snowmakers made snow, which usually indicates where you can find some of the best snow surfaces on the mountain. It also describes the existing snow surfaces in some detail. See the "Deciphering snow conditions" sidebar in this chapter.

- ✔ **Grooming conditions:** The grooming report also tells you which areas have been freshly groomed. What exactly is *grooming*? It's when the mountain's snowcats churn up any icy spots and then level and smooth the snow surface so that it looks almost like wide-wale corduroy. If there's fresh snow, grooming means it's been compacted, which is good or bad depending on whether you hate or love powder. While all green circles and most blue squares are groomed on a daily basis, many blacks and a few blues are left with moguls on them throughout the season. If a trail is marked "ungroomed" on the report, you can assume there are bumps on it. Keep in mind that the grooming routine can change from day to day, and a trail that was buffed smooth yesterday may have moguls today, and vice versa.

Deciphering snow conditions

A grooming report, or a ski report you hear on the radio or by calling a resort, uses a series of tightly defined terms to describe the snow surface.

Corn snow: A condition, usually found in the spring, characterized by large, loose granules of snow that freeze together at night, and then melt apart again during the day.

Frozen granular: A hard surface of old snow formed by granules freezing together after a rain or a period of warm temperatures.

Hardpack: When natural or machine-made snow becomes very firmly packed because of grooming or wind exposure, but has never melted and re-crystallized.

Ice: A hard, glazed, usually translucent surface created either by freezing rain, ground water seeping up into the snow and freezing, or by the rapid freezing of snow saturated with water from rain or melting.

Loose granular: This surface results after powder or packed powder thaws, refreezes, and re-crystallizes. It can also be created by machine grooming of frozen or icy snow.

Machine groomed granular: Loose granular snow that has been repeatedly groomed by power tillers so that the sugary texture is halfway between loose granular and packed powder.

Packed powder: Powder snow, either natural or machine-made, that has been packed down by skier traffic or grooming machines. The snow is no longer fluffy, but it is not so extremely compacted that it is hard.

Powder: Cold, new, loose, fluffy, dry snow that has not been compacted and is usually the product of fresh, natural snowfall at a low temperature.

Spring conditions: A snow reporting term, which is the late season equivalent of variable conditions, often with the addition of bare spots or a discolored surface from melting and traffic.

Variable conditions: A snow reporting term that means that a variety of surfaces may be encountered.

Wet granular: Loose or frozen granular snow that has become wet after a rainfall or a period of high temperatures.

✔ **Lift status:** The grooming report also tells you what lifts are open. Sometimes during the week, an area closes down a lift if there's another one nearby that serves the same terrain. This isn't usually a problem unless you hike over to a lift to find it as inert as Chef Paul Prudhomme after Thanksgiving dinner.

The report also lists the times that the lifts start running, what time the lifts close, and which lifts close early during the day.

✔ **What's open:** If it's early or late in the season, trail openings are based on sufficient snow cover. Again, that's not usually a problem, unless you ski over and find your trail of choice roped off.

Pit stop strategy

It's one of the imponderables of the universe: Why does every ski area have its restrooms in the basement? Actually, it's probably something that's better answered by your local plumber than by the Dalai Lama.

But here's some advice. Ski boots and stairs don't mix. So in the morning, go to the bathroom *before* you put your boots on. And at the end of the day, take your boots off before you head to the restroom.

During your midday bathroom breaks, take advantage of all the facilities have to offer. The hand dryers do a great job of warming and drying your gloves. Grab a paper towel and really clean off your goggles. Make a stop at the water fountain outside to replenish your fluids.

Using the Sun as a Guide

In skiing as in life, as George Harrison suggested, it's good to follow the sun. If you pay attention to the sun's location, you'll have a head start on finding the best snow as well as having the best visibility.

Following the sun

First thing in the morning, you want to find the south- and east-facing slopes. The light is the best on those slopes, and the snow may have been softened by the early morning rays.

Avoiding the sun

In the afternoon, you may actually want to avoid the sun. If it's a warm day, the sun's rays may warm the snow, and what was nice corn snow at 11 a.m. turns into mashed potatoes by 2 p.m. Now's the time for those north- and west-facing slopes. In the late afternoon you want to ski on wide-open slopes without too many shadows so you can see more easily.

Moving from Place to Place

Most of the time, skiing is about exhilaration. But sometimes, it's about transportation, merely getting from one place to the next, so you can start having some fun. If you were smart in planning your day, as I discuss earlier in this chapter, you can keep these schlepping-around-the-mountain segments to a

Starting off

If you haven't skied in a while, it's best to start off slow. That's what I do. While I usually ski black diamonds, I start off on a green or an easy blue to get used to the area and to get my ski legs back. The same goes for days when you're concerned about the weather. If it's stormy, foggy, or especially cold, try taking a lift that goes only part way up. Then if you need to add an extra layer, or you decide to just wait until the weather breaks, you won't have to ski half an hour to get back to the base lodge.

minimum. But no matter how well you plan, you're bound to encounter a few during the course of a ski day. This section is about negotiating these places safely and efficiently, so you can get on with the important matter of the day: having fun.

Catwalks

At many mountains — especially large mountains in the west — to get from place to place you have to ski narrow connecting trails sliced across the face of a slope or the top of a ridge. These are called *catwalks,* shown in Figure 10-2. They're not much fun to ski, and they can sometimes be tricky and even a little dangerous. Here's how to deal with them:

- ✔ **Avoid the edge:** The one thing you absolutely, positively don't want to do on a catwalk is fall off the edge. Catwalks usually cut across steep slopes, and if you tumble, you tumble a long way. That's why, in general, you should stay on the side of the catwalk nearest to the uphill slope. It gives you a wider margin for error. And it also sends a clear message to faster skiers behind you that if they want to pass you, they should do so on the outside.

- ✔ **Control your speed:** The key to happy catwalking is keeping your speed under control. But because most catwalks are quite narrow, you can't use your turns for speed control the way you can on a regular trail. So pull out that wedge that you used when you were just a beginner and use your edges to slow your progress.

- ✔ **Use the slope:** If you find yourself going too fast, you can ski up the uphill slope in an attempt to scrub off some speed. This is of course assuming that it's snow-covered and obstacle free.

Figure 10-2:
You don't
want to fall
off the
edge of a
catwalk.

Courtesy NSAA and Studio 404 Photography

✔ **Beware of merging skiers:** Some catwalks cross other trails or have other downhill trails that feed into them. So if you see this kind of inter-section, always check uphill for fast skiers who may not see or be looking for you.

The flats

In general, there's a good reason they call it downhill skiing. But in the ser-vice of getting from one place to another, you eventually have to cross some flat or even uphill spots. While this can be good exercise, it's generally not all that much fun. If you follow these guidelines, you can keep your slogging to a bare minimum:

✔ **Plan for it:** The best way to handle the flats is to avoid them altogether. If you're heading from one side of the mountain to the next, the best way to do it is to take a lift to the top and ski the trails that run in the direc-tion you want to go, instead of dragging yourself across the flat base area. If you're confused, or if you lost your trail map, don't be afraid to ask a ski patroller or a lift operator for the best way to get from Point A to Point B.

✔ **Keep up your speed:** If you have no choice but to take a *traverse* — a long, flat trail — speed is your friend. Say you need to head to the next lift, 150 yards away from the bottom of the trail you're skiing. As you get toward the bottom of the trail, double your present turn radius and make one big, fast, wide turn onto the flats. You want to carry as much speed as you can from the slope to the flats.

Don't worry if you feel like you're going a little too fast — you scrub off that speed quickly enough as the slope flattens out. Just check for obstacles and other skiers before you commit to this fast turn.

Remember, this fast-turn-onto-the-flats strategy *does not* apply to catwalks and other narrow traverses. For these you have to slow almost to a stop before merging and be ready to yield to approaching skiers.

✔ **Tuck:** After you're on the flats, getting into an aerodynamic tuck is one good way to maintain your speed. That's why racers do it. Most beginners tuck incorrectly, however. They bend at the waist, drop their arms, and have their ski poles sticking up like the antennae of some Alpine bug. First, it's dorky looking; second, it's not very comfortable; third, it's not very aerodynamic; and fourth, with a little bad luck, another skier could end up impaled on your pole.

For a real racer-style tuck, don't bend at the waist. Instead, crouch, getting into the Alpine version of the fetal position. Your thighs should be parallel to the ground and your torso should be resting on your thighs, your arms together and out in front of you, and your back as flat as you can get it. Position your poles parallel to your skis and the ground. Keep your head up so that you can see where you're going and avoid obstacles, other skiers, or stampeding wildebeests (just checking to see if you're paying attention).

✔ **Follow the shade:** I figured out this trick while snowboarding, where even the slightest reduction in friction can make the difference between creeping along and unbuckling your bindings and walking. If you have a long, slow traverse, aim for the shady side of the trail — the snow is icier there, which means it's a little faster.

✔ **Find the track:** Another snowboarder trick. On a well-traveled traverse, you can usually find a track made by other skiers. These tracks are harder packed than the loose snow around them and reduce the friction factor considerably.

✔ **Skate:** Even with the best traversing strategy, sometimes the flats are long enough and slow enough that you just have to add some of your own energy into the equation.

The first thing to do is skate on your skis. Push with the inside edge of one ski and slide with the other, and then do the same on the other side. This push-and-glide motion is similar to ice skating, in-line skating, and especially cross-country skate skiing. Not only does skating make it easier to get around, it's also a great drill for improving your one-footed balance and the flexion/extension motion of your leg. Good skiers moving from turn to turn, especially racers, often look like they're skating.

✔ **Poling:** To give your skating a boost — or if you can't skate yet — use your poles for propulsion, too. As you're poling on the flats, the proper hand position can make all the difference. If you grab the poles with your palm on the grip, as you do when you're skiing, you're using your triceps muscles. But if you put your palm on *top* of the grip, you can also employ the much stronger pectoral muscles in your chest.

Avoiding the Crowds

Waiting in line stinks. Skiing is all about getting out into the wilderness, alone, at one with nature, embracing the solitude. Think Jack London with an American Express card. It shouldn't be the on-snow equivalent of the DMV. Here's how you can maximize your skiing time and minimize your hanging around time.

✔ **Ski weekdays:** On Tuesday, most folks are working. If you can avoid doing likewise, you can have the mountain practically to yourself. And if there are fewer people on the mountain, the lines vary between short and non-existent.

✔ **Ski early:** Plenty of skiers sleep in. Others are hanging out in the cafeteria eating breakfast when the lifts open. Still others are navigating the rental shop. But you, if you're smart, are on the first chair of the morning. Or at least the second.

✔ **Ski through lunch:** If you insist on eating lunch at 12:30 p.m. you're going to encounter double trouble. You're going to wait on long lift lines in the late morning. And then you're going to be following the press of humanity into the cafeteria, where you can wait 15 minutes for the privilege of buying an overpriced, overcooked hamburger. And you will finish with lunch at the same time as everyone else, so — you guessed it — you're going to be waiting in long lift lines again all afternoon. So eat early, eat late, or better yet, pack a PowerBar and a piece of fruit and eat on the chairlift.

✔ **Ski the chairs:** High-speed quads (fast four-person lifts) and gondolas (enclosed lifts) are wonderful things. But so often I see this ridiculous scenario on a beautiful sunny day: 200 people waiting in line to get on the quad, and not a soul riding the triple 20 yards away that goes to exactly the same place. They wait ten minutes in line to save maybe a minute off their trip to the top.

If it's cold or snowy, by all means take the faster chair. But don't just head to the quad simply because everyone else does. Unless you *like* standing in line.

Dealing with the Weather

You know all those storms that bring all that lovely snow to your favorite resort? They also make mountain weather especially unpredictable. I can't tell you how many days I've skied in bright sunshine on one run, and found the mountain swathed in fog on the next. I've also seen a snow squall come out of seemingly nowhere, and depart just as suddenly. If you know how to handle it, this weather improvisation can add to the excitement of skiing. If not . . .

- ✔ **Dress for it:** Adopting the Boy Scout motto — be prepared — is smart when you're packing for a day of skiing. It may seem silly to be packing both spring gloves and a neck warmer or sunscreen and a rain hat, but there are many days when the temperature and sun conditions change drastically over the course of the day. And when a storm blows up in the middle of a run, you may be glad you have impromptu weatherproofing in the form of a hood and a high collar.

- ✔ **Whiteouts:** It's hard to ski if you can't see, but sometimes you have to do just that. Whiteouts are caused by a combination of fog, snow, and even low-lying clouds.

  In a true whiteout, you literally can't see where you're going. If you're caught in that situation, make your way carefully down until you can see again. Try to remember the geography of the trail — how wide is it? Are there any steep pitches? Does it turn? If other skiers are in the vicinity, you can probably hear them.

- ✔ **Fog:** If you're skiing on a foggy day, one of the best ways to enhance your visibility is to ski on a gladed trail. The trees at the trail edge not only provide some contrast and make it easier to see, they actually change the temperature enough to disperse the fog somewhat.

- ✔ **Rain:** "I'm skiing in the rain, just skiing in the rain, what a glorious feeling, I'm happy again." You're thinking that I've lost my mind, right? On the contrary. Rainy days are great days for skiing. The temperature, by definition, is moderate. The snow is invariably soft and lovely. Lift lines and skier traffic are non-existent. The key to enjoying the rain is preparation. Wear your most weatherproof clothes, and if you're planning to be out for a while, pull out the heavy artillery: a large plastic garbage bag. Just poke a hole for your head and your arms, and you have an instant poncho.

- ✔ **Wind:** You've heard of wind-chill factor? That's why skiing on blustery days isn't much fun. On a pedestrian level, a blustery day makes it colder. So much so that your risk of frostbite increases significantly on a windy day. And when it gets really windy, the resort will often close certain lifts for safety reasons, because the chairs are getting buffeted too much. So stick to sheltered lifts and trails.

✔ **Flat lighting:** As the sun begins to duck behind neighboring mountains in mid-afternoon, the lighting at a ski area can get dangerously flat. It becomes difficult to discern small changes in terrain and snow surface. The first thing to do, of course, is take off your sunglasses if you're wearing them. If you have goggles with rose or amber lenses, this is the time to try them out.

A Spotter's Guide to Trail Hazards

"Guess a snow snake got him." Snow snakes get the blame for any fall that happens for no apparent reason. But the key word in that sentence is *apparent.* Behind every fall, you can usually find some sort of explanation, usually terrain based. The key to staying upright is keeping your head up and your eyes open, and watching for spots that aren't quite white. Here's what to watch out for:

✔ **Brown spots:** If Frank Zappa were a skier, he would have warned you about the brown snow. At the beginning or end of a season or after a mid-season warm spell, brown spots start materializing on the slope. Those brown spots are bare ground, otherwise known as mud. If you hit a bare spot with any speed, what's likely to happen is that your skis stop dead when they hit the mud, but your body continues forward, at least until you do a somersault into the snow. Not fun. And if one ski gets stuck in the mud, while the other continues sliding on the snow, it's worse.

✔ **Blue or yellow spots:** This is the universal sign for ice. If you see a spot that's blue or yellow, avoid it at all costs. It's likely to be the kind of transparent ice that you could chop up and make a mixed drink with. However, understand that not all ice is going to be colored — a slope can be very white and still very, very slick.

✔ **Black spots:** Black means rocks. Little rocks are more of a problem for your skis than for you — they can put serious gouges in the bottom of your skis. Bigger rocks, or similar obstacles like tree roots, can deflect your ski, causing you to cross your tips and fall. These things can also actually grab your ski, sending you into low earth orbit, and proving once and for all that Milton Friedman was wrong: there is such a thing as a free launch.

Finding Powder

For most accomplished skiers, powder is one of the singular joys of skiing. (See Figure 10-3.) The problem, of course, is that it's in short supply. It's amazing how even a sparse crowd can track up a mountain in only a couple of hours. Here's how to maximize your chances of finding some fresh tracks:

Figure 10-3:
The joy of
powder.

Courtesy Elan

✔ **Avoid the powder pigs:** The key to powder skiing is going where the powder pigs aren't. Certain mountains have reputations that attract advanced skiers, while other trails are considered suitable for lower-level skiers. If you hear a storm brewing, head instead to the more family-oriented resort in the vicinity. Chances are the powder may last hours or maybe even days longer at the area without the hard-core reputation.

✔ **Get out early:** It's astonishing to see how quickly maybe 100 skiers can track up a whole mountain. By 10 a.m., the virgin snow is basically a memory. If you want to be a tracker, rather than a trackee, you better be on one of the first chairlifts.

✔ **Go to the intermediate area:** Beginners and lower-level intermediates, don't like powder. They fall in it a lot and wish that it were groomed. So during a snowstorm, these people often sleep in. Those are the times when you should head over to the green circle and blue square terrain, especially if there are skiable glades adjacent to the trails. You should find plenty of snow over there because most of the powder pigs stick to the more advanced terrain. After it stops snowing, however, all bets are off because the easier terrain will be groomed immediately.

Part III

Staying Safe and Getting Fit

The 5th Wave   By Rich Tennant

"The simulated mogul function isn't working, so every once in a while I'll sneak up behind you and try to knock you down."

In this part . . .

Playing safely — that's what these chapters are about. I explain skiing rules of the road and provide other smart sliding tips to help keep your skis worry free. I also show you how to get fit and stay healthy while you're skiing, as well as how to get your kids started skiing the easy way.

Chapter 11

Skiing Safely

• •

In This Chapter

▶ Skiing responsibly

▶ Riding lifts safely

▶ Co-existing peacefully with snowboarders

▶ Responding to an accident

▶ Avoiding avalanches

▶ Preventing knee injuries

• •

*W*hat's the first image that many people have of skiing? A guy sitting in the lodge by the fire with a brandy in his hand, a goofy grin on his face, and a cast on his leg. While this image isn't completely fictitious, like all stereotypes, it serves to confuse as much as illuminate.

Repeat after me: Skiing isn't that dangerous. Injuries occur with similar frequency in sports like baseball and soccer. You're far more likely to encounter a serious injury driving to the slopes than sliding on them, and resort operators, equipment manufacturers, and ski instructors are doing everything they can to make skiing even safer.

But all these people can't make skiing safer without your help. In this chapter, I describe the basic rules of safety and etiquette on the slopes. I also discuss trail designations and *Your Responsibility Code,* the rules of the road for on-snow safety. I explain how to get along with snowboarders, and give you the real facts about skiing-related deaths, avalanches, lift-related mishaps, and how you can reduce your risks of each. Finally, I talk about knee injuries and tell you how you can help prevent them.

How Safe Is Skiing?

While there is an inherent risk in skiing, the good news is that the sport is safe and getting safer. Over the last quarter century, the overall injury rate in skiing has decreased by half, from 5 injuries per 1,000 skier days to 2.5 per 1,000 today. This decrease is largely due to better equipment, more attention to safety by resorts, and aggressive skier education programs.

As you can see from the following chart, the risk of injury while skiing is comparable to many other active sports.

Sport	*Injuries per 1 million participants*
Ice hockey	37,130
Football	17,666
Skiing/snowboarding	11,383
Soccer	11,272
Baseball	10,141

The grim reality, however, is that every now and then someone is killed when skiing. When one of the victims is a member of one of America's most prominent political families, like Michael Kennedy, or an entertainer, like Sonny Bono, the incidents make national news. However, skiing fatalities are both rare and largely preventable.

To put the risk in perspective, based on fatalities per hour, you're more than three times more likely to be involved in a fatal airline crash or a fatal automobile accident than a fatal skiing accident.

According to Jasper Shealy, a professor at Rochester Institute of Technology and the nation's foremost expert on ski injuries, most skiing deaths are caused by reckless skiing. Shealy even goes so far as to suggest that these deaths shouldn't even be called "accidents." In analyzing virtually every skiing-related fatality in the United States. over the past two decades, Shealy has discovered a persistent pattern, one that hasn't changed much over time. Most victims of fatal skiing injuries

- Are young males
- Skied on an intermediate trail
- Skied at a high rate of speed
- Collided with an immovable object like a tree, rock, or lift tower

What's the take-home lesson here? You should:

- ✔ Control your speed at all times.

- ✔ Be vigilant no matter how easy the trail may seem.

- ✔ Give yourself a margin for error when skiing near trees, lift towers, and the edge of a trail.

- ✔ Avoid using any drugs or alcohol, which can impair your judgement and your reflexes, before or while skiing

Skiing Responsibly

Safety starts with you. The most important way to prevent accidents and injuries while you're skiing is to understand basic safety rules and stay on suitable terrain. In this section, I show you how to become a safe skier, as well as what to do if you do come upon an accident.

Your Responsibility Code

You remember your driver's test? The stuff about speed limits in hospital zones and hand signals for a left turn? Skiing has its own rules of the road, called *Your Responsibility Code,* drafted by the National Ski Areas Association. Fortunately, these rules are a lot more straightforward than your local traffic code. If you forget them, they can be found on almost every resort's trail map. Here are the points of the code, along with my own annotation:

- ✔ **Always stay in control, and be able to stop or avoid other people or objects:** This is skiing's golden rule. You have to adjust your speed to the conditions and slow down when it's crowded or icy. You have to stay on trails that are within your ability range (see "Understanding Trail Desginations," later in this chapter). And most of all, you have to look out for the other guy.

- ✔ **People ahead of you have the right of way. It is your responsibility to avoid them**: It may seem obvious — after all, the skiers in front of you don't have rear view mirrors — but the failure to watch for slower skiers in front of you, especially those off to one side, is a leading cause of "Where did he come from?" collisions.

- ✔ **You must not stop where you obstruct a trail or are not visible from above:** It's very easy to get caught up in the moment and just stop where you feel like it. But before you bend down to buckle your boots or whip out your cell phone, look back up the trail. If you can't easily see oncoming skiers because of a drop-off or a curve, they can't see you either.

✔ **When starting downhill or merging into a trail, look uphill and yield to others:** Think of the slope as a freeway ramp. You don't just pull out in front of a tractor trailer without at least a glance in your mirrors, do you? Think of the trail the same way. Look back uphill, and wait for a gap in traffic.

✔ **Always use devices to help prevent runaway equipment:** All modern bindings are equipped with ski brakes designed to stop them from sliding down the hill if they come off. Most skiboards and snowboards, however, don't have brakes, so be sure to wear a safety strap.

✔ **Observe all posted signs and warnings. Keep off closed trails and out of closed areas:** Ski patrollers don't close trails just because they like to string ropes. Trails are closed because of a hazard — whether it's a groomer on a slope, a big bare spot, or an avalanche danger. Ducking a rope is illegal in most states, and more importantly, doing so may get you hurt or even killed.

✔ **Prior to using any lift, you must have the knowledge and ability to load, ride, and unload safely:** If you've never ridden a particular kind of lift before, watch a few experienced riders get on and off and ask any pertinent questions. Then tell the lift operator that you're a newbie so he can slow the lift down or be ready to stop it in case you have problems loading or unloading. (More on lift safety later in the chapter.)

Understanding trail designations

All trails are not created equal. If Abraham Lincoln were a skier, that's what he would have told you. Some trails are as gently pitched as a bowling alley, while others are as steep as an elevator shaft. Some trails are as wide as a football field, and others are no wider than a football player.

As you might guess, this variety, while providing a certain level of spiciness to the skiing life, has its own safety implications. If a beginning skier were to inadvertently stumble upon a truly steep trail filled with Volkswagen-size moguls, it would be a bad thing.

How do ski areas prevent this from happening? With signs. At U.S. resorts, each trail is marked with a sign that tells you the trail name and tells you its difficulty rating.

The designations are as follows:

✔ Green circle: Easiest

✔ Blue square: More Difficult

✔ Black diamond: Most Difficult

✔ Double black diamond: For Experts Only

The National Ski Patrol

They're part cop, part paramedic, and part safety inspector. I'm talking about the members of the National Ski Patrol. Ski patrollers have the responsibility of policing safe skiing on the mountain (and the authority to pull the lift tickets of those who refuse to comply). They transport injured skiers off the mountain and perform first aid when appropriate. Perhaps most importantly, they make sure the slopes are safe for skiing by doing everything from performing avalanche control (see "Avalanche!" later in this chapter) to marking small, temporary hazards. If you see a skier in a funny-looking jacket with a chunky cross on the back, smile and say thanks. He or she is looking out for your safety.

The system seems simple, and for the most part it is. You should heed the trail markings and only ski those trails that are within your abililty level. (For more about how to rate yourself as a skier, see Chapter 7.) There are, however, two important caveats to this rule.

Designations are relative

The trail designations don't relate to some abstract difficulty scale. Although many skiers don't realize this, the designations compare the trail in question to the other trails at the same resort. Because some mountains are bigger and steeper than others, a green circle at a large western resort can be steeper than a blue square or even a black diamond at a small resort in the Midwest. And from a marketing point of view, resorts like to include a lot of blue square trails — what most people like to ski — which means that some blues may be quite green and others might be almost black.

If you're venturing to a resort you've never skied before, keep these relative designations in mind and start on a green circle (if you're a beginner) or a blue square (if you're an advanced skier). If you're not sure about a trail, ask a ski patroller, an instructor, or some other ski area employee for a more detailed description before you try it yourself.

Trails change

You must also realize that the difficulty of a trail can change dramatically from day to day, or even from hour to hour, with changes in snow conditions. A blue square trail that's a cakewalk first thing in the morning after it's been groomed can be a confection of a different kind when it gets icy at 3:00 p.m. On steeper terrain, moguls can crop up or get bigger during the course of the day.

As a rule, when the weather's warm, such as in the late fall or early spring, conditions are often icy early in the morning (the previous afternoon's slush refroze overnight) and slushy in the afternoon. During cold weather, the trails often get icier later in the day as skiers push the loose snow to the side of the trail and uncover the solid base underneath.

Being a good Samaritan

You're just cruising along, whistling a happy tune, when you see another skier lying on the ground, alone, apparently injured, on the side of the trail. What do you do?

- ✔ **Secure the area:** Remove your skis and stand them uphill of the injured skier in the shape of a giant X. (Of course, if you ever see one of these, slow down and either steer clear of the area, if the situation seems to be under control, or stop to help, if it's not.) If you're in a difficult traffic position — on the bottom of a blind drop-off or around a sharp corner — station another skier uphill to steer traffic around the accident scene.

- ✔ **Determine the extent of the skier's injuries:** Get a general idea of the skier's condition. If the skier is unconscious or disoriented, this could be a sign of a serious head injury, which, naturally, has to be treated differently than a sprained knee. Ask the victim what happened and what hurts.

- ✔ **Summon the ski patrol:** Flag down another skier and have him go to the nearest lift and have the operator radio the ski patrol. If possible, inform the ski patrol about the general nature of the injury and whether it's an emergency. Be sure to provide a good description of where you are.

- ✔ **Tend to the victim:** Obviously, your actions depend on your training and the victim's condition. If it's a serious injury or illness, then perform whatever kind of first aid you can — such as clearing the victim's airway or administering CPR — within the limits of your abilities. If it's an orthopedic injury — a sprained knee or an injured shoulder — then your role is largely providing reassurance. Don't, under any circumstances, try to move the victim, and try to discourage the victim from moving himself or herself until the ski patrol arrives.

- ✔ **Report the accident:** When the patrollers do arrive, they'll ask you a few questions about the condition of the victim and the cause of the accident if you saw it. Some states have passed laws governing skiing accidents, making it illegal to leave the scene if you're involved in an accident in which another skier was injured.

Riding Ski Lifts Safely

Ski lifts are extremely safe. Lift-related injuries can be broken down into two categories: loading- and unloading-related injuries and equipment failures.

Equipment-related failures are extremely rare; statistically speaking, you're only slightly less likely to get hit by lightning. Loading-related injuries are more common but also easily preventable. Here are some things you can do to stay safe on the lift:

- ✔ **Clue yourself in:** If you've never ridden the lift before, watch a few other skiers get on, and ask the lift operator for help if you're still unfamiliar with the lift's operation. (For more information on riding lifts, see Chapter 6.)

- ✔ **Tuck yourself in:** Make sure you don't have any loose clothing — scarves are especially dangerous — that can get caught on the lift.

- ✔ **Prepare yourself:** Loosen your boots, adjust your goggles, pull up your neck gaiter, blow your nose, and otherwise get yourself ready while you're still waiting in line. When you get to the front of the lift corral, take your pole straps off and move your poles to your inside hand.

- ✔ **Move into position quickly:** Most loading mishaps come from getting a late start. If you're not really ready — you've forgotten to take your pole straps off, for example — then you should just wait for the next chair. As soon as the chair in front of you moves past your position, you should slide up into the loading area and stop right on the red LOAD HERE mark. Remeber that different chairs load at different speeds.

- ✔ **Pay attention:** While you're loading the lift is no time to catch up on gossip. Focus on the people in front of you, the people you're riding with, the lift operator, and the oncoming chair. Don't zone out until you're actually on the chair and have pulled down the safety bar.

- ✔ **Don't reach down:** If you drop a pole or a glove while you're loading, don't bend over and pick it up. You'll probably fall. Just say "Pole!" and the lift operator will pick up the wayward piece of gear and hand it to someone on the chair behind you, who'll deliver it safe and sound to you at the top.

If a lift stops when you're on it, just sit tight. Most likely the lift is just stopped because a skier fell while getting on or off, and it should be running again in a few minutes. In the rare event of a serious mechanical problem, ski patrollers will instruct you what to do. Under no circumstances should you try to get off a lift that's stopped.

Co-existing with Snowboarders

During the early days of snowboarding, skiers got along with riders roughly the way the Hatfields got along with the McCoys. Skiers complained that snowboards would be the end of civilization as we know it, while boarders thought skiers were just hopeless old fogies. By now it's clear that snowboarding has done nothing but give skiing a long-needed kick in the pants, and snowboarding has made the sport better in any number of ways. And in another pleasant surprise, it turns out that snowboarders have a serious accident rate far below that of skiers.

On the other hand, snowboarders *are* different from skiers. They use the mountain differently, and you'll be a lot safer if you understand them. Here are some rules for co-existing peacefully with riders:

- **Watch the blind side:** Because snowboarders face sideways, they're a little like flounder — all their eyes are on one side. If you're passing a snowboarder on her *heel* side — the side without eyes — give her an especially wide berth.

- **Ignore the noise:** By their very nature, snowboards are louder than skis. On hard-packed snow an approaching snowboarder can sound like a thousand monkeys scraping a thousand windshields. But the noise doesn't mean that the rider is out of control; exactly the opposite. Learn to identify the sound and put it out of your mind the way you tune out the garbage truck first thing in the morning.

- **Watch their turn shape:** Snowboarders also tend to make differently shaped turns from skiers. They tend to make longer, wider turns that go further across the hill. When you're passing a snowboarder on an open slope, it's usually wise to give him a slightly wider berth than you might give a skier in a similar situation.

Catching Air

For many skiers — especially kids and young adults — catching air (also known as jumping) is one of skiing's great thrills. However, jumping can be dangerous. Getting air — or more accurately crashing when you land — does increase your chances of getting injured. If you do decide to jump, you must do so in a way that doesn't endanger other skiers. Remember, when you're in the air, you can't steer, and if you land on someone, they could be seriously injured or even killed, it will be completely your fault, and you could be prosecuted. Note also that many ski areas prohibit jumping altogether.

If you (or your kids) want to jump — and I'm not recommending it — here are some rules for minimizing the risk to other skiers:

- **Sight the takeoff and landing:** The first and most important safety precaution you can take is making sure that you can see the takeoff, the landing, and all the snow in between from where you start. If you can't, find somewhere else or bag it altogether.

- **Find an appropriate place:** The trail should be wide enough that approaching skiers have plenty of space to go around you. If there's too much skier traffic, you should abandon takeoff. Many ski areas have installed terrain parks, which include large and small jumps built by a snowcat. While terrain parks do help to separate would-be jumpers from skis-on-the-ground sliders, you still have to observe these safety rules.

Helmets

Is skiing a helmet sport? The Consumer Product Safety Commission thinks so. It has issued a recommendation that skiers wear helmets while on the slopes. This is the latest development in a significant pro-helmet movement in skiing. More and more adult skiers are wearing helmets. Many of the youngsters who grew up wearing helmets continue to wear them, and at a few ski areas, such as Big Sky, Montana, a few of the hot locals have donned helmets, spawning an unusual kind of copycat scenario. Helmets themselves have gotten better — lighter, more comfortable, and better ventilated — and the improvements will likely continue in the wake of upcoming helmet safety standards by the American Society for Testing and Materials (ASTM).

However, helmets aren't a panacea. Experts warn that contemporary ski helmets are effective only to speeds of about 15 miles an hour. Most serious and fatal accidents involve much higher speeds, as fast as 40 miles an hour, and the victim often incurs potentially fatal trauma to other areas besides the head.

Then you've got what's called *compensatory behavior.* This means that people who are wearing safety equipment tend to be less careful than those who aren't. Drivers wearing seat belts, for example, tend to drive faster than unbelted drivers.

Although a helmet may minimize the already small chance of suffering certain kinds of serious head injuries, it's no substitute for good common sense. In other words, make sure you use your head after you put a helmet on it.

✔ **Clear the landing:** Before you jump, you need to check the landing. Is it steep enough? (A flat landing is actually more dangerous than a steep one.) What's the snow like? Is there sufficient runout after the landing point? If I do fall, where will I land?

✔ **Recruit a spotter:** Find a friend or two to watch for approaching skiers and let you know when the takeoff and landing zones are both completely clear.

Avalanche!

Most skiers don't have to worry about avalanches. That's a good thing, too, because avalanches are among the most devastating forces in nature. Although we generally think of snow as soft and fluffy, avalanches are anything but. They can destroy whole villages, and the bodies of some skiers caught in the middle of a severe avalanche have been described by search teams as looking "like a Hefty bag filled with Jell-O." Avalanche victims who were rescued from smaller avalanches report that it's like being stuck under a few tons of concrete. It's dark and virtually impossible to move, much less dig yourself out.

What causes an avalanche?

An avalanche is caused by insufficient friction between two layers of snow. Think of an avalanche as a snow slide. It could start when a thaw-freeze cycle puts a glaze on one layer of snow, and then a subsequent heavy snowfall falls on top of the top layer. It may take several more snowfalls, but those unstable upperlayers ultimately tend to slide off. This is just one possible scenario, and I don't have the room to talk about avalanches in, um, depth.

Minimizing avalanche danger

To reduce the risk of being caught in an avalanche, follow these guidelines:

- ✔ **Stay in bounds:** This is simple. Avalanche danger within the bounds of a North American ski resort is virtually non-existent. Ski patrollers do avalanche control work on avalanche-prone areas within the confines of the ski area. Some of the control work is as simple as pushing down unstable snow ridges; other aspects are as complex as launching grenades to intentionally set off avalanches in areas of unstable snowpack. If, however, you're venturing into the backcountry outside the confines of a ski area, you need to heed a few more avalanche safety tips.

- ✔ **Educate yourself:** Read about avalanche safety and don't venture into the backcountry without an experienced guide or partner who understands how to assess avalanche dangers and respond to avalanche emergencies. Check the daily updates on avalanche danger for the area where you're going — forest rangers, patrollers at local ski areas, and backcountry ski shops are all sources of information.

- ✔ **Watch for avalanche-prone areas:** Unfortunately, the backcountry slopes that most advanced skiers like to ski — the equivalent of a black diamond at most ski areas — are also the most likely to avalanche. Shallower slopes don't have enough stored energy to slide, and on steeper slopes, the snow generally sloughs off before it can build up to a critical mass. Open bowls and chutes, as opposed to forested runs, are especially slide prone.

- ✔ **Understand search and rescue:** If you're venturing into avalanche territory, you've got to prepare for the worst. If your buddy has been buried in an avalanche, you've already screwed up horribly. But you still may be able to save his life. Avalanche victims have stayed alive for more than an hour while buried, but their chances of survival diminish with each passing minute. At a minimum, each skier must pack a shovel, an avalanche probe, and an operational avalanche beacon — a small transceiver that allows rescuers to pinpoint a buried victim quickly — and know how to use it. But of course the best avalanche survival technique is avoiding accidents in the first place.

Avoiding Knee Injuries

Why is it that skiers get carried down the mountain on a toboggan? It's not for a broken leg anymore. Modern bindings have dramatically reduced the possibility of a broken leg. The most common serious injury in skiing is a sprain or tear of one or more of the ligaments of the knee. An especially serious problem is tear of the Anterior Cruciate Ligament (ACL). This ligament is the tissue on the inside of the knee joint that connects the femur and the tibia bones. ACL injuries often follow an unusual pattern. The knee injury doesn't happen as a result of a fall. Instead, the skier hears a loud pop, and only falls because of the resulting instability of the knee.

Unfortunately, women are especially prone to ACL injuries, not only in skiing but in all activities. A combination of pelvic structure and looser joints make women particularly susceptible to this kind of knee injury.

There is some good news on the horizon for ACL injuries. On one hand, treatment for ACL injuries — which usually involves reconstructive surgery involving a graft from the patient's patellar tendon — has improved dramatically over the past decade. What had once been considered a career-ending injury for a ski racer now can be fully repaired and rehabilitated in less than a year.

But even more promising is the possibility that many ACL injuries can be prevented through skier education. Video analysis by Carl Ettlinger of Vermont Ski Safety suggested that most ACL injuries are preceded by a certain combination of body positions. He postulated that by actively teaching skiers to avoid those positions, they could reduce their chance of injuring their knees. In a pilot study, ski instructors and patrollers were instructed on how to avoid the circumstances that seem to result in ACL injuries. The results of that study were very promising. Skiers given the course showed a 62 percent reduction in ACL injuries compared to a similar group the year before.

Here is some advice from Vermont Ski Safety's Knee Friendly Skiing program. Follow this advice to help prevent knee injuries:

✔ **Avoid high-risk behavior:**

- Don't jump unless you know where and how to land. Land on both skis and keep your knees flexed.

- Don't fully straighten your legs when you fall. Keep your knees flexed.

- Don't try to get up until you've stopped sliding. When you're down, stay down.

- Don't land on your hands. Keep your arms up and forward.

✔ **Recognize potentially dangerous situations while there's still time to respond:**

Although the following elements may fall into place in almost any order during a sudden loss of balance or control, the order shown here is characteristic of the chain of events that can often put the average skier at risk:

- The skier's uphill arm is back.
- The skier is off-balance to the rear.
- The skier's hips are below her knees.
- The skier's uphill ski is unweighted.
- The skier's weight is on the inside edge of the downhill ski's tail.
- The skier's upper body is generally facing the downhill ski.

✔ **Respond quickly and effectively:**

When elements of this kind of scenario that leads to ACL injuries begin to fall into place, the ideal initial response is one that addresses as many elements as practical without limiting the skier's ability to take other appropriate measures, including any actions necessary to avoid collision with obstacles or other skiers. The following actions are a good example of an appropriate initial response:

1. Keep your arms forward.
2. Keep your feet together.
3. Keep your hands over your skis.

✔ **Correct your skiing technique:**

Many of the positions associated with knee injuries are the result of poor technique. By improving your technique, you can not only ski better but also reduce your chances of knee injury.

Chapter 12
Keeping Healthy, Getting Fit

• •

In This Chapter

▶ Dryland training for skill and fitness

▶ Stretching to prevent injuries

▶ Protecting your skin

▶ Dealing with frostbite and hypothermia

▶ Preventing altitude sickness

• •

Skiing is chicken soup for the soul. Oops, that's another book series. But though it's true that skiing can replenish the spirit, it's also true that skiing can be hard on the body. You're out in the cold. You're out in the sun. And you're engaging in an activity that's surprisingly vigorous. Think about it too much, and you're on your way to the Donner Party family reunion.

But it doesn't have to be that way. You remember what they say about an ounce of prevention? By preparing yourself before you take to the slopes and knowing a few warning signs of potentially serious problems, your days on snow can be both easy and uneventful, medically speaking.

In this chapter, I discuss the demands that skiing places on your muscles — it's more vigorous than you think. I also discuss off-season training, outlining the ways you can become a stronger, better skier without so much as setting foot on snow, and prevent injuries at the same time. I also talk about how to care for your skin — preventing everything from frostbite to sunburn. Finally, I give you some easy tips for preventing and treating altitude sickness.

Skiing Smart to Avoid Injury

Skiing is harder than it looks. If your friends don't believe you, an exercise physiologist can back you up. In studies performed at the Steadman-Hawkins Sports Medicine Foundation, researchers discovered that the demands skiing places on your muscles are unrivalled in any other sport.

To brace against the forces generated by a turn, racers held their muscles at 100 percent of maximum contraction for a virtual eternity in the neuromuscular universe. While you may not be working quite that hard while you're skiing, resisting the forces generated by a turn places demands on your body that you simply don't encounter while running or playing badminton.

What's the take-home lesson? At best, the demands of a couple of days of hard skiing can make you so sore that you can barely get up off the couch. At worst, they can result in an injury. To keep the smelly analgesic ointment away and the doctor at bay, take these few simple steps:

- **Pace yourself:** Here's an old joke: A skier sees a friend with his leg in a cast, and asks him "When did that happen?" The friend replies, "On my last run." As with all humor, there's a grain of truth in that. When you're tired, your technique gets sloppy, and your fatigued muscles have less in reserve to help you recover your balance. Ski patrollers know that most injuries occur at the end of the day, when skiers are tired and the conditions are tougher — the snow surface becomes icy or chopped up, and the light gets flatter. So, if your body's telling you it's time to call it quits, resist the temptation to try to squeeze in one more run.

- **Ski efficiently:** Learning better technique allows you to adopt a more efficient stance that uses your skeleton, instead of just your muscles, to support yourself during turns. Thus, you can focus more of your energy on important stuff — like turning your skis. To find out more about improving your skiing technique, see Chapter 7.

- **Train appropriately:** Doing some strength and flexibility training before you hit the slopes can help your body get ready to handle the demands that a day on the slopes can dish out (the following section tells you how).

Training for Skiing

Skiing is a strange sport. In many sports — golf, for example — the best training is to follow that sneaker company's motto: Just do it. You get stronger simply by playing.

But even during ski season, most folks don't get to go skiing every day, or even every week. And virtually everyone who sticks to one hemisphere has an off-season that lasts from May to November (or November to May).

You can look at this climatic constraint in one of two ways: You have plenty of time to train; or you have plenty of reason to train. Either way, it's time to hit the gym.

Skiers even have a term for working out off the slopes: *dryland training.* Two different kinds of dryland training — fitness training and skill training — work in concert to help you improve your skiing.

Fitness training

One of the best ways to become a stronger skier is simply to get stronger. You can increase the power and speed you can direct toward the task of turning the ski by building up the muscles that help stabilize your joints. Getting in shape can help you prevent injury as well. By improving your endurance, you can ski effectively more hours a day, and more days a week, which is a great way to stretch your lift-ticket dollar.

✔ **Aerobic training:** In addition to all the collateral benefits you get from increasing your cardiovascular fitness — losing weight, relieving stress, and decreasing your risk of countless diseases — aerobic exercise also helps you build the endurance you need to ski longer, and can even help prevent altitude sickness. What route you take is up to you: running, walking, cycling, and cross-country skiing can all be solid cornerstones of a dryland training program.

Before you begin any program involving strenuous exercise, remember to consult your doctor.

Weight training: Heading to the gym this summer is one of the best ways to ensure that you ski more powerfully this winter. Skiing is a total-body sport, so a balanced training regimen consisting of moderate repetitions of moderate weights for the upper body, torso, and legs is the place to start. It doesn't matter much whether you choose to use weight machines or free weights, as long as you do the exercises correctly. Doing exercises incorrectly not only reduces their effectiveness, it can actually lead to injury. So if you're not currently lifting weights, consult with a trainer at your gym or health club to help you devise an appropriate workout program and demonstrate proper technique for each exercise.

Pay special attention to your hamstrings. Studies show that over the course of a season, skiers' quadriceps muscles (the muscles on the top of the thigh) get markedly stronger, while their hamstrings (the complementary muscles on the back of the thigh) become relatively weaker. This kind of imbalance can make you susceptible to knee injuries.

Skill training

Skill training helps you become a better and more adept skier. Here I'm talking about activities that enhance your balance and your proprioceptive abilities (in English, your body awareness), and reinforce the movement patterns you use in skiing. Frankly, almost any endeavor more strenuous than playing chess can help in some way. Shooting baskets in your backyard or playing a few sets of tennis are much better than channel surfing, from a training point of view. However, a few sports, discussed in the following sections, really zero in on skiing-related skills and enhance your on-snow performance.

In-line skating

How do I train thee? Let me count the ways. Skating enhances your balance, but that's only the beginning. The gradual flexion/extension movement of your leg in a skating stride mimics almost exactly the leg movements you employ in a ski turn. And because skate wheels don't slide sideways on asphalt, the way the edge of a ski can on snow, you can get the feel of *carving*, or making a turn without any skidding. Skating can also teach you about watching where you're going, picking a line through traffic, and simply getting used to traveling faster than your legs could otherwise carry you.

Although just plain skating is great training, you can up the ante easily. Find a gentle slope, free of traffic, with smooth asphalt, get a few coffee can lids and set up your own in-line slalom course. Concentrate on making smooth, round turns, shifting your weight to the outside skate early in the turn. If you want, you can even bring a pair of ski poles — apply some duct tape to protect the metal tip — and use a pole touch (see Chapter 7) to help begin your turns.

In-line skaters can reach speeds of 15 miles an hour or more — bicycle speed. So it's smart to wear a helmet, as well as other protective gear, such as wrist guards, kneepads, and elbow pads. Remember, you can't ski better if you're wearing a cast.

Cross-country skiing

This is a no-brainer — the two sports are first cousins. For beginners, cross-country introduces the concept of sliding on snow and controlling their skis — keeping them parallel, for example. More advanced skiers can practice balancing and sliding on one foot.

The techniques for going downhill on a cross-country trail are similar to downhill skiing, but on skinny, edgeless Nordic skis even a molehill can pose a real challenge. On the other hand, downhill skiers use a cross-country-like skating technique to get from place to place when the terrain flattens out.

And of course, cross-country not only uses many of the same leg muscles, it's also one of the best ways to improve your cardiovascular fitness. For once the infomercials were telling you the truth.

The only drawback? If you can find enough snow to ski cross country, you could just as well be skiing downhill.

Ice skating

Every ski instructor's dream lesson — Wayne Gretzky, Michelle Kwan, Mario Lemieux, Nancy Kerrigan, Tonya Harding, um, never mind. But seriously, folks, figure skaters, hockey players, and just plain pond skaters usually make an easy transition to downhill skiing. Sliding forward on a metal edge on a slippery surface — what could be better training for skiing? Not much. Skating not only improves your balance, it improves your ability to control your ski's edges. And as with in-line skating, the basic stride uses many of the same muscles as a well-executed ski turn.

Mountain biking

Mountain bike champions Julie Furtado and Missy Giove are former ski racers. Why am I bringing this up? Because these two sports share similar physical and mental skills. When they're riding downhill, mountain bikers adopt a body position that's remarkably like that of skiing.

Perhaps the most important common thread between skiing and mountain biking is *line judgement* — the ability to look ahead and plot a smooth, flowing course down a trail or a slope. The idea is to aim not for the obstacles, but for the spaces between them, and few activities force you to do this as much as mountain biking does. Also, because many ski areas are open to mountain biking in the summer, you don't have to wait until November to hook up with your lift operator friends.

Stretching for Skiing

Even in 90-degree heat, most runners don't jog around the block without stretching for ten minutes beforehand for fear that they'll snap a tendon like a dried-out rubber band. Skiers, on the other hand, often head straight to the lift in sub-freezing temperatures without so much as a single stretch.

Minor injuries occur during overly vigorous stretching, however, so try to warm up a little first — just lugging your gear up to the lodge might be adequate — and remember to stretch gently.

Here are five stretches — three you do inside, two you do on the snow — which can help get you ready to ski.

- **Hamstring stretch:** Before you go outside, sit on the floor of your condo, or even in the lodge cafeteria. Extend one leg in front of you and bend the other leg, keeping the outside of the bent knee on the floor. Lean forward and grab the ankle of the extended leg. Don't curl your neck down, but instead try to move your chin toward your toes. You should feel a stretch in your hamstrings (the muscles on the backs of your thighs). Hold that position without bouncing for 30 seconds, and then repeat on the other leg.

- **Quad stretch:** Standing upright and holding onto something for balance if necessary, bring the heel of one foot up to your butt and grab your ankle with the hand on the same side. Gently pull the ankle up until you feel a stretch in your quadriceps (the muscles on the front of your thigh). Hold that position for 30 seconds and repeat on the other side.

- **Hip stretch:** Still indoors, lie flat on your back. Bend one leg up, grab your knee with both hands and gently pull it toward your opposite shoulder. You should feel a stretch in your hips and buttocks. Hold the position for 30 seconds, again not bouncing. Repeat on the other leg.

- **The A stretch:** When you're out on the snow with your skis on, stand with your feet spread about as far as they'll go. Slowly bend one knee until you feel a stretch on the inside of your non-bent leg, as shown in Figure 12-1. Hold that position for 30 seconds and repeat with the other leg.

- **X-C stretch:** Start out on snow with your skis on. Slide one ski forward, cross-country ski style, bending your forward knee until you feel a stretch in the opposite calf, as shown in Figure 12-2. Hold that position for 30 seconds and repeat on the other leg again.

No pain/no gain doesn't apply to the morning warmup. Stretching shouldn't hurt. If you reach the point of pain, you may be injuring yourself, so back off a little.

Fighting Soreness

Despite your best efforts, you may occasionally get sore after a hard day of skiing. Here are a couple of strategies for staying pain-free.

- **Keep your joints warm:** The synovial fluid that lubricates your joints is a little like the oil in your car — it gets syrupy and loses its effectiveness in cold weather. Warming up properly, and keeping your knees warm by wearing a neoprene brace while you ski, can help keep that pesky joint happy and pain-free.

Figure 12-1:
The A
stretch.

Figure 12-2:
The X-C
stretch.

✓ **Take anti-inflammatories:** After checking with your doctor, taking a non-prescription strength anti-inflammatory (such as ibuprofen) can not only ease the pain of muscle and joint soreness, it can actually help promote healing by reducing swelling.

✓ **Ice down your aches:** When you're done for the day, apply an ice pack to the sore joint or muscle. (A plastic garbage bag and the hotel's ice machine come in handy here.) Leave it on for about half an hour and reapply if the soreness returns.

These treatments are for chronic injuries and mild soreness. If you have new, acute or severe pain, consult a doctor before you continue skiing or otherwise resume activity.

Skin Care

What's a dermatologist's worst nightmare: *Vogue* proclaiming that wrinkles are in? HMOs clamping down on liposuction? A price increase on BMWs? No, a ski vacation. While a week in the mountains can do wonders for your soul, it can be hell on your skin. The slopes provide a triple whammy.

First, the sun's ultraviolet or UV rays are more intense at higher altitudes because the thinner atmosphere just doesn't filter them as well as the atmosphere at sea level does. This effect is compounded by the fact that 90 percent of the sun's rays reflect off the snow — so you can get a beach-style double dose of sun. These effects are so pronounced that it's possible to get a severe sunburn on unprotected skin in less than an hour on a sunny day at a resort in the Rockies. In short, the slopes are Sunburn City. And finally, there's the direct assault of the wind and the cold. Which means that it's Windburn City, too. What to do about it? Read on.

Protecting your skin

Following are a few common-sense suggestions on ways to protect your skin while you ski:

✓ **Use sunscreen:** Your first line of defense is sunscreen. Use a serious sunscreen with an SPF of at least 30 on all exposed skin at all times. And, yes, that means even on cloudy days, when 70 percent of the sun's damaging rays still get through. At higher altitudes, it's possible to get a sunburn even on a day where the sun hardly peeks out.

✓ **Protect sensitive areas:** Sunscreen often isn't enough on sensitive areas. Fair-skinned skiers should consider some extra protection, such as an opaque sunscreen like zinc oxide, for vulnerable areas, such as nose, ears, and lips.

✔ **Moisturize:** Your defense against windburn is moisturizer. In cold weather, your skin actually produces less of the lipids it normally uses to protect itself. So you've got to take up some of the slack. And don't forget your lips — they're especially prone to chapping in cold, windy weather, so look for a medicated lip balm that offers some protection from the sun.

✔ **Take cover:** There's a lot to be said for getting in out of the sun. A hat or a baseball cap can provide necessary shade on sunny days, but if you're feeling over-sunned, take cover. Eat lunch inside or under an umbrella, or ride the gondola instead of the chairlift.

Protecting your eyes

Just like your skin, your eyes can be damaged by the same ultraviolet rays that increase in intensity with altitude. And the reflection of sun off the snow can lead to a temporary condition commonly known as snow blindness. But it's easy to protect your eyes:

✔ **Shield them:** Your first line of defense is quality eyewear. That's why you should wear a good pair of sunglasses or goggles, as shown in Figure 12-3. They should have impact resistant lenses and offer protection from both UVA and UVB rays. See Chapter 5 for more information about eyewear.

✔ **Moisturize them:** At high altitiudes, the low humidity can sometimes make your eyes feel dry as well. This is especially a problem for contact lens wearers, so make sure you carry eyedrops with you and use them as necessary.

Figure 12-3:
Quality
sunglasses
provide
protection
against
UV-A and
UV-B rays.

Courtesy Smith Sport Optics, Inc.

Preventing frostbite

It's every non-skier's greatest fear: You go out for a happy day in the snow, and you end up looking like Beck Weathers, the guy who was saved from Everest, minus his nose and a few digits. Yes, frostbite is bad.

But frostbite is not mysterious, and usually not all that serious.

The following sections explain what symptoms to look for and how you can treat less serious cases of frostbite.

Recognizing the signs

Frostbite happens when your skin cells get frozen, literally. Preventing it is largely a matter of common sense. Here are some easy tips:

- **Cover up:** If your skin is appropriately covered, you can reduce your risk of frostbite to almost nothing. This means wearing a hat, goggles, warm gloves, and a neck gaiter. (Refer to Chapter 5 for information about accessories.) On very cold and windy days, minimize the amount of skin you leave exposed.

- **Know the symptoms:** Red, rosy cheeks aren't anything to worry about. They're actually a sign of enhanced circulation. If your skin starts getting pale, that's when you have to worry. Here are some of the early symptoms of frostbite:

  - Blanched appearance to the skin

  - Pins and needles sensation

  And the later stage symptoms:

  - Numbness

  - White patches on the skin

  - Blistering

- **Buddy up:** One of the problems with frostbite is that when you're really in danger, you don't feel it anymore. So if it's a really cold day, have your skiing partner check your face for the early signs of frostbite, and do the same for him or her. This advice applies doubly to parents. Kids may be having so much fun that they don't notice the early warning signs.

- **Inspect your extremities:** Although frostbite can occur on any part of the body, be especially vigilant in inspecting exposed skin and extremities: the tip of your nose, earlobes, and fingers and toes.

Frostbite first aid

Most cases of mild frostbite don't require medical attention. Take these steps for frostbite first aid.

1. **Get inside: Go to a warm place — like the lodge.**

   Don't start trying to rewarm the area until you get inside. If you warm the affected area while you're outside, it may refreeze, possibly damaging the tissue further. It's better to wait a few minutes and treat frostbite properly.

2. **Slowly warm the frostbitten area.**

   If you notice the early signs of frostbite, the key is to warm the area, but to do it slowly. Apply a washcloth soaked in warm water — around 100 degrees (just above body temperature) — to the affected area.

   Immersing the area in hot water, or exposing it to direct heat, such as a radiator, can actually damage the area more than the frostbite itself. Don't rub or massage the affected skin either.

3. **Get medical help, if necessary.**

   Most cases of frostbite affect only the skin and the outermost layers of tissue, and can be treated at home with the expectation of a full recovery. However, if the frostbitten area shows signs of blistering, numbness, or white patches, or if feeling and color don't return within 30 minutes, seek medical attention immediately.

If the victim shows signs of hypothermia as well as frostbite, treat the hypothermia symptoms first, because hypothermia, discussed in the next section, can be life-threatening.

Hypothermia

Hypothermia occurs when the body's core temperature drops significantly. The shock-like symptoms of hypothermia outlined below are actually the body's attempt to preserve brain function in a desperate situation: The body is losing heat faster than it can replace it. You can prevent hypothermia by dressing warmly, taking frequent rest breaks, and especially by staying dry.

Keep in mind that hypothermia doesn't occur only at exceedingly cold temperatures. If you're underdressed, and especially if you get wet, hypothermia can occur at temperatures well above freezing.

Hypothermia is a potentially life-threatening condition that demands immediate medical attention in all but the mildest cases.

The signs

The early signs of hypothermia are

- ✔ Persistent chattering teeth
- ✔ Persistent, uncontrolled shivering
- ✔ Slight confusion or lack of coordination

Later signs of hypothermia include

- ✔ Slowed respiration and heart rate
- ✔ Cessation of shivering
- ✔ More profound disorientation and lack of coordination
- ✔ Irrational behavior
- ✔ Loss of consciousness

The problem, of course, is that these symptoms make it difficult if not impossible to self-diagnose or self-treat hypothermia. That's why you need to monitor your skiing companions, especially young children.

Treating hypothermia

If someone exhibits the very early symptoms of hypothermia — essentially they feel really cold — the treatment is straightforward. Do whatever you can to make them warmer, such as putting on a hat, cinching down collars and cuffs to minimize heat loss, and find shelter immediately so they can warm up. If someone seems to be suffering from a more serious hypothermia, it's a potentially dangerous situation. Take the following steps immediately:

1. **Monitor the victim.**

   Constantly check the person's breathing and heart rate and be prepared to administer CPR if necessary. *Don't leave the victim alone.*

2. **Seek shelter.**

   Handle the person gently, but get him or her to a warm location as quickly as possible. Once inside, take off any wet or constricting clothing and replace it with dry clothing.

3. **Warm the victim.**

Cover the victim with warm blankets, making sure to dry and cover the top of the head. Applying warm packs to the neck, armpits and groin can help the warming process. If the victim is fully conscious, you can speed the warming process with warm liquids and small amounts of high-energy foods, like a candy bar.

4. **Get help.**

Understand that these steps are only first aid measures. Hypothermia is a potentially fatal condition and if the victim exhibits any symptoms beyond shivering or teeth chattering or these symptoms persist after moving the victim to a warm place, you should seek immediate medical attention from a doctor or the mountain's ski patrol.

Despite what you may remember from the cartoons about St. Bernards with brandy flasks around their necks, never give alcohol to someone with hypothermia. Alcohol can actually lower body temperature further — a good reason for postponing your imbibing until after the ski day is over.

Altitude Sickness

You have a splitting headache. You're out of breath. You're feeling more than a little queasy. All things considered, you'd rather lie down than stand up. Hangover?

Not quite. You've got altitude sickness.

Altitude sickness, formerly known as acute mountain sickness or AMS, is a condition that affects some skiers when they travel to the higher elevations — over 8,000 feet — typical of many ski resorts, especially those in the Rockies and other western mountain ranges in the United States. The cause and effect is simple: At higher altitudes, the thinner air has less oxygen, so your body just doesn't work as well as it does at sea level.

Altitude sickness can be unpredictable. It doesn't affect every person the same way, and the same person can react differently at different times at the same altitude. Altitude sickness can come on suddenly, sometimes happening immediately after arriving at the higher altitude, while at other times, the onset is delayed.

However, while altitude sickness isn't much fun, it is easily prevented.

Preventing altitude sickness

To prevent altitude sickness, follow these suggestions:

- ✔ **Acclimatize:** Your body is a remarkable machine, and it can adapt to a lot, even a chronic lack of oxygen. Your body adapts to being in a higher elevation — changing your respiration rate to move fluid to the lungs and brain— if you give it a chance. Over the long term, the body will actually begin to make more red blood cells to increase its oxygen-carrying capacity. The key is to restrict your activity in the early part of your vacation, until your body begins to acclimate.

- ✔ **Pace yourself:** Even if you're feeling fine, it's important not to overdo. Get plenty of sleep, take frequent rest breaks, and don't ski so long or hard that you're ready to drop.

- ✔ **Rehydrate:** Thin air also carries less moisture than air at sea level. The low humidity makes for great skiing — the snow tends to be light and fluffy. However, high-altitude air also saps your body of fluids — just sitting dehydrates you as much as exercising does at sea level. The moral: Drink twice as much as you would at sea level.

  When I'm at higher altitudes, I drink several large glasses of water first thing in the morning, a full bottle, or sometimes two, at each meal or rest stop, and another liter after I'm done for the day. And I also carry a bottle to sip from on the chairlift and keep a full glass of water on my nightstand.

  A portable humidifier in your hotel room or condo, left on overnight, or even a filled bathtub, can help to keep the air in the room relatively moist, and keep you from getting dehydrated while you sleep.

- ✔ **Moderation:** The low oxygen levels in the air place your body under stress, so don't add to its troubles. Fatty foods, caffeine, and alcohol, which slow down digestion and can contribute to dehydration, can also exacerbate altitude sickness.

Treating altitude sickness

In general, the treatment for altitude sickness is similar to the prevention. Reducing your activity, rehydrating yourself, and eating well usually eases most symptoms. If symptoms persist or worsen, the alternative is to return to a lower altitude — which can sometimes be accomplished with a short drive to a neighboring valley town.

Generally, altitude sickness at the moderately high altitudes of most ski resorts isn't serious. Treating the symptoms as outlined in the preceding section is generally enough. However, in rare circumstances, two very serious conditions normally associated with extreme high-altitude climbing, like the kind Jon Krakauer, author of *Into Thin Air,* did on Mount Everest, can surface at lower altitudes:

- ✔ **High-altitude pulmonary edema (HAPE):** HAPE is characterized by the lungs filling up with fluid, and, if left untreated, the victim can literally drown in his or her own bodily fluids.

- ✔ **High-altitude cerebral edema (HACE):** HACE is characterized by a fluid-induced swelling of the brain.

If altitude sickness is accompanied by a wet-sounding cough, chest pains, difficulty breathing, or some change in coordination or consciousness, seek immediate medical attention.

Allen's altitude sickness story

I can talk about altitude sickness firsthand. A few years back, I was on assignment in Snowbird, Utah. I took an early morning flight to Salt Lake City, which arrived about noon. I hopped a quick shuttle to Little Cottonwood Canyon, and by about quarter to two I had checked into my hotel and started to unpack. At this point I had two options. I could flop on the bed and watch a pay-per-view movie and then maybe mosey up to the Cliff Lodge's spectacular rooftop hot tub. Or I could try to cram in a little more than an hour of skiing in the late afternoon spring slush. I chose option B.

I took the tram to the summit, which is more than 2,000 feet higher than Snowbird's 9,000-foot base. I made a few turns through the heavy snow, but then . . .

"I don't feel so good."

I skied a little more, and I said, "I *really* don't feel so good."

I was tired, dizzy, I had a splitting headache, and most of all I was nauseous. I sat down on the snow. I lost my in-flight meal. From there on in I skied a few hundred yards. I sat down. I upchucked. And I repeated this all the way down the three-mile long run from the top. It was the longest, and, yes, worst run of my skiing career.

And it was all my fault. I was dehydrated from the flight — airplane air is notoriously dry. I was tired from catching an early flight. And most of all, I wasn't acclimated. My body didn't have a chance to adapt to the almost 12,000 foot difference in altitude between my New Jersey home and Snowbird's summit, so my body rebelled against this sudden lack of oxygen.

If I'd been just a little bit smarter and followed the advice I gave you in this chapter, I would have had an uneventful trip. But you would have missed out on a good story. The things I do for my readers!

Chapter 13

Skiing with Kids

. . . .

▶ Deciding whether your child is ready

▶ Buying kids' gear

▶ Choosing the right type of lessons

▶ Supporting your child

▶ Keeping your child safe on the slopes

. . . .

Kids and snow — they go together like peanut butter and jelly; like hide and seek; like James and the Giant Peach. Youngsters, you see, have unambiguous feelings about snow. They don't have to shovel it. They don't have to drive in it. They don't have to listen to Al Roker predict it. All they have to do is play in it.

So, naturally, kids love skiing. They don't have to buy equipment. They don't have to pay for lift tickets. They don't even have to think about orthopedic surgeons. All they understand about skiing is "Whheeee!"

That's how it should be. But the best part is that if you do your share and sweat these details for the little buggers, they let you share in the fun. To help you discharge your parental duties, I discuss everything you need to know to get your kids started skiing: I talk about the right age to start them skiing; I talk about kids' gear; I talk about the ski school programs you can enroll them in; I talk about how you can help keep them safe. I also talk about how to deal with separation anxiety when you drop them off at ski school, and how to help your kids' progress by keeping your own expectations in check.

Family Fun: The Benefits of Skiing with Your Kids

If you're a skier, you probably already know why your child should ski. But if you're a casual skier, or you've never skied yourself, the benefits of getting your whole family on snow may not be so obvious. So here's a checklist:

- ✔ **It's a family sport:** Skiing — along with other forms of snow sliding like snowboarding — is just about the best family activity there is. A five-year-old can't play a round of golf. And Grandpa isn't up for a game of tackle football. But snow sports allow little kids, big kids, parents, and even grandparents to share a day together doing something besides passing the stuffing and gravy.

- ✔ **It's fun:** You want to get your kids out from in front of the computer and the television and into the real world. Nice idea, but face it: It takes more than a game of hopscotch to lure your kids away from their video games. But skiing is so much fun that your kids may actually get excited about friction-based interfacing in three dimensions.

- ✔ **It's educational:** Skiing is a great opportunity to get your kids — especially city kids — out into nature in the wintertime and let them explore. You can even take the opportunity to teach them a little about the non-concrete world — about the water cycle, how animals adapt to winter, and so on. Best of all, you can see the wonder in their eyes the first time they spot fresh rabbit tracks or a hawk hovering overhead.

- ✔ **It's a lifetime sport:** When exactly was the last time you ran a post pattern? Hit a curve ball? Or scored a goal? Unlike most of the other sports that kids learn when they're young, skiing is something they can do when they're 20, and 50, and 70. It is, as they say, a gift that keeps on giving.

Knowing When Your Child Is Ready to Start Skiing

You're better equipped to judge your child's readiness than I am because it really depends on your kid. A few kids can rip up the slopes when they're three. Others really need to wait until they're six.

As a rule, if your kid is ready for regular school, she's almost definitely ready for ski school, too. However, both physical and psychological considerations enter into the decision.

Physical development

In one way, skiing is more like soccer than like baseball. It doesn't take a tremendous amount of coordination, so almost any kid who can walk can have fun at some level. But on the other hand, skiing takes strength — more strength than you think — and many otherwise spunky little kids have less strength than you think. Pay close attention to what your child can and can't do, so you set him up for success on the ski slopes.

Holding a wedge

Many young kids — under the age of five — lack the muscular development to hold their skis in a wedge, the toes-in position that helps beginning skiers to turn and slow down. (See Figure 13-1.) They can understand the concept and can do it while they're standing still, but once they start moving, the skis seem to have a mind of their own. The instructor can tell you whether this is the case.

Figure 13-1:
Bigger kids can hold a wedge; some smaller ones can't.

Courtesy Booth Creek Resorts

If your child can't hold a wedge when she's moving, she's not really ready to ski the mountain because she won't be able to turn or control her speed. But she can still join in the fun, as long as you keep your expectations in check. To a 4-year-old, just sliding on the snow by the lodge is real skiing. Quite frankly, young kids probably have just as much fun playing in the snow — throwing snowballs and building snowmen with you or with their ski school classmates — as they do actually skiing. So, as long as she is having fun, don't worry too much about your child's early progress. Every future Olympic champion started off making snow angels.

Coordination

While it's much easier than hitting a baseball, skiing takes coordination. But while little kids naturally develop leg strength as they grow, coordination develops through experience. So by exposing your kids to skiing early, they'll naturally develop the ability to balance on sliding objects, cue into their feet, and to judge speed and distance.

If your older child is at a stage where he tends to fall over his own feet, don't worry too much. At first, he may have a tough time with the balance and coordination necessary for skiing, but mastering the necessary skills can actually help a child develop body sense, not to mention self-confidence.

Psychological development

Is your child ready for anything? New experiences? A few bumps and bruises? Footwear that's not quite as comfy as her Arthur sneakers? That's good.

Is your child able to concentrate and focus on new tasks? That's good, too.

Skiing is relatively easy to learn, but as with most things, it becomes more fun the better you get at it. Although kids catch on quicker than adults, even tiny skiers have a learning curve. So a kid should have enough patience to stick it out through a few rough patches. You can help by doing the following:

- Telling your child, in a funny, positive way, about how you learned to ski

- Setting up reasonable expectations for accomplishing ski milestones such as riding the lift (maybe not the first day), and skiing from the very top of the mountain (not for a while)

Don't think that your child has to be a budding Evel Kneivel to learn to ski; cautious children often catch on very quickly because they tend to listen closely and follow directions.

The motivation factor

"If a kid doesn't want to learn to ski, you can't make 'em." That's what Yogi Berra would say if he were running a children's ski school. The real X-factor in determining whether a kid is ready to learn to ski is motivation. If your kids are really excited about going skiing — whether it's because they saw Kermit doing it on *Sesame Street,* or one of their friends went skiing, or, most of all, because they see that you're excited about it — they'll pick up the skills they need in a hurry. So, if your child expresses interest in learning to ski, take advantage of this opportunity and take her skiing before she gets hooked on the latest video game instead.

On the other hand, if you're pushing your child into doing something he really doesn't want to do — your let's-go-skiing suggestions are eliciting more than token resistance — reconsider your own motivation. A kid who really doesn't want to ski simply won't, and forcing the issue only sets up a classic "You will/I won't" scenario, which should be reserved for homework and feeding the dog. If he insists on staying home during a day trip, or playing video games in the lodge for part of the family vacation, it's probably smart to let him. When he sees how much fun everyone else is having, he'll want to join in soon enough.

The fear factor

Just like adults, kids can get scared on the slopes. While your fears may be more reality based — centering around a trip to the orthopedic surgeon — a kid's fears are just as real and can be just as debilitating.

With younger kids, it's often a fear of a new situation. They sometimes have fears you don't fully understand but can alleviate. Like not knowing how they'll find you later (Tell them you'll pick them up before lunchtime) or that they'll fall off the chairlift (they're not going on the big chairlift today).

Older kids, on the other hand, are more like adults. They won't admit that they're scared of anything. But if you sense that they are, don't come right out and ask them "Are you scared?" That won't work. You can, however, after skiing a steep section, or riding a particularly high chairlift, say "Hey, that was kind of scary," to suss out their reactions and initiate a dialogue. If your child is having trouble with a certain kind of terrain or snow condition — say, narrow trails or hardpacked snow — it may be a technique flaw that's holding her back. In this case, an afternoon in ski school may be just what the doctor ordered.

Gearing Your Kids Up

The great thing about kids — and the problem when it comes to buying ski equipment — is that kids are always growing. Boots that fit perfectly this season are likely to be two sizes too small next year. Same with skis and ski clothes. This can be frustrating — and expensive. But you can find ways to get your kids outfitted without ending up in the poor house.

Small boots, tiny skis

The natural temptation is to buy something that's a size too big with the thought that your child will grow into it. Don't do it. Skis that are too long are hard to control, and boots that are too big make skiing virtually impossible. If your child is skiing with gear that's the wrong size, she won't have fun. That's bad. Or she could get hurt. That's worse.

How do you know if gear is the right size? Here are some tips:

- **Boots:** Boots should basically fit like sneakers — with a little bit of toe-wiggle room. If you're trying on boots with a kid who can't give you meaningful feedback, try taking the liner out of the boot shell so you can see exactly where the kid's toes are. And, if possible, buy boots with buckles that your child can use without your help. Find out more about boots and the basics of boot fitting in Chapter 2.

- **Skis:** Children's skis should be no longer than the distance from the ground to the kid's shoulders. Shaped skis turn more easily than traditional straight-sidecut models (see Chapter 3 for more info about ski design), but for little kids, the construction isn't all that important. They'll ski better on the Kermit skis they like than on the Mickey Mouse skis that might be your first choice.

- **Bindings:** Bindings should be easy for the child to step into — if not out of — on her own. And make sure that the DIN settings (see Chapter 3 or ask your ski shop) go low enough for your child's weight.

- **Poles:** Little kids don't use them. As I explain in Chapter 1, poles are largely a crutch, albeit a necessary one, for adult beginners. Kids don't need them, and are apt to be distracted by their poles at best, or use them as weapons at worst.

Tiny skis can be expensive. But they don't have to be like saving for a college education. Here are some ways to save money while getting your kids outfitted for skiing.

✔ **Renting:** If you're just starting out or you ski only infrequently, renting skis is the way to go. You pay for the day or the week, return the skis when you're done, and if your kids need a bigger size the next time, you just ask for that size.

The rental shop can be a stressful place (see Chapter 1). So, if you're renting for both you and your kids, consider making two separate trips to the rental shop, if possible: one for them, one for you. Failing that, at least bring a couple of toys to keep the young 'uns occupied while you wait in line.

✔ **Leasing:** Many ski shops address the growing kids issue, too. For considerably less than the price of buying gear, they lease you a set of equipment for the season. If you plan to ski a lot, this is a good alternative because it's cheaper than renting every time, and you avoid the hassles of the rental shop.

✔ **Ski swaps:** Many ski areas run ski swaps — essentially Alpine flea markets — in the fall, and these tend to be especially good places to find gear for kids. Look for gear that's not abused — check the bases of skis for big gouges and the soles of boots for significant wear. Of course, make sure that the fit is right. And factor in the price of a binding check and tune-up — $25 or so — into any ski purchase.

✔ **Hand-me-downs:** If you've got kids of different ages, or friends with older kids, there's no reason why your littler ones can't use their outgrown gear. Again, make sure that anything you inherit is in good condition and really fits.

If you get skis from a source other than a ski shop, make sure to take them to a ski shop to have the bindings checked and adjusted. Be sure to take along the boots as well as the skis because the shop needs them to do a binding check.

Should my child wear a helmet?

Many ski areas not only recommend ski helmets for children, they actually require them if a child is enrolled in a season-long program. And that's probably a good idea. (See Chapter 11 for more about helmets.) Many of the caveats that apply to adults don't apply to children — generally they can't get going fast enough to be involved in the kind of crash where a helmet doesn't help. And, because they're smaller, children are also far more likely to collide with other skiers, another situation in which a helmet offers significant protection. If you do get a helmet for your child, make sure that it fits properly, and that he can still see to the sides and hear clearly.

Kids' clothing: Dressing for success

An instructor's observation: Kids routinely show up at ski schools with adequate equipment (it came from the rental shop, after all) but totally inadequate clothing. I can't count how many times I had a kid in my lesson with woolen mittens or no hat, or so bundled up that she literally couldn't move.

> ✔ **Layer them:** "I'm too hot!" "I'm too cold!" Count on hearing one or both of those from your child at least once during the course of a day on skis. Make sure the kids wear enough layers that they, or you, can provide do-it-yourself climate control. (See Chapter 4 for the lowdown on layering.)

> ✔ **Waterproof them:** Especially for little kids, who spend lots of time *in* the snow, as opposed to *on* it, waterproof clothing may be just as important as warm clothing. That's why sweat pants and woolen mittens are a definite no-no. Plan to bring along at least one, and preferably a few, extra pair of nylon gloves to change into when pair number one gets wet.

> Little kids will often let their hands go cherry red, and eventually sickly white — because they're wet and frozen —without ever complaining. So make sure their mittens are waterproof and that they will really stay on. And knit mittens are an absolute no-no.

> ✔ **Don't overdress them:** Skiing is an active sport. If kids are bundled up so much that they can barely move, they won't ski very well — or have much fun doing it. And, if they get so sweaty that they get soaked, they'll get colder than if they were underdressed.

> ✔ **Watch for loose clothing:** Scarves, drawstring hoods, and hats with dangling tassels can be dangerous because they get caught on chairlifts. So buy a neck gaiter instead of a scarf and otherwise check your child for loose ends before sending him out on the slopes.

> ✔ **Protect them from the sun:** Because of the high altitude and the way that the sun reflects off the snow, you should apply — and reapply — high-SPF sunscreen to all of your child's exposed skin, even on overcast days. Your child also needs eye protection: sunglasses or goggles. Sunglasses are usually a little easier to deal with, and if you add a colorful elastic strap, your child will not only be able to keep them on, she'll want to.

Helping Your Kids Learn to Ski

Should you teach your kid to ski? In a word, no. You don't try to teach your kid long division, do you? There are an abundance of good reasons to leave that sort of thing to paid professionals. Here are a few reasons to leave teaching skiing to the pros as well:

- **Ski school is fun:** Ski instructors have one big disadvantage compared to, say, math teachers: Their students don't have to be there. Good instructors realize this pretty quickly and make their classes fun. Most ski school lessons are a cross between gym class and recess. Most parent-teaching-progeny lessons are a cross between a little league baseball practice and a lecture about taking out the garbage.

- **Instructors understand skiing:** It's actually pretty easy to slide down the bunny slope. So easy, in fact, that little Briana may pick up some bad habits that make skiing more challenging terrain more difficult. Instructors nip bad habits in the bud and stress solid movement patterns that can serve your child as well next season as they do this week.

- **Instructors understand kids:** Kids' instructors can capture kids' imaginations. (See Figure 13-2.) They've got more games than Blue's Clues. They learned them during instructor training and constantly exchange new ones with other teachers. On the other hand, you'd make them up as you went along. They also explain things in age-appropriate ways that kids can understand and relate to. Plus, they're so excited about skiing that it's contagious.

- **You get to go skiing.** A lesson is a perfect time for you and your kids to have a little quality time apart. Seize the opportunity to take a romantic chairlift ride with your spouse or catch up with a friend. Then, when Junior's lesson is over, you're ready to give him all the attention he deserves.

The following sections explain what you *can* do to help your child learn to ski.

Courtesy Booth Creek Resorts

Figure 13-2:
A good kids'
instructor
loves
children
and knows
skiing.

Make it a positive experience

Now that you've decided — I hope — to enroll your child in ski school, here are a few ways to make sure that your child has a positive lesson experience.

✔ **Be positive:** Kids take their cues from you. If you seem worried or ambivalent, they pick up on it like a gossip columnist on a celebrity romance.

✔ **Be informative:** Tell your children what's going to happen. Show them the kids' learning area (probably where you see the four-foot high ply-wood frogs). Tell them you'll drop them off with a nice teacher, and that you'll leave for only a little while. Let them know that they'll have fun playing in the snow. Remind them that you'll be back soon, and that they can show you what they learned and then you'll all go to the lodge for cookies and hot cocoa. When you finish telling them how much fun they'll have, encourage them to ask questions.

Don't neglect this little orientation session for older kids; they may seem blasé but they can be even more concerned about what they'll encounter in a new situation than their blissfully oblivious younger siblings.

✔ **Be firm:** When you drop your child off at a lesson, often the first thing you see is tears. "Mommy, I want to ski with you." "Daddy, don't go!" Resist the temptation to stick around. Most kids are upset for a few minutes, but before too long, they're having too much fun to miss you. But if you give them any indication that you're wavering — should I stay or should I go — they'll be that much more likely to mount profound and prolonged resistance. So give them a big hug, tell them about how much fun they're going to have, let them know when you're going to be back, and then leave.

As for allaying your own anxiety level, some ski schools let you call from a cell phone or a lodge phone to get a report, or will give you a beeper. Even if a resort isn't wired, they can get a message to you by some low-tech means, like posting it on a message board near the lift that you're riding. Some resort day care centers also have one-way mirror/windows, so you can come back in 20 minutes and ease your mind with a peek, without rekindling your child's separation anxiety.

✔ **Be gone:** It's very tempting to hang around the beginner area so you can see your children. The problem, of course, is that if you can see them, they can see you. Parents who stick around distract the class — kids look to their parents for approval or keep trying to leave the lesson. So take this opportunity to go off and take a few runs alone or with your spouse. Then come back just before the end of the lesson and let your child show off. This is also the time to talk to the instructor and get the lowdown, not only on how your kid is doing, but on what the lesson covered, and what kind of games they played so that you can incorporate that into your family ski session.

Remember that these are just guidelines. Kids are all different, and you know more about how yours react than I do. Dropping your child off at ski school is very similar to leaving him with a new babysitter or on the first day of nursery school. So you should do the same things you've found to work in those situations.

Don't take a lesson with your kid

Do you go to school with your kid? Of course not. If you did, you'd place performance pressure on your child and compete with the teacher for little Jared's attention. Those reasons, plus the fact that kids and adults learn differently and at different paces, are the exact reasons you shouldn't try to take ski lessons with your child. If you want to take a lesson, take an adult lesson. If you've got an older child and the ski school supervisor tries to put you in the same group, politely suggest that you'd like to be separated. It gives you the chance to hear, "That young lady is your daughter? Oh, I thought she was your *sister*."

Some resorts, however, offer special parent/child lessons for smaller kids. These are mostly for parents who know how to ski, but want to learn games and exercises they can do with their kids. And these, of course, are fine.

Pick the right kind of program

Nowadays, it seems that kids' ski schools have more course offerings than a small university — certainly more options than those for adults. But while the names may change from resort to resort, the basic categories stay pretty much the same.

Group lessons

Small groups; other kids; playing in the snow: What could be better?

Little kids especially have fun in groups. Games like Red Light/Green Light and Duck, Duck, Goose work better with a handful of kids. Older children may be a little less likely to get into the games and be more sensitive to how they're doing compared to the rest of the class, but group lessons give kids of all ages a set of realistic expectations. When they watch their classmates slip around and fall, they realize that they're not the only one who can't zoom around the mountain the first time they put skis on.

The format also fits into a well-planned ski day. A half-hour of getting ready, an hour-and-a-half in the lesson, and an hour or so of post-lesson skiing with Mom and Dad is an appropriately full and exciting morning for most kids.

Private lessons

If you've got the kind of kid who thrives on personal attention — she learned to conjugate a sentence only after a one-on-one tutoring session with the teacher — consider a private lesson.

It's usually better to start with a group lesson, but if your little snow bunny doesn't seem to be thriving in a group environment, hits some kind of technique roadblock, or has decided for some reason — real or imagined — or another that he's scared, it may be time for a private lesson.

When you're booking the lesson, make sure to explain to the person at the desk why you're doing it, and a little about your child's personality, so your kid gets hooked up with an appropriate instructor.

All-day programs

It's the ski school equivalent of preschool. Depending on the age group, these groups combine a little skiing with a lot of babysitting or vice-versa. Kids go through the program in small bunches, grouped by age and ability. Ski lessons are punctuated by potty breaks, hot cocoa breaks, lunch breaks, and video breaks. Whether this kind of program will be an adventure or an ordeal will depend on your child. If she can manage the separation anxiety, these programs are great ways for younger or more inexperienced kids to get up to speed while you and your older kids get in some skiing. Many resorts also offer half-day programs that afford both you and your child a nice balance between personal discovery and family time.

Race programs

Many small areas have season-long weekend race programs, which are kind of the on-snow equivalent of Little League. These are similar to the all-day programs but most of the kids are eager and accomplished skiers who are raring to go in the morning, and whine after the last run. But don't be fooled by the racing label. The kids like the go-fast cachet, but the menu generally includes a lot of free skiing, a few drills, and a run or two down the race-course.

Day care programs

Having a child too young to ski — one who can't stand or walk — doesn't mean you have to postpone your skiing. Many ski areas have day care programs that, in most states, have to meet the same standards as regular day care programs. Remember to book ahead, especially during holidays, because a day care slot can actually be harder to get than a condo reservation.

How long should ski school be?

If you're gone too long, your kids get anxious, especially in a strange setting, and that's not the best way to sell them on the skiing experience. If your child took a week of long, teary days before he got used to nursery school, you might think twice about enrolling him in an all-day ski school program. By the time he's adapted to the new routine, you're ready to leave, and all he'll remember about skiing is missing Mommy and Daddy.

Daily morning doses of two or three hours are a good place to start for most kids. After three hours, exciting and new experiences can get old in a hurry.

Helping Pre-Teens Enjoy Skiing

While you're busy worrying about the little kids, your pre-teenager probably has her own sets of issues. Pre-teens may look tough, but they're surprisingly sensitive. What comes across as boredom or token resistance — "Skiing is sooo lame" — may be masking a real sense of insecurity.

Adolescents are very attuned to the reactions of their peers, and would rather die than look foolish in front of other kids their own age. Their bodies are changing as well, and that can often translate into clumsiness. Here are some ways to help pre-teens and adolescents learn to ski with a minimum of trauma.

- **Bring a friend:** Often pre-teens resist going on a ski trip because it takes them away from their friends. The easy way to combat this is to invite a friend along — instant support group.

- **Support them, subtly:** Kids are smart. If you gush, they realize they're being had. So comment in a low-key way — "You know, you're skiing that run better than you did last year" — or even bring in some actions to support your words — "If you're interested, we can sign you up for the Junior Racing program."

- **Bribe them:** Well, not exactly. But at that age kids can be very materialistic. And the promise of a cool pair of skis or a new jacket if they stick out, say, five ski lessons, can be a powerful incentive.

Pacing the Day

Kids are like old Camaros — they've not good at conserving energy. They go and go and go and go. Then they run out of gas. Kids can get tired especially quickly at high altitude. It's your responsibility to help your kids pace themselves.

- **Start the day at a reasonable hour:** If it's a long trip, don't plan to ski your first day. Arrive early, and let everyone chill out and get a good night's rest. If your kids are enrolled in a morning lesson, get an early enough start that you can eat breakfast and not have to rush around. But if you're skiing on your own, you don't have to be on the slopes the moment the lifts open.

✔ **Take frequent breaks:** Every hour or so plan to go back to the lodge for a few minutes. These are great opportunities to take care of potty needs, rehydrate with juice or hot cocoa, reapply sunscreen, and, if possible, rest.

✔ **Go in to lunch early:** Kids burn through those waffles fast. So make sure they refuel before they run out of gas. And consider mealtimes when scheduling lessons: Don't book a lesson at noon if that's when the kids usually eat lunch.

✔ **Knock off early:** Children are used to going flat out until the bell. But hey, you've got the car keys, so you decide how much is enough. If your kids seem pooped, suggest going back to the condo for a video, or maybe a dip in the hotel pool.

✔ **Play in the snow:** Kids love to play in the snow. (See Figure 13-3.) Adults love to play in the snow. So schedule some time to do just that. Make snow angels. Have a snowball fight. Build a snow tarantula. A ski vacation is an opportunity to celebrate winter, so take advantage of it.

Figure 13-3: Playing in the snow should be a part of every ski day.

Courtesy Sport Obermeyer, Ltd.

The burden of expectations

Although it may not seem like it, your kids really do want to please you. They live for your approval. Which is why it's important to temper your expectations when you take your kids skiing. Your job is to walk the fine line between being encouraging and oppressive.

Here's a quick Ed Koch checklist — How am I doin'?

Is your kid . . .

✔ **Improving?** Kids are little learning machines. They almost can't help but get better at things. But if your child really is not getting better, it may be a sign that he doesn't want to.

✔ **Scared?** Older kids will feign boredom so they don't have to admit they're afraid.

✔ **Bugging you to come back?** This is the acid test. If kids are excited about something, they bug you until they get it. If the youngest ones in your family are the driving force behind your ski trips, congratulations, you've got a bunch of skiers on your hands.

If the answers to these questions are yes, nominate yourself for Parent of the Year. Or at least buy your kid a season pass — you know he'll use it.

Keeping Your Kids Safe

As a parent, the only thing you want more than for your kids to have fun, is for them to be safe. And despite its reputation, skiing is actually quite safe. (See Chapter 11 for more about ski safety.) In the sections that follow I address two special concerns for small skiers: speed control and lift safety.

When they're skiing too fast

Kids like to ski fast. Too fast, sometimes. Too fast for Mom and Dad's peace of mind. Here are a few ways to notch down the throttle on your little speed demons that don't involve screaming, yelling, or threats of grounding.

✔ **Make a slalom course:** It's possible that your kids don't turn because they don't know how. If they're lacking basic skills, put them in a class. If you think they just need a little practice try this: Find a spot on the side of a beginner hill. Collect a few small, non-threatening objects like brightly colored coffee can tops and lay out a little slalom course on the snow, then run some friendly, family slalom trials.

✔ **Play follow the leader:** The rules are simple. You lead and your kids follow. They have to follow your path, and they can't pass you. Your priority is to ski slowly, and make controlled turns that end up pointed across the hill. (For more about controlling your speed with turns, see Chapter 8.)

✔ **Count the turns:** Pick out a point a few hundred feet down the slope — a tree, a lift tower — and challenge your child to see how many turns they can make between here and there. Play Name That Turn: "I can make 15 turns between here and there." "Well, I can make 20." Have them count out loud to keep things on the up-and-up.

Child safety on a ski lift

With a few exceptions, ski lifts weren't built with kids in mind. So, you need to be at least as careful with your kids going up the hill as going down. For more information on general lift safety, see Chapter 6.

If possible, small kids should always ride with an adult. They're less likely to swing the chair or do something else silly and potentially dangerous. Little kids are also easily distracted and can forget lift-riding basics like lifting the safety bar. They've even been known to fall asleep during a lift ride.

✔ **Speak up:** Most lift operators are trained to be on the lookout for kids who may have trouble getting onto the lift, but they can't read your mind. If this is your first time riding the lift with your child and you're not a strong skier yourself, let the lift operator know. She can slow the lift down, and be ready to stop it if either of you fall.

✔ **Scoot up:** Most lift-loading mishaps begin when you, the skier, get too late a start. All of a sudden, you're doing a Buster Keaton routine — and you're Buster Keaton. Make sure you have your poles off and are ready to slide into the loading area. You be the traffic cop to your kid. Say, "After the people in front of us get on, we're going to take the next chair. Ready? Let's go."

✔ **Sit back:** When you're safely on the chair, sit back and encourage your little one to do likewise. The seats and safety bars on most chairlifts were designed with big people in mind, and if a little kid leans too far forward and slides under the safety bar, it's possible, although not likely, that he could fall off.

✔ **Split up when you unload:** Just before the top of the lift, make a brief unloading plan with your child. If he's sitting to your right, suggest that he turn to the right when he gets off, while you go straight or slightly to the left. If your child is still prone to falling while getting off, make sure you remind him to peek over his shoulder before getting up so he doesn't get hit by an approaching chair.

Part IV
Getting Away

The 5th Wave   By Rich Tennant

"We did a lot of altitude training before coming out here. It wasn't easy either—there's only one roof-top restaurant and bar where we live."

In this part . . .

Whether you want to get away for a day or spend a week in the snow and sun, these chapters help you plan the perfect ski country getaway. You can find out how to choose a resort and how to minimize the hassles of getting there by plane or by car.

Chapter 14

Planning a Perfect Day (Or Weekend) Trip

In This Chapter

▶ Managing a day or weekend trip

▶ Deciding on your length of stay

▶ Listening to great tunes while you're on the road

▶ Driving in winter conditions

From vacation to vacation — that's no way to live. Or, more to the point, that's no way to ski. If you restrict all your skiing to week-long vacations, you end up skiing only five, maybe ten, days a year. And that's just not enough.

A short ski trip, whether it's just for a day or a long weekend, is the perfect antidote to utility bills, school projects, and checking your e-mail. It's a chance to call your own snow day, to celebrate winter, to let things — mostly yourself — slide. And while an impromptu ski getaway is great, a well-planned ski getaway without couldas, shouldas, or wouldas is even better.

In this chapter, I tell you how to get ready on the spur of the moment. I discuss how to decide where to go and how long to stay. I give you advice on how to drive safely during the winter and even have some fun on the road. I even talk about how to get to the slopes if you don't have a car or an airline ticket. So, if you're ready to leave your other concerns behind, get ready to plan an escape.

Getting Ready for a Day Trip

A day trip is a little like a bank job: It's important to make a quick getaway. And a quick getaway is easier if you've got your ducks in a row. Here are a few ways to help make that happen.

✔ **Pack the night before:** Make sure to do the groundwork before you turn off Letterman. Pack your ski bag. Get your ski clothes out. Brown-bag a lunch. If you live in a place where it's safe to do so, put your skis on the car rack. Heck, you can even pour yourself a bowl of Rice Krispies. (Although if you want it to snap, crackle, and pop at you, wait until the next morning to add the milk.) In short, do everything you can the night before to help you get on the road without undue delays.

✔ **Get an early start:** You set your alarm every day of the week for some silly reason like going to work or getting the kids off to school. Just do the same on a ski day, and as you're about to whack the clock radio, wrap your mind around the happy thought that you won't be punching the clock today, you'll be making turns.

✔ **Mount your ski rack:** Yes, I know you do your taxes on April 14 and buy all your gifts on Christmas Eve. But don't wait until just before you leave to put your ski rack on the car. It's a job for daylight when you're in no particular hurry.

If you try to do it the night before, Murphy's Law dictates that you'll drop one small, vital nut into the snow or a pile of leaves in the dark. For more information on ski racks, see Chapter 5.

Picking Your Destination

When you're going on a short trip, whether for a day or a weekend, the process of picking the destination changes significantly. Suddenly, "close" becomes almost as important as "great." Here's how to plan your trip to maximize the fun and minimize the hassle.

What kind of mountain?

What makes a perfect short trip mountain? Great skiing. You want a place that offers the kind of terrain you want, whether it's easy cruising runs or steep bumps. Smaller mountains can actually be better, because you spend less time getting from place to place, and you won't have to leave any terrain unsampled. You do, however, also want to be able to cram as much skiing into as short a time as possible, so fast lifts — or short liftlines — take on additional importance as well.

Remember that a lot of the factors that make bigger — and more distant — resorts popular for longer vacations, aren't such a factor in a shorter trip. If you're only skiing a day or two, variety of terrain isn't really that important, and off-the-slope diversions — from great restaurants to great views —don't really enter into the equation. For info on planning a longer ski vacation, head to Chapter 15.

How far?

The key to a great weekend trip is optimizing your driving-to-skiing ratio. Obviously, spending, say, 12 hours in the car to ski nine hours is not smart. A one-to-one ratio sets the outside limit for your distance. For a day trip, more than about two and a half hours each way is too much. For a weekend trip, five hours each way reaches the point of diminishing marginal returns.

How long?

How long should you stay away? That's a matter between you and your dogsitter. But seriously, you do have to decide whether you're going to take a day trip or extend it to a long weekend.

A ski trip is yet another of those cases where it pays to buy in quantity. To prove it, I calculated the number of driving hours and the number of skiing hours for a typical two-day weekend trip and a three-day non-holiday long weekend trip. Tables 14-1 and 14-2 show the results.

Table 14-1	Two-Day Trip	
	Driving	*Skiing*
Friday night:	3 hours	0
Saturday:	0	6 hours
Sunday:	4 hours	4 hours
Total:	7 hours	10 hours
Ski to schlep ratio: 1.43:1		

Table 14-2	Three-Day Trip	
	Driving	*Skiing*
Friday night:	3 hours	0
Saturday:	0	6 hours
Sunday:	0	6 hours
Monday:	3 hours	6 hours
Total:	6 hours	18 hours
Ski to schlep ratio: 3:1		

Snowed in

Even if you only have time for a two-day trip, do yourself a favor and clear your calendar for Monday. It doesn't happen often, but it does happen — getting snowed in, that is. You don't want to be faced with that conundrum that Mick Jones of the Clash elucidated so elegantly on "London Calling": *Should I stay or should I go?* To paraphrase the esteemed Mr. Jones' argument — "If I stay there will be trouble" — if you've got important business scheduled for Monday morning, calling in with a bad case of powder sickness might not be the best career move (see "Career Opportunities" on *The Clash*).

On the other hand, Mr. Jones, if he were a skier, might have countered, "If I go it will be double." Indeed, if you decide you have to get back to work come hell or high snowbank, you face a double whammy. First, you miss that rarest of commodities, a Monday morning powder day. And two, you face that gnarliest of automotive nightmares, a drive back in a Sunday evening snowstorm. So by putting off those gotta-be-there-or-else meetings until Tuesday during the winter, you can put off this kind of Solomonesque (or is it *Salomonesque*?) predicament.

As you can see, your hassle to fun ratio more than doubles when you add an extra day. When you get into the intangibles, the scale shifts even more decisively toward the longer excursion. With some serious traffic, the Sunday drive home can easily take more than an hour longer than the same drive on Monday. Plus, in truth, you can get in even more hours of quality skiing on Monday than you do on Saturday or Sunday, with shorter lift lines and virtually nobody on the slopes or in the cafeteria.

From a monetary point of view, a three-day trip makes a lot more sense than a two-day one. For the purposes of Table 14-3, I assume your hotel is $60 a night on Friday and Saturday and $50 on Sunday night, it's a 175 mile drive at 32 cents a mile, and that weekend lift tickets are $40 and midweek tickets are $30.

Table 14-3	Two Against Three	
	Two-Day	*Three-Day*
Lodging:	$120	$170
Driving:	$56	$56
Lift tickets:	$80	$110
Total:	$256	$336
Cost per skiing hour:	$25.60	$18.66

The bottom line: You save almost seven dollars an hour by making a long weekend trip. Your actual mileage may vary, as they say, but it's pretty clear that a non-holiday three-day weekend is a good deal. Save up those personal days and plan to put them to good use this winter.

Hitting the Road

Few activities are linked as closely as driving and skiing. They go together like hop and scotch, like toga and party. But if you've got the right attitude, the time in the car doesn't have to be complete drudgery. You can catch up with your spouse, your family, or yourself. If you've got someone to share the driving with, you can catch up on your sleep.

Packing the car

Loading up for a ski trip is a little different than packing for the beach, where the biggest tragedy is forgetting the sunscreen or that big, blue inflatable shark. When you drive in the winter, there's always the possibility, however small, that you may get truly stranded.

In that case, some smart preparation can mean the difference between a cold, uncomfortable night and a real tragedy:

- **A full gas tank:** Even if you're like Kramer on *Seinfeld,* the King of the Land of E, you run a big risk in running on fumes toward ski land. You don't want to run out of fuel in the cold, in the dark, on a country road, thirty miles from the next gas station. If you do get stranded, by the weather or some other kind of breakdown, you find out very quickly that the heater only works when the engine is running.

- **A windshield scraper:** Buy a good one, because a scraper that shatters in the cold isn't much better than no scraper at all.

- **Windshield washer fluid:** It's truly amazing how quickly road salt and sand can build up on your windshield, even days after a storm. And if you can't clean the haze off, you may just as well be driving in a white-out. New wiper blades also help you see clearly.

- **A flashlight:** For reading maps, checking under the hood, or just getting the key into the lock at the condo.

- **Food and water:** If you do get temporarily stranded, having a little to munch on can make it a lot more bearable. If you're unlucky enough to get stranded big-time, those emergency rations can mean the difference between having a great story to tell, and being a not-so-great story for the person who finds what's left of you in the spring.

Music to drive by

What's the difference between a long boring drive and a great road trip? Tunes! Great music makes the miles roll by. It can also help you get revved up for a great day of skiing, prepare for a cozy evening in front of the fire, or keep you from falling asleep behind the wheel. Here are ten of my all-time favorite road-tripping records:

✔ **Elvis Costello**, *This Year's Model:* Impassioned, angry, but with a sense of humor and a kernel of idealism, this proto-punk classic is perfect for trying to make up for lost time after a traffic jam.

✔ **Miles Davis**, *Cookin' With the Miles Davis Quintet:* Swings enough to serve as a wake-up call, yet mellow enough for a late night drive. Don't miss John Coltrane's turn on "My Funny Valentine."

✔ **Los Lobos**, *Kiko:* America's best band — sorry Deadheads — provide lyrical imagery set to a relentless, Latin-tinged groove. It's beat poetry of a different kind.

✔ **Bob Dylan**, *Bringing It All Back Home:* If the surrealistic whimsy of "Subterranean Homesick Blues," the cerebral sensuality of "She Belongs to Me," or the driving venom of "Maggie's Farm" don't get to you, then this sentiment from Dylan's liner notes should: "I would not want to be Bach. Mozart. Tolstoy. Joe Hill. Gertrude Stein or James Dean/they are all dead." You don't have be a ski patroller to know that dead men don't ski.

✔ **Sly and the Family Stone**, *Greatest Hits:* From "Family Affair" to "Thank You Falletinme Be Mice Elf Again," Sly Stewart packs more groove per minute into this collection than any other disc ever assembled.

✔ **Lucinda Williams**, *Lucinda Williams:* Her dad Miller is one of the great poets of the 20th century, and this set of blues-flavored folk proves that Lucinda's a chip off the old block. Her version of "Passionate Kisses" puts Mary Chapin-Carpenter's to shame, and "Side of the Road" is simply one of those songs that's so good you wish you wrote it.

✔ **Bruce Springsteen**, *The Wild, the Innocent, and the E-Street Shuffle: Born to Run* may be the more obvious choice, but *The Wild and the Innocent* has that magic that happens only when an artist's reach just barely exceeds his grasp. And besides, you never hear the ten-minute long, "Incident on 57th Street" on the radio.

✔ **Cowboy Junkies**, *The Trinity Sessions:* As intimate as a whisper in your ear, this is one of the all-time great after-midnight records, with Margot Timmins sounding like she's singing just for you. "200 Miles," a blues about driving (as opposed to a driving blues) is particularly apropos.

✔ **Bob Marley**, *Catch a Fire:* Backed by the Wailers, Marley proves why he's one of the most transcendent figures in popular music. Joyful and wise at the same time, "No Woman, No Cry" carries that all-important message: Live in the moment.

✔ **Sonny Terry and Brownie McGee and Lightning Hopkins**, *Blues Hoot:* On blues harp and guitar respectively, Terry and McGee play the two-man game better than Scottie Pippen and Michael Jordan, while Mr. Hopkins hammers on his Gibson like *he* invented rock and roll, and he's out to set the record straight.

✔ **A bag of sand or kitty litter:** It's instant traction. If you get stuck, shovel around your wheel wells and sprinkle some of the rough stuff in the direction you hope to be traveling.

✔ **A shovel:** For helping to dig your car out of a parking space or, if you're really stuck, for clearing out the area around the tailpipe so you don't get carbon monoxide poisoning.

✔ **A space blanket:** In terms of warmth per ounce, it's unbeatable.

✔ **A cell phone:** Not only to call for help if you're stranded, but also to call for road conditions and weather updates (generally available from your local state police) before you leave and while on route.

Driving in winter

In the skiing business, people hang onto this myth of the Perfect Winter. In this perfect winter, it snows two feet every Thursday night and stops first thing Friday morning, which gives the plows just enough time to do their business in time for you to drive up on clean, dry roads on Friday night and ski under perfect blue skies on Saturday morning. Unfortunately, this is likely to happen just after Elvis shares his recipe for deep-fried peanut butter and banana sandwiches with space aliens on the *Today* show.

Until that happens, you're going to have to deal with driving in the snow every now and then. Unfortunately, driving in the snow is not nearly as fun as skiing in it, but it is a fact of life for skiers. Follow these simple tips and your trip will be safer and less stressful.

Prepare your car

Before you head off on a ski trip, give your car the once over. Make sure all the lights are clean and working. Clean the windshield, windows, and mirrors.Check that the windshield washer fluid is full. If you're heading into an area where you may need tire chains — such as over a steep mountain pass — make sure you have them and know how to use them.

Pay attention

One of the major causes of accidents is not paying attention. Dialing your cell phone, yelling at your kids, or eating a breakfast burrito can all distract you from the task at hand. If you're unlucky enough to hit a patch of black ice while you're trying to multi-task, you can find yourself on the automotive equivalent of the Tilt-a-Whirl.

In search of the right ski car

Beefy tires. High ground clearance. Lots of luggage space. Four-wheel drive. You'd think that a sport utility vehicle might make the perfect ski vehicle. Think again. State troopers in snowy states can tell you that a disproportionate number of the cars that slide off the road are four-wheel-drive sport utilty vehicles. Four-wheel drive helps you get going when the traction is low, like when you're inching your way up a snowy hill. But it really doesn't do much good in keeping the car on the road in a turn when the road is slick. Because of their greater weight and higher center of gravity, SUVs are actually less manueverable and take longer to stop than cars. Compounding the problem is that most sport ute drivers don't realize this, and drive faster because they're overconfident.

The moral of the story: If you do buy a sport ute, realize that you still have to drive slowly and gently when the roads are slick, or you'll need that four-wheel drive to help haul your vehicle out of a ditch.

Or you might consider one of the increasing numbers of all- or four-wheel-drive sedans and small wagons made by companies like Subaru, Audi, and Volvo. They've got enough traction to weather almost any snowstorm, and yet they're more maneuverable than sport utes on both slick and dry roads.

Slow down

Cars are governed by physics — centrifugal force, inertia — things like that. Go into a turn too fast on a slippery road and you'll likely overpower the moderate amount of friction that keeps the car pointed where you want it to go. The result can be a close encounter between your front fender and a silver spruce. Slowing down to 40 may cost you a couple minutes, but driving too fast can cost you a lot more.

Be gentle

When you're driving on ice or snow, imagine that your car is on a tightrope. Slamming on the brakes, turning the steering wheel sharply, or any abrupt movement from you is likely to upset the car's delicate balance.

Brake for animals

Look at the woods, lovely, dark, and deep on either side of the two-lane road. Remember who lives there: Bambi and Bullwinkle. Although we humans live in fear of grizzly bears and great white sharks, the cold hard fact is that, because of their nasty habit of running in front of automobiles, deer are responsible for more human deaths in the United States than any other animal. Not as common as deer, moose are even more dangerous, because a large one weighs almost as much as your car.

The answer? Be vigilant. Scan the sides of the road, especially at sundown when animals tend to be most active. If the road is four lanes, move to the left lane so that you have more time to react to an animal crossing the road.

Stay with the car

Yes, mishaps do happen. Whether it's a small accident or serious car trouble, winter is a bad time to be left with an immobile automobile. But don't panic. Most of those stories that end up in Great Cannibalism Tales start with a basic little mistake — the wilderness equivalent of wandering off to see what that noise was in a *Friday the 13th* movie. If you're stranded, stay with the car. Put up an emergency triangle, put a sign in your back window, and sooner rather than later, a car will come by and help you. Even if you're on a deserted road, where the plows aren't expected for a while, your car still provides shelter.

Other Ways to Get There: Skiing by Mass Transit

It may not be exactly ideal from an environmental point of view, but driving is by far the easiest way to get to the slopes. However, that doesn't mean it's impossible to go skiing if you're car-free. It does mean that you've got to use your ingenuity. Here's how:

- **Bumming a ride:** Don't have a car? Despair not, fair skier. You've got friends who have cars, right? The most obvious way for the car-less to get a day of skiing in is to simply tag along with someone who's driving. Think of it as carpooling Alpine style. In this scenario, there's a lot to be said for being proactive. Don't wait for an invitation, go ahead and make some plans. Do the legwork and reserve a room, get driving directions, and work out the arrival and departure logistics. After all, every ski trip needs a catalyst, and there's no reason it can't be you. And, if you expect to be invited again, be sure to chip in for the gas.

- **Taking the bus:** Many metropolitan ski shops run ski trips as a service to their customers. The itinerary usually consists of leaving early for a nearby mountain and getting back the same evening. These trips are usually quite inexpensive, and if you figure in the wear and tear on your car, they may actually be cheaper than driving. In a few places, notably Salt Lake City, you can actually take a city bus to a ski resort for just a few dollars.

- **Hopping a train:** During the '30s and '40s, ski trains were almost as chic as luxury liners, and, hey, James Cameron never made a movie about them. In the '90s, ski trains seem poised for a comeback. New train services are running up the east coast from New York to Vermont and through parts of Colorado and hook up to shuttle buses sponsored by the resorts. Trains tend to be a little more comfortable than buses, and often have a rolling party atmosphere. Pass the noisemakers.

Chapter 15

Planning Your Vacation

• •

▶ Choosing a resort

▶ Picking a date

▶ Deciding where to stay

▶ Asking the right questions before you book

• •

*P*lanning a ski vacation is like waging a war: It takes organization and commitment and heavy artillery and. . . . Actually, it's not really much like that at all. No, planning a ski vacation is more like solving a differential equation: You've got a series of variables and when you change one, the others change, too, and then you've got your imaginary numbers. . . . Come to think of it, it's actually completely different. I've got it! Planning a ski vacation is really like performing brain surgery: It takes precision and daring and a really, really sharp chisel. No, no, never mind. . . .

Actually, planning a ski vacation is like, well, planning a ski vacation. But the key word is *planning*. Sure, you can just call up your travel agent, give her your credit card number, and tell her to book you someplace snowy. But if you want to have a truly great vacation — and remember, you're the one defining *great* — you've got to do a little soul searching, followed by a bit of research.

Because no resort is all things to all people — and if one were, it'd be too darn crowded — finding the perfect vacation spot is a matter of setting priorities. That's what this chapter is about.

In the pages that follow, I help you ask the right questions — including some you probably never thought of — before you book your vacation. I discuss the merits of different kinds of resorts. I talk about the crucial resort amenities: snowmaking and lifts. I give you a list of questions to ask before you book any vacation. Plus, for you, I reveal my all-time-best secret for saving money while getting the best snow and the best weather of the year.

Deciding Where to Go

Where should I go on vacation? That's a question ski writers get asked a lot. When someone asks me that question, I say, "Where should I live? How should I invest my IRA money? And by the way, what should I order for dinner tonight?" The answer to all of these questions, of course, is "It depends." (Actually, in the interest of expediency and politesse, I usually skip right to "It depends.")

There *is* no best ski area, any more than there's a best movie, a best investment, or a best food. The right choice for any given trip depends not only on you and your needs and preferences, but on your mood.

What type of skier are you?

To help you establish your own list of priorities, take this quiz.

1. **At 7:45 on the second morning of a ski vacation, I'm**

   A. Sleeping in.

   B. Slurping up cereal.

   C. Checking out the local forecast on the Weather Channel.

   D. Nursing my hangover from the night before.

2. **I stop for lunch when**

   A. I've got reservations.

   B. The kids get hungry.

   C. Stop for lunch?

   D. All my new buddies are ready to eat.

3. **If I were a snow-sliding celebrity, I'd be**

   A. Oprah Winfrey.

   B. Melanie Griffith.

   C. Jonny Moseley.

   D. One of the Beastie Boys.

4. **When I'm done skiing I want to**

   A. Go shopping.

   B. Get the kids some dinner.

   C. Ice my knees and take some ibuprofen.

   D. Head to happy hour.

5. My aprés-ski beverage of choice is

    A. A microbrewed pale ale.

    B. Apple juice.

    C. Gatorade.

    D. A tequila shot.

6. When my vacation is over, I want to have a great story about

    A. Beautiful views and perfect weather.

    B. Justin's first day on skis.

    C. That gnarly tree run.

    D. Dancing on the bar.

If most of your answers were As, consider yourself a **casual skier**. You're looking for a vacation where you ski, rather than a skiing vacation. The size of the mountain isn't all that important, certainly not as important as its location. Fast lifts are nice because you won't want to get cold and you want to squeeze in a lot of skiing so you can do other things as well. Look not only at the resort itself, but the town around it. Are there good restaurants? Cool non-skiing attractions? Good shopping? Consider off-mountain lodging. A bed-and-breakfast may be right up your alley.

If most of your answers are Bs, you must be a **family skier**. So you want an area with good kids' programs. In general, a smaller mountain works better for families with young children, simply because the smaller acreage makes it harder for the kids to get really lost. A self-contained base area where most of the attractions are a short walk away may work better than having to schlep into a ski town.

If most of your answers are Cs, you're a **hardcore skier**, as serious about the sport as Jerry Seinfeld is about breakfast cereal. You want a mountain that offers great snow and a lot of terrain. That probably means a big place. Aprés-ski amenities aren't that important — a few restaurants and a hot tub, and you're happy. You may want to check out clinic or camp programs that can help you improve your skiing and hook you up with other serious skiers.

If most of your answers are Ds, you're a **social skier**. A ski vacation is your chance to cut loose. You probably want to head to a ski town where you have a chance to meet people — both locals and fellow vacationers. Ask the locals about special events, which can get a lively area hopping even more. You probably don't want to head to a family resort, because you don't want to run the risk of having a crying two-year-old put a damper on a romantic evening or impromptu party.

Picking a Mountain

Each mountain comes with its own charms and drawbacks. In this section I discuss some of the choices you need to make in deciding on a destination.

Big or small?

Big mountains offer variety, as shown in Figure 15-1. They often offer trails ranging from the easiest greens to white-knuckle double blacks — that's a good thing when you've got a week to explore them all. On the other hand, at a big mountain, the logistics can get pretty complicated, especially if you're traveling in a group. "Let's meet for lunch in the lodge" leads to "*Which* lodge? There are four." You need to make similar decisions about which lift, which trail, and sometimes even which mountain.

Figure 15-1: Big mountains give you plenty of terrain to sample.

©Mark Maziarz, Park City

Small mountains offer less in the way of terrain. However, if you're a beginner, you don't *need* a lot of terrain. The bunny slope at even the smallest area provides plenty of challenge for your first couple of days on skis. Small mountains are less intimidating, and their size makes it far easier to find where everything is and how to get from one place to the other.

SKI SPEAK

"Daddy, where does snow come from?"

At a lot of resorts, snow comes from a snowgun. But I'm getting ahead of myself.

The first thing you need to make snow is, of course, water. Most ski areas have a pond or some other water source nearby and a series of pipes that can draw water from the source to the slopes.

The other ingredient in manufactured snow is air. So, air hoses — looking like the ones firefighters use — run up the hill alongside the water pipes.

The third ingredient is cold. While snowmakers can actually make snow when it's slightly above freezing (the same way that Mother Nature can), it does have to be within a few degrees of 32 degrees Fahrenheit to make snow.

The water pipes and air hoses meet at a snowgun, which sprays both water and air in a carefully measured ratio, based on the ambient air temperature and humidity. The result: artificial snow. See the accompanying figure.

The cool part is that by adjusting the proportions, a resort's snowmaking crew can optimize the snow for the weather and for a specific trail's needs. Early in the season, for example, snowmakers blow heavy snow over the bare ground so that it compacts into an icy, almost concrete-like base. Later in the season, when the base is built and the temperature drops, the groundspeople blow a light, fluffy snow that skis very much like Mother Nature's finest.

One difference exists between artificial snow and natural snow: Manufactured snow doesn't have that distinctive no-two-alike snowflake pattern. Examined under a microscope, artificial snow crystals actually look like rice grains.

Courtesy NSAA and Studio 404 Photography

Kid friendly or adult centered?

Many ski areas are waking up to the fact that some of their most important customers don't have credit cards. I'm talking about kids. Ski resorts are going out of their way to add family-friendly accommodations, plus activities and programs for kids — from snow-tubing to nature walks. For older kids, they're opening game rooms and alcohol-free dance clubs, starting lessons later to accommodate late-sleeping teens, and even staging nocturnal snowboarding competitions.For more information about skiing with kids, see Chapter 13.

If you're not traveling with kids, you may want to steer towards a resort that has a more sophisticated flavor: More candlelight dinners and fewer booster seats.

An old town or a new resort?

Which came first, the ski area or the town? No, this isn't a riddle. It's a serious consideration when choosing a vacation destination.

The resort came first

Many newer resorts were built in the middle of nowhere, and the town, or at least the non-skiing amenities, popped up around it. These resorts tend to be very well planned, self-contained, and easy to get around in. Restaurants are close to the lodging, which is close to the lifts, and you usually find ample parking. These places can be a little shy on local color. Few locals actually live at the resort, which means that you're likely to find three T-shirt shops for every drugstore. This type of ski area is not quite Disneyland, but it's a ski resort with the emphasis on *resort*.

The town came first

In places where the town came first, your vacation comes with a large slice of local color. You can tour the local mine or the maple sugar farm and gaze at Victorian houses that were built before modern skiing was even invented. Plus, the enthusiasm of the locals, most of whom live there at least in part for the skiing, is infectious. On the other hand, the town wasn't built with vacationers in mind, so things may be a bit spread out, and you won't be able to, say, charge your dinner to your room tab.

By car or by air?

That's pretty much your choice. The trade-off is pretty simple: Driving is generally less expensive; flying is quicker and allows you to cover far more ground and thus ski farther afield. For more information about flying to a ski destination, see Chapter 16. To find out more about driving in winter, see Chapter 14.

A baker's dozen of other questions

There are no stupid questions, only stupid mistakes. If I had a dollar for every time I heard that. . . . Except it's true. The following list gives you some of the questions you should ask before you fork over your credit card number so you don't end up making a stupid mistake.

- ✔ What's the closest airport?
- ✔ Is there more than one airport that serves the resort?
- ✔ Is there a shuttle to the resort from the airport?
- ✔ Is there plenty of parking, and is it free?
- ✔ What other resorts are nearby? How can I get there? Can I use my lift ticket at them?
- ✔ Does the room price include lift tickets or a discount on lift tickets?
- ✔ Can I ski to the lift from my room/condo? If not, is there a shuttle bus?
- ✔ Is there a pool or a hot tub?
- ✔ Is there a gym or a health club?
- ✔ Does the resort have any evening programs for children? Adults?
- ✔ Does the area offer day care? Do I need to reserve a spot in advance?
- ✔ How cold does it get there during January (or February or April)?

Analyzing an area's infrastructure

While ski school programs and restaurants and views routinely enter into a vacation choice, a few less glamorous but equally important considerations — if I were an urban planner, I'd call them the infrastructure — should enter into your decision.

Snowmaking facilities

You buy insurance for all kinds of things: auto insurance in case you're in a car wreck; health insurance in case your gall bladder goes bad.

Well, think of snow-making equipment as insurance for your vacation — that's how ski areas look at it.

In general, most ski areas were built in places where lots of snow falls. And most weeks and most years, lots of snow does fall. But Mother Nature being oblivious to commercial concerns, sometimes the first big dump of the year happens the week after Christmas vacation instead of the week before. (And at some resorts, particularly those in the mid-Atlantic region, that first big dump doesn't come at all.) Thus, snowmaking is your insurance that there will be something to ski on when you get there. Obviously, this is a much more important consideration if you're planning to ski in early December than if you're going in mid-February. So, before you book your vacation — especially an early-season one — ask about an area's snowmaking capacity.

Lifts and gondolas

High-speed lifts can be wonderful: They slice your waiting-in-line time significantly to let you get in more runs per day, so when it's cold out, you spend more time skiing and less time shivering your way up the mountain. See Figure 15-2.

Figure 15-2:
Gondolas
are fast
and offer
protection
from the
weather.

©Heavenly Ski Resort, Steve Barker

In praise of slow chairlifts

Let me tell you a secret. I *like* riding chairlifts. For me, riding a lift holds many of the same charms as watching a baseball game. It's a great opportunity for conversation — about skiing, about the weather, about life. You can snuggle with your significant other, catch up with a friend, or introduce yourself to a stranger — "Great day, huh?" is always an appropriate icebreaker. You rush around the other 51 weeks of the year. On your ski vacation, you can afford to take your time.

Some skiers judge a resort as much by the speed and number of its uphill conveyances as by its terrain, snow, or customer service. I think this is a mistake. At most resorts, the waits are short enough during the week that high-speed lifts are more of a luxury than a necessity and if you've got a whole week of skiing, getting in enough runs by 11:30 a.m. to tire you out for the day is a dubious accomplishment at best.

Picking the Date

In many ways, *when* you go is almost as important as *where*. The character of a place changes according to the weather and the number of skiers.

Holiday skiing

Sometimes, of course, the date is picked for you. If you've got school-age children, you can only go during school vacations. In that case, plan to make your reservations early and be prepared to pay a premium rate for rooms and lift tickets.

But if you don't have those scheduling constraints, be smart and avoid the weeks when those families are skiing — usually after Christmas and the Martin Luther King birthday and President's Day holidays. Remember that the dates for school vacations vary by region, so be sure to ask before you book. Spring breaks, however, are usually too late in the season to draw large crowds — or peak season pricing — and represent a great opportunity for a family on a budget.

Spring skiing

Pssst. Come over here. Closer. Wanna hear the best-kept secret in winter sports? Spring skiing. Few people know it, but the skiing is better — no, make that best — after the vernal equinox. Here are some of the reasons why.

✔ **It's warmer:** You're much less likely to encounter a day where it's ten degrees Fahrenheit, or ten below zero, at the end of March than in the middle of January.

✔ **It's snowy:** Understand this: Virtually every ski area in the U.S. closes, not for lack of snow, but for lack of skiers. Places like Vail and Aspen routinely boast 100-inch bases when they close in early April — a snowpack which often lasts until mid-summer.

✔ **It snows:** As if that weren't enough, April, and especially March, are among the snowiest months of the year in many mountain ranges. So your chances of hitting a powder day are often just as good after the equinox as before.

✔ **The days are longer:** In the morning, the sun's been warming the snow long before you get on the lift. And in the afternoon, you can knock off skiing at 3:30 and still have a solid two hours of sundeck time.

✔ **It's less crowded:** When the crocuses start to bloom, most folks run into the garage and unearth their golf clubs. It doesn't matter to them that the greens are brown and the wind speed is more appropriate for hang gliding than hitting straight drives or, for that matter, that the skiing is better than it's been all year. No, the very same people who were happy to ski on mud in early December are off playing golf or tennis or whatever just when the days get warmer (if not warm) and the snow is still plentiful. Take a moment to reflect on their loss. . . . Then give thanks for the fact that they won't be invading your personal space in the lift line.

✔ **It's cheaper:** Can you say off-peak? For this reason, ski resorts go out of their way to keep their skiers away from the siren song of warm-weather pursuits. They cut prices on lift tickets. They cut prices on rooms. They host special events, complete with plenty of free giveaways.

Choosing Your Accommodations

Where you sleep can make as big a difference in your vacation as where you ski. At most mountains, you have a fair amount of choice as to what kind of accommodations you book. Here's a look at some of the basic options and the pros and cons of each.

Hotels

You've stayed at one of these before, right? Cable TV, a couple of brass lamps, ice machine down the hall. Well, for better or for worse, hotel rooms aren't that much different in ski country — except the view's better.

Pros

Staying in a hotel means low hassle and low effort. You've only got one room to deal with and the maid comes every day to empty your trash, clean the bathroom, and make the bed. (Why can't it be like this at home?) Hotels also offer plenty of other amenities, from a pool, maybe a hot tub, to room service.

Cons

Even a medium-size hotel room can get a little claustrophobic after a week. Lack of a kitchen forces you to eat out or subsist on snack foods. (Pass the chips, please.) And a hotel is often the most expensive option, especially if you're traveling with a family or a group.

Condominiums

During the '80s, it was practically a sport within a sport to see how many condominiums you could build at your resort. Most of these condos are available for rental on any given night.

Pros

You've got virtually all the comforts of home, and then some. Most condos have a full — and fully equipped — kitchen, a fireplace complete with its own wood pile, and even a closet full of board games for the kids. If you're coming with a big family or a small group, you can actually save some money compared to staying in separate hotel rooms, especially if you factor in the savings associated with cooking. And most condos are designed with ski in/ski out access, so they're especially convenient to the slopes.

Cons

Condos come with at least some of the responsibilities of home, too. Most condos don't have maid service, so you have to make your own bed, take out the garbage, and clean out the kitchen when you're done.

Bed-and-breakfasts

What a wonderful idea: Buy a big house in the mountains and, in the winter, rent out some of the rooms to skiers who share your appreciation for antiques and powder days. What may be even better is to be the visitor rather than the visitee and, for a reasonable nightly rate, have the charm without the leaky roofs and the termite problems.

Pros

Can you say quaint? If you're looking for a little country charm when you get back from a long day at the slopes, a B&B is just the ticket. It's a little like staying at a friend's house, except that you don't have to bring a gift unless you want to. B&Bs are often a little less expensive than other lodging options.

Cons

By definition, a house built in the nineteenth or even the eighteenth century is likely lacking some modern conveniences. Forget about the whirlpool; you may even have to share a bathroom with other guests. Because virtually all B&Bs are down the proverbial road a piece from the ski area, you can forget about ski in/ski out convenience, too. You generally have to use your car to get to the slopes.

Seasonal rentals

If the skiing bug really bit you hard, you may want to consider a seasonal rental — also known as a ski house. Essentially, you and a bunch of friends rent a house just down the road from your favorite ski area from November until, say, April.

Pros

Because you pay up front, you're likely to ski almost every weekend to make sure you get your money's worth. Also, whether you're organizing a house with friends or taking a slot in a preexisting house, your housemates are likely to give you the kind of education, skiing and otherwise, that you can't get at Princeton.

Cons

At its worst, a ski house can be a little like that house you had in college: fights over who gets the bedroom with the door, biology projects in the refrigerator, and at least one roommate who keeps forgetting to write a check for the utilities. Then you've got those Saturday night toga parties (which side of the ledger these events end up on is up to you).

Adding Variety to Your Vacation

Just because it's a ski vacation doesn't mean you have to spend every minute skiing. Or if you really do want to spend every minute skiing, that doesn't mean you have to ski at one resort until you know every trail like it was your backyard. In this section, I show you how to add a little spice to your vacation.

Taking a detour to another resort

Ski resorts generally lie in mountain ranges, with one mountain as close to another as commuters on the subway. The proximity can make it practical and fun to sample one resort while you're staying at another. Sometimes two resorts — like Smugglers and Stowe in Vermont and Snowbird and Alta in Utah — are so close together that you can actually ski from one to the other. In other cases, the next resort is only a short drive away. New England, Lake Tahoe, and Colorado's Front Range all have resorts within a virtual stone's throw of each other. Adding a one-day detour to another resort is a great way to add a little variety to your vacation. In many cases, neighboring areas actually have programs that allow you to use the same lift ticket at each resort.

Planning a day off from skiing

Progress is a wonderful thing. The advent of high-speed lifts allows you to ski a lot.

The not-so-bright side of that equation is that you can actually ski too much. You can get burned out. If you're not in shape (see Chapter 12 for information about fitness), you can actually get injured.

So factor in an extra day when booking your vacation. If you feel like you need permission to take a rest day during the middle of your vacation, consider this a note from your mother. If you're booking a six-day, five-night package that starts on Sunday, figure on taking Tuesday or Wednesday off to go shopping, try some other winter sport, or just chill out and recharge your batteries. Your body and your mind will thank you for the break. See Chapter 19 for ideas about what to do when you're not skiing.

Just the ticket

Just because you're chilling out doesn't mean that the time is ticking off your lift ticket. Most areas offer flexible ticketing programs that allow weekly guests to ski multiple days, even if they're not consecutive days. Some areas have instituted "smart ticket" policies, which allow you to pay by the ride. Your lift ticket is essentially a debit card, which you swipe at a turnstile at each lift, and points are subtracted for each lift ride.

In short, you pay for as much as you ski, which is a good deal if you don't plan to ski much. For more serious skiers, who'll ski many runs in a day, a conventional pass is still a better deal.

Chapter 16

Skiing Through Airports

· ·

In This Chapter

▶ Putting the right thing in the right bag

▶ Booking your flights

▶ Avoiding delays

▶ Getting to the resort

· ·

*W*hat's the most important invention in the history of skiing? The fiber-glass ski? The detachable quad lift? The stretch pant? For my money, it's the jet airliner. The advent of commercial aviation means that you can live in Florida or Texas or anywhere else where snow is something you see only on the Weather Channel, yet hop on a flight and be in Utah, Colorado, or even the Swiss Alps by the end of the day. Talk about instant gratification.

This whole transcontinental airline system is mighty convenient for skiers; however, airlines weren't built with winter sports in mind — skis don't fit into the overhead baggage compartments, and airports in Jackson Hole and Telluride don't do non-stop 747 traffic. And, the fresh snow that every skier prays for can make getting to a ski resort a nightmare.

If you want to get to your mountain destination with as little hassle as possi-ble — on time, with your baggage in hand, and without spending a fortune — you've got to do a little planning and remember a few simple, but important, tips.

In this chapter I talk about packing properly, so that lost luggage becomes an inconvenience, not a disaster. I discuss how to book a flight to get the best possible fare and minimize your chances of getting stranded. I talk about the ups and downs of commuter flights. I tell you how to deal with delays, cancel-lations, and other unpleasant surprises. Finally, I fill you in on how to get to and from the airport. So buckle your seat belts, stow your tray table, and get ready.

Packing Properly

Here's a sad story. A few years ago, I was writing an article about an extreme skiing camp. One of my fellow campers had encountered an epic bit of misfortune. She was flying into Colorado from New York and changed planes in Denver. The bad news: She went to Crested Butte, Colorado, but her luggage went to Jackson Hole, Wyoming. The worse news: In her lost luggage were her skis, her boots, all her ski clothes, and even her contact lenses. This meant that she had to ski the first day and a half of her dream vacation at one of the most challenging mountains in America, with some of the country's best skiers, in borrowed clothes, rental boots, demo skis, and glasses that kept fogging up. In short, 20 percent of an expensive trip was compromised (if not ruined) by poor packing.

She assumed "It won't happen to me." But it did.

Don't make the same mistake. When you're packing for a ski trip, organize your gear on the assumption that your luggage will be delayed or even lost — eventually, you'll be right. I would no more check my ski boots than a diabetic would check his insulin supply.

Under the seat in front of you: Carrying your essentials on board

The first order of business is to find a boot bag small enough to meet the airlines' carry-on luggage size restrictions, but large enough to carry almost everything you need for a day of skiing. Then figure out what you absolutely, positively can't be without, and don't let it out of your sight. You're not going to be able to carry everything you'd like to, so do some triage, with the most important items — things not easily begged, bought, or borrowed — getting priority handling. If you carry your necessities, you don't have to worry about baggage handlers sending your stuff to a different time zone.

Here's what I pack in my carry-on bag, listed in order of importance:

- Ski boots
- Contact lenses
- Knee brace
- Ski pants
- Gloves
- Socks
- A set of thermal underwear

    ✔ Hat

    ✔ A change of underwear

I wear my ski jacket and fleece on board, so I'm pretty much good to go. Notice that the first three items on my list are, if not quite irreplaceable, pretty much custom-made for me. The next couple itmes are relatively high-ticket items. Then come the things I can do without in a pinch but that I have an emotional attachment to — my on-snow equivalent of a security blanket.

In short, I pack enough to be able to survive for a day (or in a worst-case scenario, a full vacation) without having to go shopping first thing in the morning. The couple essentials I'm omitting — sunscreen, goggles — are easily available at any resort ski shop.

Your priorities are probably a little different than mine, so make your own list. But whatever your essential something is, if you put it in your checked luggage and your bags are lost or delayed, don't say I didn't warn you.

Packing your skis

Skis are long, clumsy, and relatively fragile. You may think that combination of characteristics would cause lots of problems for airlines. Happily, it doesn't. No U.S. airline charges a surcharge for checking skis, assuming that you're otherwise within the excess baggage limits. And strangely, skis seem less likely to get lost or damaged than conventional luggage.

I put my skis in a cheap, old ski bag — basically a large nylon pouch that doesn't look as if it's worth stealing. I clip the skis together base to base, with a band around the tips to keep the bases from rubbing together. Then I do a little strategic packing. I put a pair of sweat socks over the tails, wrap a sweatshirt around the bindings, and generally pad the skis with T-shirts and other clothes that may come in handy during the trip but that I'm not overly concerned about keeping wrinkle-free.

Baggage handlers don't put skis on the baggage carousel. Your boards head straight to the oversize baggage area at the side of the luggage area. In most ski-town airports the oversize baggage area is pretty obvious, but you may have to ask where it is when you get home.

Before you walk away with a pair of skis, be sure to match the tag to the claim check, because many ski bags look alike.

Don't worry if you get bumped — or volunteer — and take a later flight. Your skis should get locked up in the baggage area, so you don't need to be concerned about them.

Fare Thee Well: Booking the Right Flight

Passenger aviation in the '90s is a mixed bag. On the one hand, airfares are as low as they've ever been. On the other hand, the hassle quotient is probably higher than it's ever been with crowded airplanes, fare restrictions, and cancellation charges.

Looking at it macroeconomically, you're paying non-cash costs. But being smart and prepared can help keep you from dipping into your wallet or tearing out your hair. In the following sections, I give you some tips for getting where you want to go, when you want to go, for the price you want to pay.

Commit early

There's always a catch. The catch to those Denver-for-$195 fares is that the airlines put aside a limited number of seats at that price. The airlines also limit the number of seats for folks cashing frequent-flier miles. So, if you want the lowest fare possible, plan in advance and book your flight as soon as you book your lodging. You may also want to check with a ski tour operator or a travel agent who specializes in ski vacations. They can sometimes come up with cheaper flights and better itineraries to ski-town airports.

Understand that while it's a traveler's prerogative to change his mind, change doesn't come cheap when you're involved with an airline. Most discount fares are non-refundable, and even changing your itinerary slightly usually incurs a moderate fee.

Fly early

How can a thunderstorm in Dallas disrupt your flight from New York to Denver? It's easy, actually. Remember that the plane you're getting on has to fly to you from somewhere. If you're flying at 5:00 in the afternoon, your airplane probably already flew three or four flight segments before you even get on board. So, a delay earlier in the day at any of four other airports can affect your flight. If the plane runs into a time-consuming mechanical problem or a lengthy weather delay, your flight can actually be cancelled for lack of an airplane, even when it's sunny where you are and sunny where you're going.

Although you can't control the weather, you can reduce your chances of getting caught in commercial aviation's domino effect. The way to do that is to fly early in the day. If you're taking a flight at 9:00 a.m., the airplane probably arrived the evening before, which all but eliminates the possibility of a delay in some other city postponing your departure.

Psst ... Want a free ticket?

How do you get a free vacation? By raising your hand. Because airlines do overbook and are reluctant to bounce passengers off a plane against their will, airlines often offer you a significant incentive for taking a later flight. The key is not to jump at the first offer. Usually, the airline starts with something like a $100 travel certificate (hardly worth a few hours of your time), but as it gets more desperate — the plane's full and ticketed passengers still pacing around the boarding area — it ups the ante. It's routine to get as much as $300 in airline scrip, and I've seen the amount get up to $500 or more. With today's low airfares, that can buy you a whole round trip ticket and pay for part of a friend's.

If you're late for a flight — because of traffic or a delayed connecting flight — try putting your name on the volunteer's list. If the flight's packed and you're late, you probably won't get on it anyway, and if you checked in after the cutoff time, the airline is only obligated to give you a meal voucher and a seat on a later flight. Of course, volunteering is a good strategy only if your itinerary is flexible enough to absorb the change. Before you raise your hand, find out just how big the inconvenience is going to be. If you're going to miss the last flight into your destination (which means you miss a day of skiing) or the last shuttle bus to your resort (which means a $250 cab ride), an airline voucher is no bargain.

Flying early in the day also has other advantages. It gives you some maneuvering room in case you face a delay on the next leg in the trip, or the airline makes you an enticing offer because it overbooked your flight. (See the "Psst ... Want a free ticket?" sidebar.) If everything goes well, remember that the earlier you arrive at the resort, the sooner you can start having fun.

Arrive early

Airlines simply aren't as mellow as they used to be. Everything from security concerns — "May I see two forms of picture ID, please?" — to overbooking have made arriving at the airport ten minutes before they shut the doors (as I used to do) a risky business. The fine print on your ticket states that the airline can give away your seat if you don't check in far enough in advance, and the more crowded the flight, the more likely an airline is to strictly enforce its policy. Bring a book and plan to get to the airport at least an hour before flight time. Showing up early is especially important for your return flight. A small commuter plane, which is often the only airborne way out of a ski town, is much less likely to have an empty seat for you if you arrive late than a jumbo jet.

The Saturday-night-stay-over ski vacation

If you booked a flight lately, you know that in order to get the lowest fare — make that *any* cheap fare — you have to stay over Saturday night. Requiring a stay-over separates bargain-hunting vacationers from business travelers on expense accounts, which is why every vacation naturally includes a Saturday night stay-over.

But what about your next business trip? If you're flying to, say, Denver or Salt Lake City on business during the winter, you have a classic win-win scenario. You can point your rental car in the direction of one of the local ski resorts, and snag a day or two of epic skiing on the weekend after you finish with business. By invoking that Saturday night stay-over, you look like a hero to your office manager because you saved $600 on the airfare. But what if you get snowed in on Sunday? In that case, buddy, you're on your own.

Go direct

Murphy's Law being what it is, you should look at every plane change as another opportunity for a delay or a mix-up. Eliminate as many variables as possible and opt for non-stop flights whenever you can. Fly directly to the resort, non-stop, if you can. If you do have to transfer to a commuter flight, make sure that your flight to the hub is non-stop. If possible, to try transfer in a snow-free city — like Dallas or San Francisco — instead of Denver or Chicago.

Making Connections

It's a fact of life: The big cities that are home to big hub airports generally don't have ski resorts in their backyards — even Denver is a couple of hours' drive away from the big Rocky Mountain resorts. So, changing planes is all but inevitable, and you, and every other skier, had better figure out how to get around an airport. The following sections give you tips for zooming through airports when you've got ten minutes to make your next flight, and for killing time when you've got two hours to wait.

Tight connections

You were a little skeptical of your itinerary in the first place — a half-hour to change planes is cutting it a little close. Now that your first-leg flight is sched-uled to depart 15 minutes late, you're really sweating. How do you maximize your chances of making your connecting flight with two minutes to spare (instead of missing it by two minutes)? The idea is to be as efficient as possible. Here's how:

- ✔ **Request a seat close to the front of the plane:** The fewer people between you and the doors, the quicker you can be on your way to your next flight. If you're booking a tight connection, try to get a front row aisle seat. If you can't do that, arrive early at the airport and explain your predicament to the representative at the counter.

- ✔ **Have your stuff ready:** Put your book or your laptop computer away before the plane begins its descent, and remember to zip the carrying case so that things don't go flying when you start running.

  It's even a good idea to get your jacket from the overhead bin. You want to be able to start heading for the jetway as soon as that Fasten Seatbelts sign goes off.

- ✔ **Know where you're going:** Listen when the flight attendant makes connection announcements just before landing. Jot down both your arrival gate and the connecting gate. Then look at the back of the in-flight magazine and figure out the shortest distance between those two points.

- ✔ **Run:** Why do I always wear sneakers on the plane? So that I'm always ready to break into a 400-meter sprint, just in case my connection becomes too close for comfort. If you're in good shape, a run is probably faster than a moving walkway, or even a short shuttle train ride. It's no fun to run through airports, but three minutes of anaerobic hell is better than three hours of hanging out in the airport food court.

Loose connections

Sometimes, your itinerary gives you plenty of time to kill at an airport. Other times, despite your good intentions, you miss the connecting flight by five minutes and have to wait a couple of hours for the next flight.

The key is to plan for this contingency. Larger airports are like the most boring mall in the world — a few tacky stores and a food court designed to serve a captive audience — but most tiny ski-town airports don't have anything more exciting than a small snack bar and a newspaper machine.

Stock up on distractions before you leave home. Bring a magazine. Bring a book. Bring two books. Bring a portable CD player. Bring your laptop computer. (Remember to plug it in while you're waiting in the terminal.) Bring your knitting. Whatever you bring, make sure that it can keep you amused for at least a couple of hours. Sooner or later, you'll be very glad you brought something.

Bumping back

Okay, it's happened. You've been bumped, or your flight's been delayed or cancelled. What do you do now? First, stay calm. Then follow these suggestions:

- ✔ **Re-book:** See that long, rapidly growing line of irate flyers converging on the counter? Walk right past it and head to a pay phone. Call the airline reservations number. The key to getting on the next flight is quick action, and the reservations person on the phone has exactly the same capabilities to rearrange your itinerary as the person at the counter, but she'll be able to do it faster and more efficiently.

- ✔ **Negotiate:** After you're booked on another flight, make sure you get what's coming to you. If the delay is clearly the airline's fault, explain politely but firmly how valuable your time is and how much this delay is costing you. Most airlines give you a meal voucher if the delay is a short one. They may upgrade you to business class, if they have the room. If the delay involves an overnight stay, make sure the airline pays for the hotel, meals, and the transfers back to the airport. Not getting the answers you want? Remember these magic words: May I speak to your supervisor?

Puddle Jumping: A Commuter Flight Primer

Most ski towns don't have large multinational companies, big convention centers, or any of the other things that make airlines fly jumbo jets there. So like it or not, you often have to hop a commuter flight to your final destination. Generally, commuter flights aren't all that bad. But they are subject to a few problems that you normally don't encounter on jumbo jet flights:

- ✔ **Weight restrictions:** To keep the Federal Aviation Administration happy, small airplanes have very strict weight restrictions. Skiers often have heavy luggage. I think you can see where this is going. In an effort to avoid bumping passengers, commuter airlines often bump luggage to a later flight. On rare occasions, an airline may actually bump passengers, too.

- ✔ **Overbooking:** On a jetliner, overbooking rarely becomes your problem. Airlines are reluctant to bump you involuntarily, and they merely up the ante until they get a couple of volunteers from among the other 200 passengers, and you get on the flight. Not so on commuter flights. If there are only 18 seats and 20 passengers, then there's a problem, and it can quickly become *your* problem. The ounce of prevention? Get to the gate well in advance. Airlines generally bump passengers in the reverse order of their arrival.

- ✔ **Turbulence:** It's a matter of physics: Smaller airplanes are affected more by turbulence than larger planes. If you're at all prone to motion sickness, be prepared. Skip the airport food before going on board, and bring along your favorite airsickness remedy, whether it's ginger snaps, an accupressure band, or a scopolamine patch. Early morning and late afternoon flights seem most prone to hitting turbulence, so take that into account when planning your itinerary.

- ✔ **Diversions:** Chew on this one a while: You pick a resort because it snows a lot there. The problem, of course, is that it may snow while you're trying to get there. If it's dumping while you're flying, your flight may end up being diverted to another airport.

First, keep the problem in perspective — even in mountain towns, snow-related winter diversions are less common than thunderstorm-related diversions in the summer.

If a storm does crop up while you're en route, the airline will do everything it can to get you where you're doing. Generally, the airline diverts a commuter plane to the nearest passable airport and then tries to bus you to your final destination. This, of course, can be a little time consuming, but there's usually no better alternative. And it's better than getting diverted in a jumbo jet, where you can end up in Omaha when you want to be in Denver.

Heading Resortward

You finally land, and you can almost smell the fresh powder. Except for the small matter of getting from the airport to the resort. You've got two choices: driving yourself, or having someone drive you.

Shuttle buses

You can usually find a shuttle bus service, generally privately operated, which runs between the resort and the nearest airport. Sometimes the ride's short (it's about half an hour from Salt Lake City to Snowbird), and sometimes the drive is longer. (Figure on a couple of hours from Denver International to the larger Colorado resorts.)

Shuttle services are generally economical and run frequently, and most destination resorts are set up so that you can get along very nicely without a car.
After you book your flight, call the resort and get information on the shuttle —
you generally have to make a reservation. Make sure you know where the
meeting place is, and hit the ATM before you leave. You sometimes have to
pay cash, and for the longer rides, a shuttle service can run $60 or more.

It's good form to tip the driver, especially if he had to wait for you or helps
you schlep your luggage. Five dollars is about right, although feel free to tip
more if he goes above and beyond the call of duty.

Don't forget to book your return trip, allowing yourself a little cushion to get
to the airport on time.

Rental cars

If you're getting in at an odd hour, or you just can't bear the thought of being
car-less — even on vacation — then a rent-a-car is the way to go. For most
vacationers, renting a car is just a matter of grabbing the cheapest little sub-
compact they can find and driving away. But when you're venturing into ski
country, you have a few other things to consider:

- ✔ **Ski storage:** You can put skis inside the car, but it's not a good idea. In
  the event of an accident, a pair of skis can become dangerous projec-
  tiles. (I was involved in an accident with a rent-a-car once, and two pair
  of skis still attached to a roof rack ended up 100 feet down the road from
  the car.) And, if you're not careful, the metal edges can slice up the
  upholstery. For a nominal fee, you can get a roof-mounted ski rack —
  money well spent.

- ✔ **Weather worthiness:** If you're heading into snow country, you need a
  car that's not going to slide around. A four-wheel-drive vehicle can make
  winter driving easier, although it's no substitute for skill and common
  sense. If a storm is brewing, ask about snow tires or even tire chains.
  (For more info on winter driving, see Chapter 14.)

- ✔ **General readiness:** Check the little things before you pull out of the lot.
  Are the windshield wiper blades fresh and clean? Is the windshield
  washer fluid full? Do the defrosters, both front and rear, seem to work? Is
  there an ice scraper in the trunk? An emergency triangle? Take a few
  minutes to familiarize yourself with the controls. Find the windshield
  washers, the emergency flashers, and the fog lights if the car has them.

After you give your vehicle the once-over, it's time to head to the mountains
and start making some turns and having fun.

Part V
The Part of Tens

The 5th Wave   By Rich Tennant

"Well, it's partially their fault for putting a restaurant that close to the chairlift."

In this part . . .

*E*veryone loves a list. In the chapters that follow, you discover some ski slang, meet some of skiing's greatest athletes, and find out about things to do when you're not skiing. And as an added bonus, I tell you how to score a free lift ticket.

Chapter 17

Top Ten Skiing Slang Terms

• •

All cultures have their own rich languages, and skiing is no exception. Skiing slang has been especially enriched in recent years by a cross-pollination with another related dialect, snowboard-speak. Anthropologists have noticed with great interest that many of the most vivid terms deal with falls and potential falls, although further research on this topic is required.

Beater: (n.) 1) A tumbling fall in which the skier rolls head over heels. syn. Starfish, describing a beater with limbs fully extended. 2) A rusty car that can be used for transportation to the slopes. "After he took that beater, he was more banged up than my old beater Gremlin."

Bluebird: (adj.) Description for a day with skies so sunny and blue and snow so perfect that it can't be improved upon. "I'm so glad I called in sick on Tuesday — it was totally bluebird."

Bulletproof: (n., adj.) Describing snow so icy that it's virtually unedgeable. Legend has it that on one particularly icy day at Stowe, a skeptical skier actually fired a .45 caliber bullet from point blank range and found the surface to be not only figuratively bulletproof, but literally so. "The stuff on the North Face froze up overnight, and this morning it's bulletproof."

Death cookies: (n.) Chunks of ice about the size of a chocolate-chip cookie, churned up by a groomer in an unsuccessful attempt to groom a bulletproof slope. Also called *frozen chicken heads*. "Exhibition was just chock-full of death cookies this morning."

Fat: (adj.) An all-purpose description for something excellent, especially deep snow conditions. "Was that fat or what?" Linguistic note: Some skiers — mostly Phish fans — still insist on the archaic spelling *phat*, which should be confined to the titles of circa-1995 rap records.

Figure 11s: (n.) Going straight down a trail without making a single turn, sometimes because of a beginner's inability to turn and sometimes in an expert's quest for maximum speed. A reference to powder skiing competitions in which skiers shadow each other's turns, leaving tracks that look like a figure eight. "He just flashed the couloir, doing a figure 11 from top to bottom."

Hospital air: (n.) A jump that carries the risk of significant personal injury and if landed improperly would necessitate the need for immediate medical care. (See Figure 17-1.) "Rob would routinely huck 30-footers; he seemed to thrive on hospital air."

Figure 17-1:
Hospital air
in action.

Courtesy Sport Obermeyer, Ltd.

Huck: (v.) To jump off a cliff or cornice, the verb phrase usually completed with a pseudo-disparaging reference to one's corporal being. "Did you see Kristen huck her carcass off that cliff?"

Sketchy: (adj.) Describes terrain or conditions that are difficult or unpleasant to ski, especially if they're borderline dangerous, such as extremely icy (see bulletproof) conditions or areas with many exposed rocks (chocolate chippy). "I checked it out, but I decided it was too sketchy."

Yard Sale: (n.) A fall in which the victim loses multiple pieces of equipment, especially within view of a chairlift, with the resulting gear-littered slope resembling a yard sale. "Yo, how much did you take in with that yard sale?"

Chapter 18

Ten Ways to Ski Free

• •

*E*verybody, but everybody, wants a free lift ticket. And while the lift ticket that's gratis, *por nada*, on the house is an elusive animal, that's part of what makes scoring one so appealing. Here are ten entirely legal ways that you can ski for free. However, because specific offers at specific resorts are subject to change without notice, appearing and disappearing from season to season, and even from week to week, I'm giving you some general guidelines. To get the details, call the ski area of your choice as well as the state or regional resort association, which often sponsors discounts and promotions that resorts are sometimes reluctant to publicize. As they say, buy a woman a lift ticket and she'll ski for a day, teach her to score a free one and she'll ski forever.

Be young

At many resorts, kids ski free all year. Of course, the young un's have to be accompanied by a ticket-buying adult, and the cutoff age varies from resort to resort.

Be old

Many resorts offer free lift tickets to vintage skiers, usually those over the age of 70. Be prepared to show some sort of ID that proves how old you are. A note from your mother, however, is strictly optional.

Have a gimmick

Ski areas have a sense of humor. They occasionally give away lift tickets just to see what people would do. Do you have a good memory? On Martin Luther King's birthday at one resort, if you recite the full text of his "I Have a Dream" speech, you get a free lift ticket. At another place, reciting the Gettysberg Address on Lincoln's birthday gets you a free one.

Go to Crested Butte

In an effort to attract early and late season skiers to the town's lodging and restaurants, this central Colorado resort slashed prices to the bare bone and beyond. In recent years, Crested Butte has offered free lift tickets until December 1 and after April 1.

Learn to ski

In the great American tradition of the free sample, many resorts and resort associations offer a way for beginners to try skiing without cost or obligation. These packages usually include rentals and a lesson as well as a lift ticket. Significant restrictions, however, do apply. These promotions are limited to certain dates, and are good only for learn-to-ski packages. But you can't beat the price.

Buy in bulk

Skiing is not dissimilar to paper towels — if you buy a lot all at once it's cheaper. All resorts sell multi-day tickets — two-, three-, or five-day passes — that are much cheaper than buying a series of single day passes. At many areas you can buy a book of tickets — say ten — in advance. The savings are usually significant enough that at least one day of skiing is essentially free.

Bring a friend

This is simple. At many ski areas, if you bring a first timer for their first day on skis, you can get a voucher for a lift ticket for yourself. Most ski areas have group sales departments, and among the incentives they offer are free tickets for the organizer of the group.

Ski a lot

You've heard of frequent flier cards? Well how about a frequent skier card? At many resorts, skiing begets more skiing (or more to the point, buying lift tickets begets more lift tickets). If you accumulate enough points under a resort's affinity program, you can trade them for free lift tickets.

Buy a season ticket

At many ski resorts, season passes are so cheap that the break-even point is 20 days or less, so if you ski a lot, you can practically ski half the season for free. A few areas are selling season tickets so cheap — around $200 if you buy well in advance — that even a vacationer could take advantage of the deal.

Volunteer

You know those people who stand around the resort on weekends in their mountain-issued jackets, answering questions, giving directions, and generally being courteous? Well, come Monday most of these mountain ambassadors go back to being accountants, carpenters, or school teachers. That means that you too could volunteer for this kind of program, which usually doesn't pay, but does carry with it a free lift ticket.

If you're not prepared to make a season-long commitment, resorts also need volunteers for special events — races, festivals, and even the Special Olympics — and those volunteers usually get to ski free for the day.

Chapter 19

Ten Things to Do When You're Not Skiing

• •

Ski vacations are about a lot more than skiing these days. High-speed lifts make it possible to cram a day's worth of skiing into a few hours and a week's worth of skiing into a few days. Which means that you have more than enough time to discover the other kinds of fun that most ski areas have in store for you. Here's a sampling.

Hot tubbing

After all, skiing is a water sport, albeit on frozen, crystalline water. So what better way to relax than in a fluid medium at the other end of the temperature scale? There's something downright decadent about wearing your bathing suit when it's 25 degrees outside — and that's where every proper hot tub should be: outside. What's my nomination for the best hot tub in skidom? The one on the roof of Snowbird's Cliff Lodge, which features breathtaking views of the mountain's most radical terrain.

Ice skating

You don't have to be Kristi Yamaguchi, or Wayne Gretsky for that matter, to enjoy sliding on a slightly different kind of frozen surface. Skating isn't about doing double axels or splitting two defenders, it's about the Norman Rockwellesque joy of being able to stand up, even if it's like a newborn fawn, on two little metal blades and then warming up with some hot chocolate and a hug.

Boutiquing

Sometimes you have to go to the source. And if you're looking for the real deal — whether it's cowboy boots, maple sugar candy, or Native American blankets — it's often easier to find in a ski town than on Madison Avenue. That goes double if it's a skiing-related item, like that perfect parka, or goggles that are simply great.

Snowshoeing

Forget Nanook of the North. Today's feather-light snowshoes are more like New Balance running shoes for deep powder. But it's about more than just exercise. Snowshoes are also the perfect tool for exploring the woods that surround many ski areas. Running through a stand of aspens, on the lookout for animal tracks, is way more interesting than waiting for the odometer on the health club treadmill to flip from 2.8 miles to 2.9 miles.

Cross-country skiing

Cross-country is a kinder, gentler form of snow sliding. It's less demanding of reflexes and courage than downhill, but it places bigger demands on your cardiovascular system. And in the wilderness, there are no lift lines. This makes cross-country skiing the perfect change-up on a ski vacation for those times when you want to raise your heart rate and lower your blood pressure.

Dog sledding

Who's the world's greatest athlete? Forget about Michael Jordan. I nominate those hearty canines that can run faster than any human marathoner in sub-zero temperatures for eight hours a day — day after day with hardly a whimper. No, I'm not suggesting that you mush in the Iditarod, but some ski resorts offer dog sled tours that range from an hour-long sample to an overnight excursion. It's the ideal way to throw your vacation to the dogs.

Snow tubing

If you're looking for the thrill without the skill, snow tubing is just the ticket. It's deliciously simple: you, the slope, an inner tube (like the one you'd find inside a truck tire) and gravity. Most areas these days have snow tubing parks with specially designed runs, some even sporting their own rope tows. Tubing is often a nighttime activity, which means it can be a supplement to, rather than a substitute for, your skiing. Kids especially love tubing.

Sledding

Ski area sledding can be anything from a three-year-old on the little hill outside your condo, to racers careening down black diamond trails on their cresta sleds at speeds approaching the legal limit. Whatever the speed, it's good, clean fun. You should be careful, though. Sleds can get going pretty fast, and lack the steering and stopping capabilities of skis. That's why it's wise to limit your sledding to designated-sledding areas that are free of obstacles.

Ski biking

Haven't had your fill of playing with gravity? Well now many resorts are offering ski bikes — think of a mountain bike with skis where the wheels would be. You wear skiboards on your feet when you ride, and simply steer with the handlebars. The sensation is a little like skiing, a lot like mountain biking, and as much fun as either.

Outletting

Pay retail? You? Why I'm sure you would sooner wear a pair of Gucci knock-offs. Factory outlet stores, featuring deals on everything from skiwear to housewares to designer sportswear have cropped up in and around ski towns like crabgrass on a newly seeded lawn. North Conway, New Hampshire, is, in fact, one of the factory outlet capitals of the Northeast.

Chapter 20

Ten Ski Jocks
You Should Know

• •

*I*n the United States, ski racing and other ski competitions such as moguls, aren't like baseball. Racers get their moment in the sun every four years when the Olympics roll around. But they're tremendous athletes, great skiers, fun personalities, and exciting to watch. Here's my personal all-time ski jock team.

Stein Eriksen

This classy Norwegian won gold and silver medals at the 1952 Olympics and three golds at the 1954 World Championships. So much for his qualifications as the best skier of his day. But the legend that is Stein came into his own after his racing days were done, when stints at Boyne Mountain, Michigan, Sugarbush, Snowmass, Park City, and Deer Valley allowed him to establish skiing as a sport of grace and charm, both on the snow and off it.

Billy Kidd

With a catchy name, an easygoing style, and speed that allowed him to beat Europe's best on their own terms, Kidd put skiing on the map in the United States. No American man had ever won an Olympic medal in skiing before the Innsbruck games of 1964, when Kidd won silver in slalom and his teammate Jimmie Heuga won bronze. Kidd later won the gold in combined at the World Championships in Val Gardena, Italy, in 1970. He remains one of the sport's best ambassadors, skiing with guests at his adopted mountain, Steamboat, whenever he's in town. Just look for the quiet smile and the big Stetson cowboy hat, probably the most recognizable trademark in skiing.

Jean-Claude Killy

This dashing Frenchman was skiing's last triple threat. On home snow during the 1968 Winter Olympics in Grenoble, France, Killy matched Toni Sailer's 1956 feat of winning all three Alpine events: the slalom, the giant slalom, and the downhill. A two-time winner of the overall World Cup title, Killy was able to uphold skiing's glamorous image singlehandedly, long after he retired from racing, having won everything in his 20s. More recently Killy has taken on a different kind of Alpine challenge, first running the 1992 Olympics in Albertville, France, and then working as director of the Tour de France bicycle race.

Franz Klammer

"Klammer's going to do it." The call from Bob Beattie of the downhill in the 1976 Innsbruck Olympics turned millions, including yours truly, onto ski racing. Before thousands of screaming hometown fans, the Austrian great put together the run of his life, throwing caution to the wind, flirting with disaster at every turn, but somehow managing to stay upright and collect a gold medal. It came at a time when he was a colossus who dominated downhill competition. By the time he retired, Klammer had won 25 World Cup downhills. But no win was as memorable as that gold in Innsbruck.

Phil and Steve Mahre

Twin brothers from Washington State, Phil and Steve set the standard for American ski racers. Racers like Billy Kidd had shown that Americans could win at ski racing; the Mahres proved they could dominate. Phil won three straight overall World Cup titles in the early 1980s, an accomplishment that was capped at the 1984 Olympics when he took gold and Steve took silver in slalom. Phil, with 27 World Cup wins, is the most successful American racer in history, and Steve, with 9 wins, is the second winningest among the men.

Tamara McKinney

Before there was Picabo, there was Tamara. Still the only American woman to win the overall World Cup title (in 1983), McKinney was a powerhouse on the world skiing scene throughout the 1980s. She won the World Cup slalom title in 1984 and the GS title in 1981 and 1983 and inspired the generation of racers, and ordinary skiers, who followed. In a sport where a single World Cup win can establish your resume, McKinney chalked up 18, second only to Phil Mahre in U.S. racing history.

Jonny Moseley

This young Californian turned skiing new-school, with a snowboard-inspired move that captured not only the imagination of skiers everywhere but also the gold medal in the moguls competition at the 1998 Nagano Olympics.

Figure 20-1:
Olympic gold-medalist Jonny Moseley.

© Scott Markewitz, American Skiing Company

Picabo Street

Picabo Street is all talent and full of exuberance and has a ravenous appetite for winning and for living. At the 1994 Winter Games in Lillehammer, she shocked the competition with a silver medal run in downhill. Proving that was no fluke, the following season she became the first American skier to win a World Cup downhill title — and then repeated the feat in 1996. Street's career seemed threatened by a crash that resulted in surgery to repair her knee and long months of rehab. But she roared back to the racecourse only weeks before the 1998 Nagano Olympics to win gold in the Super-G. Only a few weeks later, she suffered another devastating crash, this time shattering her femur and ripping more ligaments. Picabo was still recovering throughout the 1999 season but planned to return to racing in 2000.

Alberto Tomba

"I'm in training, so I'll stay up 'til two with three women instead of staying up 'til three with two women." That's the way this brilliant Italian racer pursued his career. He playfully dubbed himself the Messiah of skiing, but in reality he was a rock star. The joke was that he ate, smoked, and partied too much, but come race day, Tomba was always ready. He was the first skier to win medals in three Olympics (1988, 1992, and 1994) and to win the same Olympic event twice (the GS in 1988 and 1992). But nothing expresses his dominance as much as this stat: 50 career World Cup wins. Tomba went out with as much style as he'd ever shown, winning the last race of his career, the final slalom of the 1998 season.

Donna Weinbrecht

Only one woman could be first, and she was Donna Weinbrecht. She won gold in the first-ever Olympic mogul competition in Albertville in 1992. By that time, though, the beautiful, unpretentious New Jersey native had already dominated mogul skiing. Weinbrecht helped found her high school ski team and after graduation moved to Killington and taught herself to ski bumps. She won dozens of World Cup competitions and five World Cup titles while representing the United States for more than a decade. Most of all, Donna proved that a largely self-taught ski bum from the suburbs could become a star.

"... and the agony of defeat"

To American audiences, he may be the most recognizable competitive skier in the world, but hardly anyone knows his name. For decades, the opening credits to ABC's *Wide World of Sports*, which featured a ski jumper cartwheeling off the take-off ramp, begged any number of questions. Who was that skier? His name is Vinko Bogataj, and he was actually a very accomplished ski jumper. What happened to him? Bogataj not only survived that spectacular fall, but he did so with only minor injuries.

Part VI
Appendixes

The 5th Wave   By Rich Tennant

"Okay—here they come. Remember, it's a lot like catching salmon, only spit out the poles."

In this part . . .

Where are the best places to ski in North America? Do you want to find a local or not-so-far-away ski area from your home? Look no farther than the appendixes in this part.

I also include a handy skiing glossary to help you understand any terminology you may find confusing or have never heard.

Appendix A

The Top Ski Areas in North America

• •

*N*ow that you understand the ins and outs of buying gear, of skiing better, and of planning a vacation, all you need is a place to do it. This list is meant to give you a flavor of each resort, a thumbnail sketch that will let you know if this is a place that you might consider for a vacation. It's not meant to be a guidebook — there's simply not enough space for that.

I've covered most of the usual suspects — popular resorts that skiers discuss a lot — as well as a few less well-known gems. But just because it's not on this list doesn't mean that a ski area isn't worthy of your consideration. In Appendix B, I list contact information for more resorts, and you can have a great time at any one of them.

To learn more about these and other resorts, consult any of the numerous guidebooks on your bookstore shelves, or a magazine, which includes feature stories about resorts, as well as an annual travel guide in one of the early fall issues, which includes a list similar to this one.

As an added bonus, at the end of this appendix I've included five top ski areas in Europe.

Far West

Aleyska

Alaska is America's last frontier, and this emerging resort captures that pioneer spirit, not with cowboy theme restaurants but with a true sense of adventure. The mountain, like the state, is breathtakingly large, but there's plenty of terrain for beginners and intermediates. It's low-altitude, high-latitude location means that altitude's not a problem and toward the end of the season, the days are longer than at any resort in the lower 48 states.

Heavenly

Skiing across state lines? That's what you can do at this Lake Tahoe resort which lies on the border between California and Nevada. (See Figure A-1.) In addition to solid and scenic skiing, Heavenly also features breathtaking views of the lake, and après-ski gambling at Nevada's nearby casinos.

Figure A-1:
Heavenly
features
postcard-
perfect
views.

© Heavenly Ski Resort

Mammoth

Surfing and skiing on the same day? At Mammoth, the mega-mountain located a few hours from Los Angeles, this can almost be a reality. This aptly named mountain is annually among the leaders in skier visits because of its size and variety. Its infrastructure is due for a facelift soon.

Mt. Bachelor

Endless winter — it's every skier's dream. At this central Oregon resort, it's almost a reality. The snowfall (and the snow itself) at Mt. Bachelor is so heavy that the season generally lasts until mid-summer. This makes for enticing possibilities in the sports-mad town of Bend — skiing in the morning, and whitewater rafting in the afternoon.

Northstar at Tahoe

Customer service is the name of the game at this mid-size resort in California's Sierra Nevada mountains. The terrain has solid cruising runs, and with everything from free mini-clinics to flexible ticketing to man-made moguls, it's the kind of mountain where no stone goes unturned. Home to possibly the most beautiful public restroom in all of skiing.

Squaw Valley

One of the true skiers' mountains of North America, Squaw is home to some of the most famous — and most photographed — skiing in the U.S. KT-22, so named because that's how many kick turns it took to descend it when the resort opened, is arguably the sport's most fabled bump run. And the for-experts-only Palisades have served as the backdrop for many extreme skiing exploits.

Intermountain

Alta

If you want a trip down memory lane, skiing-wise, Alta is the place. This Utah resort doesn't have much in the way of high-speed lifts, and it still doesn't allow snowboarders. But the snow is as light, fluffy, and plentiful as anywhere in the U.S., and the dirt-cheap lift ticket may be the best bargain in U.S. skiing.

Deer Valley

If luxury is what you're after, then Deer Valley is the place. Founded by legendary racer Stein Eriksen, this resort features some of the poshest accommodations, the most refined cuisine, and the toniest shops in all of skiing. The skiing is soft as well, with immaculate grooming of the fluffy Utah powder.

Grand Targhee

The problem with learning to ski powder is that deep snow and hairy terrain often go together. If you're an aspiring powder pig, Targhee should be on your short list. This low-key Wyoming resort happily runs contrary to the steep and deep trend, featuring abundant snowfall and lots of moderate ungroomed terrain.

Jackson Hole

This wild and wooly Wyoming resort is definitely a place to test your mettle. It's one of those few areas where even an advanced skier should start out on green circle terrain and work his way up. It's located near Yellowstone, where snowmobile tours are available. Jackson Hole also offers the opportunity for other kinds of wilderness exploring.

Park City

This Utah area features plenty of gladed, groomed trails for cruising the day away, along with some off-piste challenges. The annual Sundance film festival — call in advance for tickets — has become one of the most important events in American independent cinema.

Snowbird

A majestic mountain that often gets pounded with powder, this Utah area isn't for everyone. Its steeps are breathtaking and its expert runs as challenging as can be, but if you're not at least a solid intermediate skier, you may be frustrated by the lack of moderate-to-easy terrain.

Sun Valley

Founded in the heart of Hemingway country back when Papa was still scribbling, this venerable Idaho resort is still tremendously appealing. It sports a wide variety of terrain, exceptional views, and lifts and base lodges that are second to none. It's hard to get to, but that only serves to keep the crowds down.

Taos

Are you an expert skier? Well, if you want to put yourself to the test, Taos is the place. This New Mexico resort specializes in steep, narrow chutes, and near vertical bump runs. Its ski weeks are one of the best ways for advanced skiers to improve their skill at handling challenging terrain. One of the last holdouts, Taos doesn't allow snowboarders.

Mid-Atlantic

Camelback

Thanks to the interstate highway system, Camelback is one of the top day trip areas in the east. Only 90 minutes from New York and about as far from Philadelphia, it features fast lifts that let you get in a lot of skiing in a little bit of time. Camelback also offers night skiing, which allows you to extend your sliding.

Hunter Mountain

If you're in midtown Manhattan and get the ski jones, but you still have to be home for dinner, Hunter is a solid first choice. Located in the Catskills, just over two hours from the city, it features varied terrain, fast lifts, and, yes, one of the best snowmaking systems anywhere. On weekends it can resemble Times Square, but on weekdays, it's a guilty pleasure.

Mountain Creek

Just 40 minutes outside of the Big Apple, this suburban New Jersey area has undergone a change of ownership and a facelift. The former Vernon Valley Great Gorge has moved upscale, but it still sports a surprising amount of terrain, and snowmaking that can compete with almost any resort.

Ski Windham

Not far from Hunter, this Catskill resort has a much different vibe. If Hunter is a Mustang, Ski Windham is a minivan. It's modern, efficient, and family-oriented, having the feel, if not the terrain, of a mellow western resort a little more than two hours from Manhattan.

Snowshoe

A ski resort south of the Mason-Dixon Line? You betcha. This West Virginia resort features significant vertical and gets snow aplenty (just watch the Weather Channel). When Mother Nature doesn't cooperate, it cranks up one of the best snowmaking systems around.

Whiteface

Home of the skiing events in the 1980 Olympics, this Lake Placid resort has more vertical and better expert terrain than anywhere else in the mid-Atlantic, and many New England resorts. It also features a myriad of off-day options, from the mellow — ice skating — to the adrenalized — bobsledding on part of the Olympic run.

Midwest

Boyne Mountain

Sex on the slopes? That's what you can find at Boyne Mountain, the Michigan mountain that is the home of the nation's first six-person (or sextuple) chair-lift. Drawing skiers from all over the Midwest, Boyne overcomes its lack of big vertical and Rocky Mountain powder dumps with efficient lifts, excellent snowmaking, and well-designed programs for everyone from first timers to fledgling Picabo Streets.

New England

Attitash

Located on the outskirts of North Conway, New Hampshire, this American Skiing Company-owned resort has seen significant growth in recent seasons. The Bear Peak expansion opens up some fine cruising terrain and the new Grand Hotel is one of the largest and poshest in the state.

Bretton Woods

A cruiser's paradise, this New Hampshire area features wide-open, consistently pitched slopes that make you feel like you're a better skier than you really are. Adding to that feeling is the impeccable grooming, which ranks among the best in the East.

Cannon

This brawny New Hampshire day area features New England skiing at its unvarnished best. Steep, narrow, and imposing, its Front Four offer the mountain's most apparent challenge, but the narrow trails that play hide and seek through the woods offer a change-up for less-accomplished skiers.

Cranmore

Home of North America's first ski school, this low-key Booth Creek-owned resort features a combination of wide-open cruising terrain and some classic New England-style winders. It also features a wide variety of sliding alternatives, from skiboarding to snowbiking. North Conway's Route 16 has some of the best outlet shopping in the East and is only a couple of GS turns away from the mountain.

Jay Peak

Only a few GS turns from Canada, this northern Vermont resort is known for its abundant snowfall and its excellent tree skiing. It was one of the first mountains to institute a boundary to boundary policy, meaning that all terrain, wooded or not, is open whenever there's sufficient snow. And while many resorts offer tree skiing for advanced and expert skiers, Jay has a wide variety of glades for intermediates.

Killington

Imagine Manhattan moved five hours north. On weekends, this popular Vermont resort is busier than Grand Central Station, and after the lifts close, the action shifts to party-hearty bars and restaurants that line the access road. And like New York, it's big and there's something for everyone, from ample beginner terrain to world-class moguls.

Mad River Glen

Ski it if you can. That's the motto of this throwback resort. The trails are narrow and ungroomed, the lifts are slow, and snowboarders are strictly prohibited. It's not a place for a beginner or a cruiser, but if you want a glimpse of what skiing was like 50 years ago, this Vermont resort is your own personal way-back machine.

Mount Snow

This southern Vermont resort with acres of blue squares of all descriptions is perfect for the intermediate skier. A new Grand Summit Hotel anchors the base area and new high-speed quads have improved congestion problems. But if you're skiing Mount Snow on a weekend or holiday, you may want to check out the adjacent Haystack area, which features mellower skiing and fewer crowds.

Okemo

As one of the few independently owned resorts in New England, Okemo serves up skiing family style with condos and kid-friendly eating galore. The mountain itself is solidly mid-sized, with a variety of terrain, all in a manageable package. When you encounter a typical New England freeze-thaw cycle, you may appreciate Okemo's reputation for unparalleled grooming.

Smuggler's Notch

Family-friendlyness is mostly a matter of attitude, and Smuggler's has that down pat. This northern Vermont resort caters to children of all ages, with a wide variety of on- and off-slope activities and programs. However, the terrain — especially the tree-skiing on Madonna mountain — is more than kid's stuff.

Stowe

Can a ski area be curmudgeonly? Stowe has a certain streak of Yankee independence that befits its rugged face. Trails like Goat, the centerpiece of the mountain's legendary Front Four, are true classics in a rough-hewn New England way, and the Chin offers epic off-trail skiing for experts willing to hike. An interconnect to Smuggler's Notch adds options to your vacation.

Stratton

Is there a snowboarder in your pack? Then consider a Stratton vacation. This southern Vermont resort is rider-friendly in the extreme. It features wide trails with even pitch, a great halfpipe, and little amenities like strap-in benches at the top of the lifts. Every spring it plays host to one of the biggest events in North American snow sliding: the U.S. Open Snowboarding Championships.

Sugarbush

How times change. During the 1970s, serious skiers dismissed Sugarbush, referring to it as Mascara Mountain. Now, it's home to some of New England's hardest hardcores, with steeps, trees, and the craggy, improvisational terrain that defines extreme skiing Eastern-style.

Sugarloaf

A true skier's mountain: Sugarloaf is worth the drive into the heart of Maine's moose country. It has plenty of challenging steeps, and the Snowfields, when they are open, provide one of the few Eastern equivalents of Western bowl-type skiing. Spring is the best time to visit Sugarloaf, as both the thermometer and the snowpack on the snowfields creep up as the season wears on.

Sunday River

One of the most remarkable success stories in U.S. skiing, this Bethel, Maine resort was once a small struggling day area on the verge of bankruptcy. Then new owner Les Otten began a massive expansion campaign that transformed it into one of the largest and most popular resorts in the East, featuring accommodations of all shapes and sizes, and a virtual smorgasbord of terrain options.

Waterville Valley

Only a short drive from Boston on I-93, Waterville matches a variety of terrain, including some of New England's first and best terrain gardens, to a mellow, family style ambiance. The modern base village is charming and well thought out, but it's a shuttle bus ride, or a short drive, away from the lifts.

Wildcat

Located in the shadow of Mount Washington, Wildcat offers New England skiing at its untamed best. The narrow, winding trails are a throwback to the early days of skiing, although the lifts, snowmaking, and grooming have all been updated. Since it's located in the White Mountain National Forest, there is no on-site lodging in the area.

Rocky Mountain

Arapahoe Basin

Want to get higher? This Front Range mountain sits at a greater altitude than most of its neighbors, which means that much of A-Basin's terrain consists of open bowls above tree line. It gets more snow and holds it better, which means that it's usually one of the last resorts in the region to close for the season.

Aspen

Attitude is everything. That could be the de facto motto of this classic Colorado area. The skiing is serious, and the shopping and the schmoozing are even more so. While you don't have to wear Bogner or Prada, Aspen's not the place to go skiing in jeans and a Green Bay Packers jacket. Nearby Snowmass is less demanding, both of your skiing skills and of your social skills.

Breckenridge

Think of Keystone only more so. Breckenridge is a little bigger than its sibling in the Vail Empire and has a somewhat wider variety of terrain, although not much above tree line. Breckenridge also has a lot more in the way of extracurricular activities, located near a small but swinging mining town.

Copper

Do you have separation anxiety? More than most mountains, this modern, efficient resort is able to compartmentalize its terrain, with most green circles in one area, blue squares in another, and black diamonds somewhere else. If you've got a group of skiers of similar ability levels, this is a plus. If "I'm taking this black diamond and I'll meet you at the bottom" is your group's unofficial motto, then it may not be such a good idea.

Crested Butte

Can you say split personality? The North Face at Crested Butte (accessible only by t-bar) sports some of the most challenging steeps at any North American resort. However, the lower part of the mountain features a variety of user-friendly cruising runs. And the town, a mining settlement adorned with lovely Victorians, is one of the most charming in all of skiing.

Keystone

Compact and easy to negotiate by Rocky Mountain standards, Keystone was designed with intermediate skiers in mind. It features wide trails, consistent pitches, impeccable grooming and lots of snow. The compact base area is kid friendly, but doesn't feature much après-ski action. The addition of the Outback area adds an expert dimension to the mountain. Owned by Vail, a Keystone ticket is also good at Vail and Breckinridge.

Steamboat

Seeking sybaritic skiing? Steamboat doesn't sport the steeps of some of its Colorado neighbors, but it gets as much snow as anywhere, and much of it tends to be fluffy and light.The tree skiing in widely spaced aspens is as good as it gets. The town, which lays claim to being the birthplace of American snow sliding, features a rough-hewn charm that's doubled during the annual Winter Carnival in January.

Telluride

The centerpiece of this Central Colorado resort features a formidable mountain with steeps, bumps, and some cruisers too. Add a smattering of local charm — it's located in a quaint former mining town — and it's no wonder that it attracts serious skiers and celebrities alike.

Vail

Vail is the resort that all others compare themselves to. It's got acres of buffed cruising terrain, and with the addition of the Back Bowls, some truly compelling expert terrain as well. And after you're done on the slopes, wander around Vail Village to sample some of the best restaurants and swankiest shops in all of skidom.

Canada

Lake Louise

Clank. That was the sound of your jaw dropping at Lake Louise's scenery. This British Columbia resort is not only the largest single mountain resort in Canada, it's also arguably the prettiest mountain in North America, ringed by glaciers and lakes that are bluer than B.B. King. No on-mountain lodging, but the nearby Chateau Lake Louise looks like a castle without the drawbridge, and the town of Banff offers lodging and restaurant options.

Mt. Tremblant

Once upon a time Mt. Tremblant was merely a small area just outside Montreal. Then Intrawest, the Canadian-resort giant, pumped in mega-bucks — more than $100 million. The result is a completely new base village, a slew of fast lifts, and a new status as a destination resort. This resort is a relative bargain given the U.S./Canadian exchange rate.

Whistler/Blackcomb

Don't let a drizzly day at the base convince you to sleep in at Whistler/Blackcomb. It can be pouring at the base, but as you ride the gondola up this giant British Columbia resort, it's likely to change into snow by mid-mountain, and powder by the time you get to the top. The summit is only 6,000 feet, which means that altitude is a non-factor. The skiing itself has a wide-open, almost European feel, and more terrain than you can sample in a week.

Europe

Chamonix

If there were daily prayer sessions for extreme skiers the world over, they would genuflect in the direction of Chamonix, France. The place is the world center for steep. Mountaineers, skiers, and parapenters all cross paths here. And there can't be a more neck-craning view of the mountains than in down-town Chamonix. Nevertheless, normal skiers can find almost limitless skiing, too.

Cortina d'Ampezzo

In all of Europe, Italy arguably has the best food, the best atmosphere, and the greatest understanding of how to enjoy life. It seems almost unfair that it also has some of the best skiing, but it's true. Tomba, after all, is Italian (how could he be anything else?). This resort in the southern Alps combines a chic town with dramatic, sharp-edged mountains that could fill many years' worth of skiing.

Kitzbuhel

This Austrian resort has something no other ski area in the world does: the Hahnenkamm. This is the most famous ski-racing course in the world, and winning there is like winning at Centre Court in Wimbledon — except that a grass tennis court can't kill you. In addition to world-class skiing for all ability levels, Kitzbuhel has world-class wurst eaters and world-class schnapps drinkers. In short, it has the best of the wurst.

Val D'Isere and Tignes

Here's a secret: The most gargantuan U.S. ski resort is utterly Lilliputian in comparison to the resorts of the Alps. And no place can rub it in the face of Vail the way these separate resorts that serve the same mountains in France can. They have around 120 lifts — not trails, lifts — and untold thousands upon thousands of acres of off-piste skiing, which served as the backdrop to the 1992 Albertville Olympics.

Zermatt

For many Americans, skiing is practically synonymous with Switzerland, and Switzerland is just another word for Zermatt. Lying in the shadow of the Matterhorn, the town is a bastion of European charm while the ski terrain is immense and varied. The vertical drop is 7,000 feet. Need I say more?

Appendix B

Ski Areas in the United States

● ●

*T*he following is a state-by-state list of member areas of the National Ski Areas Association

Alabama

Cloudmont Ski & Golf
Mentone, AL
Phone: (256) 634-4344
Website:
www.cloudmont.com/cloudmont

Alaska

Alyeska Resort
Girdwood, AK
Phone: (907) 754-2285

Eaglecrest Ski Area
Juneau, AK
Phone: (907) 586-5284
Website: www.juneau.lib.ak.us/
eaglecrest/eaglcrst.htm

Hilltop Ski Area
Anchorage, AK
Phone: (907) 346-1446

Mt. Eyak Ski Area
Cordova, AK
Phone: (907) 424-7766

Arizona

Arizona Snowbowl
Flagstaff, AZ
Phone: (520) 779-1951
Website:
www.arizonasnowbowl.com

Mt. Lemmon Ski Valley
Tucson, AZ
Phone: (520) 885-1181

Sunrise Ski Resort
McNary, AZ
Phone: (520) 735-7669

Williams Ski Area
Williams, AZ
Phone: (520) 635-9330

California

Alpine Meadows Ski Area
Tahoe City, CA

Phone: (530) 583-4232
Website: www.skialpine.com

Badger Pass
Yosemite, CA
Phone: (209) 372-1000

Big Bear Mountain Ski & Summer Resort
Big Bear Lake, CA
Phone: (909) 585-2519
Website: www.bearmtn.com

Bear Valley Ski Area
Bear Valley, CA
Phone: (209) 753-2301
Website: www.bearvalley.com

Big Air Winter Park
Green Valley Lake, CA
Phone: (909) 867-2338
Website: www.gobigair.com

Boreal Mountain Playground
Truckee, CA
Phone: (530) 426-3666
Website: www.borealski.com

Dodge Ridge Ski Area
Pinecrest, CA
Phone: (209) 965-3474
Website: www.dodgeridge.com

Donner Ski Ranch
Norden, CA
Phone: (530) 426-3635
Website: www.donnerskiranch.com

Granlibakken Ski Area
Tahoe City, CA
Phone: (530) 583-4242

June Mountain Ski Area
Mammoth Lakes, CA
Phone: (760) 648-7733
Website: www.junemountain.com

Kirkwood Resort Company
Kirkwood, CA
Phone: (209) 258-6000
Website: www.skikirkwood.com

Mammoth Mountain Ski Area
Mammoth Lakes, CA
Phone: 888-4-Mammoth
Website: www.mammoth-mtn.com

Mountain High Resort
Wrightwood, CA
Phone: (760) 249-5808
Website: www.mthigh.com

Mt. Shasta Ski Park
Mt. Shasta, CA
Phone: (530) 926-8600
Website: www.skipark.com

Mt. Waterman Ski Lifts, Ltd.
La Canada, CA
Phone: (626) 440-1041
Website: www.aminews.com/waterman

Northstar-at-Tahoe
Truckee, CA
Phone: (530) 562-1010
Website: www.skinorthstar.com

Plumas-Eureka Ski Bowl
Quincy, CA
Phone: (530) 836-2317

Royal Gorge Ski Resort
Soda Springs, CA
Phone: 800-500-3871
Website: www.royalgorge.com

Shirley Meadows Ski Area
Wofford Heights, CA
Phone: (760) 376-4186

Sierra Summit Mountain Resort
Lakeshore, CA
Phone: (209) 233-2500
Website: www.sierrasummit.com

Sierra-at-Tahoe Ski Resort
Twin Bridges, CA
Phone: (530) 659-7453
Website: www.sierratahoe.com

Ski Homewood
Homewood, CA
Phone: (530) 525-2992

Ski Sunrise
Wrightwood, CA
Phone: (760) 249-6150
Website: www.skisunrise.com

Snow Summit Mountain Resort
Big Bear Lake, CA
Phone: (909) 866-5766
Website: www.snowsummit.com

Snow Valley Mountain Resort
Running Springs, CA
Phone: (909) 867-2751
Website: www.snow-valley.com

Snowcrest At Kratka Ridge
La Crescenta, CA
Phone: (626) 583-9477
Website: www.aminews.com/
snowcrest

Soda Springs Ski Area
Truckee, CA
Phone: (530) 426-3666

Squaw Valley Ski Corporation
Olympic Valley, CA
Phone: (530) 583-6985
Website: www.squaw.com

Sugar Bowl Ski Resort
Norden, CA
Phone: (530) 426-9000
Website: www.sugarbowl.com

Tahoe Donner
Truckee, CA
Phone: (530) 587-9444
Website: www.aminews.com/donner

Colorado

Arapahoe Basin
Arapahoe Basin, CO
Phone: (970) 468-0718
Website: www.arapahoebasin.com

Aspen Highlands
Aspen, CO
Phone: (970) 925-1220
Website: www.skiaspen.com

Aspen Mountain
Aspen, CO
Phone: (970) 925-1220
Website: www.skiaspen.com

Beaver Creek Resort
Vail, CO
Phone: (970) 949-5750
Website: www.snow.com

Berthoud Pass Ski Area
Winter Park, CO
Phone: (303) 569-0100
Website: www.berthoudpass.com

Breckenridge Ski Resort
Breckenridge, CO
Phone: (970) 453-5000
Website: www.snow.com

Buttermilk Mountain
Aspen, CO
Phone: (970) 925-1220
Website: www.skiaspen.com

Copper Mountain Resort
Copper Mountain, CO
Phone: (970) 968-2882
Website: www.ski-copper.com

Crested Butte Mountain Resort
Mt. Crested Butte, CO
Phone: (970) 349-2390
Website:
www.crestedbutte-ski.com

Cuchara Mountain Resort
Cuchara, CO
Phone: (719) 742-3163
Website: www.cuchara.com

Eldora Mountain Resort
Nederland, CO
Phone: (303) 440-8700
Website: www.eldora.com

Howelsen Hill Ski Area
Steamboat Springs, CO
Phone: (970) 879-8499

Keystone Resort
Keystone, CO
Phone: (970) 496-2316
Website: www.snow.com

Loveland Ski Area
Georgetown, CO
Phone: (303) 569-3203
Website: www.skiloveland.com

Monarch Ski and Snowboard Area
Monarch, CO
Phone: (719) 539-3573
Website: www.skimonarch.com

Powderhorn Resort
Mesa, CO
Phone: (970) 268-5700
Website: www.powderhorn.com

Purgatory Resort
Durango, CO
Phone: (970) 247-9000
Website: www.ski-purg.com

Silver Creek Ski Resort
Granby, CO
Phone: (970) 887-3384
Website: www.silvercreek-resort.com

Ski Cooper
Leadville, CO
Phone: (719) 486-3684
Website: www.skicooper.com

Snowmass Ski Area
Aspen, CO
Phone: (970) 925-1220
Website: www.skiaspen.com

Steamboat Ski & Resort Corp.
Steamboat Springs, CO
Phone: (970) 879-6111
Website: www.steamboat-ski.com

Sunlight Mountain Resort
Glenwood Springs, CO
Phone: (970) 945-7491
Website: www.sunlightmtn.com

Telluride Ski & Golf Company
Telluride, CO
Phone: (970) 728-6900
Website: www.telski.com

Vail Mountain
Vail, CO
Phone: (970) 476-5601
Website: www.snow.com

Winter Park Resort
Winter Park, CO
Phone: (970) 726-5514
Website: www.skiwinterpark.com

Wolf Creek Ski Area
Pagosa Springs, CO
Phone: (970) 264-5487
Website: www.wolfcreekski.com

Connecticut

Mohawk Mountain Ski Area
Cornwall, CT
Phone: (860) 672-6100
Website: www.aminews.com/mohawk

Mount Southington Ski Area
Southington, CT
Phone: (860) 628-0954
Website:
www.mountsouthington.com

Whitewater Mountain Resorts
Middlefield, CT
Phone: (860) 349-3454
Website: www.PowderRidgect.com

Ski Sundown, Inc.
New Hartford, CT
Phone: (860) 379-9851
Website: www.skisundown.com

Woodbury Ski Area
Woodbury Center, CT
Phone: (203) 263-2203
Website:
www.woodburyskiarea.com

Georgia

Ski Sky Valley
Sky Valley, GA
Phone: (706) 746-5302
Website: www.skyvalley.com

Idaho

Bogus Basin Ski Resort
Boise, ID
Phone: (208) 332-5100
Website: www.bogusbasin.com

Brundage Mountain
McCall, ID
Phone: (208) 634-7462
Website: www.brundage.com

Lookout Pass Ski Area
Wallace, ID
Phone: (208) 744-1392
Website: www.skilookout.com

Pebble Creek Ski Area
Inkom, ID
Phone: (208) 775-4452

Pomerelle Ski Area
Albion, ID
Phone: (208) 673-5599

Schweitzer Mountain Resort
Sandpoint, ID
Phone: (208) 263-9555
Website: www.schweitzer.com

Silver Mountain Ski & Summer Resort
Kellogg, ID
Phone: (208) 783-1111
Website: www.silvermt.com

Soldier Mountain Ski Area
Fairfield, ID
Phone: (208) 764-2526

Sun Valley Company
Sun Valley, ID
Phone: 800-786-8259
Website: www.sunvalley.com

Illinois

Chestnut Mountain Resort
Galena, IL
Phone: 800-397-1320
Website: www.chestnutmtn.com

Ski Snowstar
Taylor Ridge, IL
Phone: (309) 798-2666
Website: www.skisnowstar.com

Villa Olivia Ski Area
Bartlett, IL
Phone: (630) 289-1000

Indiana

Paoli Peaks, Inc.
Paoli, IN
Phone: (812) 723-4696
Website: www.skipeaks.com

Perfect North Slopes
Lawrenceburg, IN
Phone: (812) 537-3754
Website: www.perfectnorth.com

Ski World, Inc.
Nashville, IN
Phone: (812) 988-6638
Website:
www.nashvilleindiana.com/
attractions.html

Iowa

Fun Valley
Montezuma, IA
Phone: (515) 623-3456

Mt. Crescent Ski Area
Crescent, IA
Phone: (712) 545-3850

Sleepy Hollow Sports Park, Inc.
Des Moines, IA
Phone: (515) 262-4100

Sundown Mountain Ski Area
Dubuque, IA
Phone: (319) 556-6676
Website: www.webfire.com/
sundown

Maine

Black Mountain of Maine
Rumford, ME
Phone: (207) 364-8977

Lost Valley Ski Area
Auburn, ME
Phone: (207) 784-1561
Website: www.lostvalleyski.com

Mt. Abram
Locke Mills, ME
Phone: (207) 875-5003
Website: www.mtabram.com

Saddleback Ski Area, Inc.
Rangeley, ME
Phone: (207) 864-5671

Shawnee Peak Ski Area
Bridgton, ME
Phone: (207) 647-8444

Spruce Mountain Ski Club Inc.
Jay, ME
Phone: (207) 897-4090

Sugarloaf USA
Carrabassett Valley, ME
Phone: (207) 237-2000
Website: www.sugarloaf.com

Sunday River Ski Resort
Bethel, ME
Phone: (800) 543-2SKI
Website: www.sundayriver.com

Massachusetts

Blandford Ski Area
Blandford, MA
Phone: (413) 848-2860
Website: www.skiblandford.org

Blue Hills Ski Area
Canton, MA
Phone: (781) 828-5090

Bradford Ski Area
Bradford, MA
Phone: (978) 373-0071

Brodie Mt. Ski Resort
New Ashford, MA
Phone: (413) 443-4752
Website: www.skibrodie.com

Butternut Basin
Great Barrington, MA
Phone: (413) 528-2000
Website: www.butternutbasin.com

Eaglebrook School
Deerfield, MA
Phone: (413) 774-7411

Jiminy Peak - The Mtn. Resort
Hancock, MA
Phone: (413) 738-5500
Website: www.jiminypeak.com

Nashoba Valley Ski Area
Westford, MA
Phone: (978) 692-3033

Otis Ridge
Otis, MA
Phone: (413) 269-4444

Ragged Mountain
Easton, MA
Phone: (603) 768-3475
Website: www.ragged-mt.com/ski

Ski Ward Ski Area
Shrewsbury, MA
Phone: (508) 842-6346

Wachusett Mountain Ski Area
Princeton, MA
Phone: (978) 464-2300
Website: www.wachusett.com

Michigan

Alpine Valley Ski Area
White Lake, MI
Phone: (248) 887-2180

Apple Mountain Ski Area
Freeland, MI
Phone: (517) 781-0170

Boyne Highlands Resort
Harbor Springs, MI
Phone: (616) 526-3000
Website: www.boyne.com/
index-bhigh.htm

Boyne Mountain Resort
Boyne Falls, MI
Phone: (616) 549-6000
Website: www.boyne.com/
index-bmt.htm

Cannonsburg Ski Area
Cannonsburg, MI
Phone: (616) 874-6711

Crystal Mountain Resort
Thompsonville, MI
Phone: 800-968-4676
Website: www.crystalmtn.com

Indianhead Mtn. Resort
Wakefield, MI
Phone: 800-3INDIAN
Website: www.indianheadmtn.com

Mt. Holiday Ski Area
Traverse City, MI
Phone: (616) 938-2500

Mt. Holly Ski Area
Holly, MI
Phone: (248) 634-8260

Norway Mountain Ski Resort
Norway, MI
Phone: 800-272-5445
Website: www.norwaymountain.com

Nub's Nob Ski Area
Harbor Springs, MI
Phone: 800-SKI-NUBS
Website: www.nubsnob.com

Otsego Ski Club
Gaylord, MI
Phone: (517) 732-5181

Shanty Creek
Bellaire, MI
Phone: (800) 678-4111
Website: www.shantycreek.com

Ski Brule
Iron River, MI
Phone: (800) 362-7853
Website: www.skibrule.com

Snow Snake Mountain Ski Area
Harrison, MI
Phone: (517) 539-6583

Swiss Valley Ski Area
Jones, MI
Phone: (616) 244-5635

The Homestead Resort
Glen Arbor, MI
Phone: (616) 334-5000

Timber Ridge Ski Area
Gobles, MI
Phone: (616) 694-9449

Minnesota

Afton Alps Ski Area
Hastings, MN
Phone: (651) 436-5245

Andes Tower Hills
Kensington, MN
Phone: (320) 965-2455

Buck Hill
Burnsville, MN
Phone: (612) 435-7174
Website: www.skibuck.com

Buena Vista Ski Area
Bemidji, MN
Phone: (218) 243-2231
Website: www.bvskiarea.com

Giants Ridge Golf & Ski Resort
Biwabik, MN
Phone: (218) 865-4143

Hyland Ski and Snowboard Area
Bloomington, MN
Phone: (612) 835-4250

Lutsen Mountains
Lutsen, MN
Phone: (218) 663-7281
Website: www.lutsen.com

Mount Frontenac Ski & Golf
Frontenac, MN
Phone: (800) 488-5826

Mount Kato Ski Area
Mankato, MN
Phone: (800) 668-5286
Website: www.mountkato.com

Powder Ridge Ski Area
Kimball, MN
Phone: (800) 348-7734
Website: www.powderridge.com

Spirit Mtn. Recreational Area
Duluth, MN
Phone: (800) 642-6377
Website: www.aminews.com/
SpiritMt

Welch Village Ski Area, Inc.
Welch, MN
Phone: (651) 258-4567
Website: www.welchvillage.com

Wild Mountain
Taylors Falls, MN
Phone: (800) 447-4958
Website: www.wildmountain.com

Missouri

Hidden Valley Ski Area
Eureka, MO
Phone: (314) 938-5373

Snow Bluff Ski Area, Inc.
Brighton, MO
Phone: (417) 376-2201
Website: www.snowbluff.com

Snow Creek Ski Area
Weston, MO
Phone: (816) 640-2200

Montana

Big Mountain Ski & Summer Resort
Whitefish, MT
Phone: (800) 858-3930
Website: www.bigmtn.com/resort

Big Sky Ski and Summer Resort
Big Sky, MT
Phone: (800) 548-4486
Website: www.bigskyresort.com

Bridger Bowl Ski Area
Bozeman, MT
Phone: (800) 223-9609
Website: www.bridgerbowl.com

Discovery Ski Area
Anaconda, MT
Phone: (406) 563-2184

Great Divide
Marysville, MT
Phone: (406) 449-3746

Lost Trail Ski Area, Inc.
Conner, MT
Phone: (406) 821-3508

Marshall Mountain
Missoula, MT
Phone: (406) 258-6000

Montana Snow Bowl
Missoula, MT
Phone: (406) 549-9777
Website: www.montanasnowbowl.com

Red Lodge Mountain
Red Lodge, MT
Phone: (406) 446-2610
Website: www.montana.net/
rlmresort

Showdown Ski Area
Neihart, MT
Phone: (800) 433-0022
Website: www.skishowdown.com

Teton Pass Ski Area
Fairfield, MT
Phone: (406) 467-3664

Nevada

Diamond Peak Ski Resort
Incline Village, NV
Phone: (702) 832-1177
Website: www.diamondpeak.com

Heavenly Ski Resort
Stateline, NV
Phone: (775) 586-7000
Website: www.skiheavenly.com

Las Vegas Ski & Snowboard Resort
Las Vegas, NV
Phone: (702) 385-2754

Mt. Rose Ski Tahoe
Reno, NV
Phone: (702) 849-0704
Website: www.skirose.com

New Hampshire

Attitash Bear Peak
Bartlett, NH
Phone: (603) 374-2368
Website: www.attitash.com

Balsams Wilderness
Dixville Notch, NH
Phone: (800) 255-0600
Website: www.thebalsams.com

Black Mountain Ski Area
Jackson, NH
Phone: (603) 383-4490
Website: www.blackmt.com

Bretton Woods Ski Area
Bretton Woods, NH
Phone: (603) 278-5000
Website: www.brettonwoods.com

Cannon Mountain
Franconia, NH
Phone: (603) 823-5563
Website: www.cannonmt.com

Cranmore Mountain Resort
North Conway, NH
Phone: (800) SUN-N-SKI
Website: www.cranmore.com

Dartmouth Skiway
Hanover, NH
Phone: (603) 795-2143
Website: www.dartmouth.edu/
~skiway

Gunstock Area
Laconia, NH
Phone: (800) GUNSTOCK
Website: www.gunstock.com

King Pine Ski Area
East Madison, NH
Phone: (603) 367-8896
Website: www.purityspring.com

Loon Mountain Recreation Corp.
Lincoln, NH
Phone: (603) 745-8111
Website: www.loonmtn.com

McIntyre Ski Area
Manchester, NH
Phone: (603) 624-6571

Mt. Sunapee Ski Area
Newbury, NH
Phone: (603) 763-2356
Website: www.mtsunapee.com

Pats Peak
Henniker, NH
Phone: (888) PATS-PEAK
Website: www.patspeak.com

Ski Whaleback, Ltd
Lebanon, NH
Phone: (603) 448-1489
Website: www.whaleback.com

Tenney Mountain
Plymouth, NH
Phone: (888) TENNEY2
Website: www.tenneymtn.com

Waterville Valley Ski Resort Inc.
Waterville Valley, NH
Phone: (800) 468-2553
Website: www.waterville.com

Wildcat Mountain Ski Area
Jackson, NH
Phone: (603) 466-3326
Website: www.skiwildcat.com

New Jersey

Craigmeur Ski Area
Newfoundland, NJ
Phone: (201) 697-4500
Website: www.atplay.com/
craigmeur/index.html

Hidden Valley Ski Resort
Vernon, NJ
Phone: (973) 764-4200

New Mexico

Angel Fire Resort
Angel Fire, NM
Phone: (505) 377-6401
Website:
www.angelfireresort.com

Pajarito Mountain Ski Area
Los Alamos, NM
Phone: (505) 662-5725

Red River Ski Area, Inc.
Red River, NM
Phone: (505) 754-2382
Website:
www.taoswebb.com/redriver

Sandia Peak Ski Area
Albuquerque, NM
Phone: (505) 856-6419
Website: www.sandiapeak.com

Ski Rio
Costilla, NM
Phone: (505) 758-7707
Website: www.skirio.com

Ski Santa Fe
Santa Fe, NM

Phone: (505) 982-4429
Website: www.skisantafe.com

Taos Ski Valley, Inc.
Taos Ski Valley, NM
Phone: (505) 776-2291
Website: www.taoswebb.com/
skitaos

Triple M-Mystical Mountain
Cloudcroft, NM
Phone: (505) 682-2205

New York

Belleayre Mountain Ski Center
Highmount, NY
Phone: (914) 254-5600
Website: www.belleayre.com

Big Tupper Ski Area
Tupper Lake, NY
Phone: (518) 359-7902
Website: www.bigtupper.com

Bristol Mountain Ski Resort
Canandaigua, NY
Phone: (716) 374-6000
Website: www.bristolmt.com

Catamount Ski Area
Hillsdale, NY
Phone: (518) 325-3200
Website: www.catamountski.com

Cockaigne Ski Area
Cherry Creek, NY
Phone: (716) 287-3223
Website: www.cockaigne.com

**Double 'H' Hole in the Woods
Ranch for Critically Ill**
Lake Luzerne, NY
Phone: (518) 696-5676

Gore Mountain Ski Area
North Creek, NY
Phone: (518) 251-2411
Website: www.goremtn.com/gore

Greek Peak Ski Resort
Cortland, NY
Phone: (607) 835-6111
Website: www.greekpeak.net

Holiday Mountain Ski Area
Monticello, NY
Phone: (914) 796-3161

Holiday Valley Resort
Ellicottville, NY
Phone: (716) 699-2345
Website: www.holidayvalley.com

Hunter Mountain
Hunter, NY
Phone: (518) 263-4223
Website: www.huntermtn.com

McCauley Mtn. Ski Center
Old Forge, NY
Phone: (315) 369-3225

Peek 'n Peak Resort & Conf. Ctr.
Clymer, NY
Phone: (716) 355-4141
Website: www.pknpk.com

Ski Plattekill Mountain Resort
Roxbury, NY
Phone: (607) 326-3500
Website: www.plattekill.com

Ski Tamarack
Colden, NY
Phone: (716) 941-6821

Ski Valley
Naples, NY
Phone: (716) 374-5157

Ski Windham
Windham, NY
Phone: (518) 734-4300
Website: www.skiwindham.com

Snow Ridge Ski Area
Turin, NY
Phone: (315) 348-8456
Website: www.snowridge.com

Swain Ski Center
Swain, NY
Phone: (607) 545-6511
Website: www.swain.com

Thunder Ridge Ski Area LLC
Patterson, NY
Phone: (914) 878-4100

Titus Mountain, Inc.
Malone, NY
Phone: (518) 483-3740

Whiteface Mountain Ski Center
Wilmington, NY
Phone: (518) 946-2223
Website: www.orda.org

North Carolina

Appalachian Ski Mountain
Blowing Rock, NC
Phone: (828) 295-7828
Website: www.appskimtn.com

Beech Mountain Ski Resort
Banner Elk, NC
Phone: (828) 387-2011
Website: www.skibeech.com

Cataloochee Ski Area
Maggie Valley, NC
Phone: (828) 926-0285
Website: www.cataloochee.com

Hawksnest Golf & Ski Resort
Banner Elk, NC
Phone: (828) 963-6561
Website: www.hawksnest-resort.com

Sapphire Valley Ski Area
Cashiers, NC
Phone: (828) 743-1164
Website: www.members.aol.com/svma/index.htm

Scaly Mountain Ski Area
Scaly Mountain, NC
Phone: (828) 526-3737

Sugar Mountain Ski Area
Banner Elk, NC
Phone: (828) 898-4521
Website: www.skisugar.com

Wolf Laurel Ski Slopes
Mars Hill, NC
Phone: (828) 689-4111
Website: www.skiwolflaurel.com

Ohio

Boston Mills/Brandywine Ski Resort
Peninsula, OH
Phone: (330) 467-2242
Website: www.bmbw.com

Clear Fork Ski Area
Butler, OH
Phone: (419) 883-2000
Website: www.richnet.net/cfslope

Mad River Mountain
Bellefontaine, OH
Phone: (937) 599-1015
Website: www.skimadriver.com

Snow Trails Ski Resort
Mansfield, OH
Phone: (419) 756-7768
Website: www.snowtrails.com

Oregon

Anthony Lakes Mtn Resort, Inc.
North Powder, OR
Phone: (541) 856-3277
Website: www.anthonylakes.com

Hoodoo Ski Area
Sisters, OR
Phone: (541) 822-3799
Website: www.hoodoo.com

Mt. Ashland Ski Area
Ashland, OR
Phone: (541) 482-2897
Website: www.mind.net/snow

Mt. Bachelor, Inc.
Bend, OR
Phone: (541) 382-2442
Website: www.mtbachelor.com

Mt. Hood Meadows Ski Resort
Mt. Hood, OR
Phone: (503) 337-2222
Website: www.skihood.com

Mt. Hood Ski Bowl
Government Camp, OR
Phone: (503) 272-3206
Website: www.skibowl.com

Timberline
Timberline, OR
Phone: (503) 272-3311
Website:
www.Timberlinelodge.com

Willamette Pass Ski Corp.
Eugene, OR
Phone: (541) 345-7669
Website: www.willamettepass.com

Pennsylvania

Alpine Mountain Ski Area
Analomink, PA
Phone: (570) 595-2150
Website: www.alpinemountain.com

Big Bass Lake Community Assn.
Gouldsboro, PA
Phone: (570) 842-6388

Big Boulder Ski Area
Blakeslee, PA
Phone: (570) 722-0100
Website: www.big2resorts.com

Blue Knob
Claysburg, PA
Phone: (814) 239-5111
Website: www.blueknob.com

Blue Marsh Ski Area
Bernville, PA
Phone: (610) 488-7412

Blue Mountain Ski Area
Palmerton, PA
Phone: (610) 826-7700

Boyce Park Ski Area
Pittsburgh, PA
Phone: (724) 327-8798

Camelback Ski Corporation
Tannersville, PA
Phone: (570) 629-1661
Website: www.skicamelback.com

Doe Mountain
Macungie, PA
Phone: (610) 682-7100

Elk Mountain Ski Resort, Inc.
Union Dale, PA
Phone: (570) 679-4400

Jack Frost Mountain
Blakeslee, PA
Phone: (570) 722-0100
Website: www.big2resorts.com

Mount Tone Ski Area
Lake Como, PA
Phone: (570) 798-2707
Website: www.mttone.com

Mystic Mountain
Farmington, PA
Phone: (724) 325-5569

Pocono Ranch Lands Property Owners
Bushkill, PA
Phone: (570) 828-2326

Seven Springs Mountain Resort
Champion, PA
Phone: (814) 352-7777
Website: www.7springs.com

Shawnee Mountain Ski Area
Shawnee-on-Delaware, PA
Phone: (570) 421-7231
Website: www.shawneemt.com

Ski Big Bear At Masthope Mountain
Lackawaxen, PA
Phone: (570) 685-1400

Ski Denton
Coudersport, PA
Phone: (814) 435-2115
Website: www.skidenton.com

Ski Liberty
Carroll Valley, PA
Phone: (717) 642-8282
Website: www.skiliberty.com

Ski Roundtop
Lewisberry, PA
Phone: (717) 432-9631
Website: www.skiroundtop.com

Ski Sawmill Mountain Resort
Palmyra, PA
Phone: (570) 353-7521
Website: www.skisawmill.com

Tussey Mountain Ski Area
Boalsburg, PA
Phone: (814) 466-6810
Website: www.tusseymountain.com

Whitetail Resort
Mercersburg, PA
Phone: (717) 328-9400
Website: www.skiwhitetail.com

Willowbrook Ski Area
Belle Vernon, PA
Phone: (724) 872-7272

Rhode Island

Yawgoo Valley Ski Area
Slocum, RI
Phone: (401) 294-3802

South Dakota

Terry Peak Ski Area
Lead, SD
Phone: (605) 584-2165
Website: www.terrypeak.com

Tennessee

Ober Gatlinburg Ski Resort
Gatlinburg, TN
Phone: (423) 436-5423
Website: www.obergatlinburg.com

Utah

Alta Ski Area
Alta, UT
Phone: (801) 359-1078
Website: www.altaskiarea.com

Beaver Mountain Ski Area
Logan, UT
Phone: (435) 753-0921

Brian Head Resort
Brian Head, UT
Phone: (435) 677-2035
Website: www.brianhead.com

Brighton Ski Resort
Brighton, UT
Phone: (801) 532-4731
Website: www.skibrighton.com

Deer Valley Resort Company
Park City, UT
Phone: (435) 649-1000
Website: www.deervalley.com

Elk Meadows Ski & Summer Resort
Beaver, UT
Phone: (888)-881-7669
Website: www.elkmeadows.com

Park City Mountain Resort
Park City, UT
Phone: (435) 649-8111
Website:
www.parkcitymountain.com

Powder Mountain, Inc.
Eden, UT
Phone: (801) 745-3772
Website: www.members.aol.com/
powdermtn/utah.html

Snowbasin Ski Area
Huntsville, UT
Phone: (801) 399-1135
Website: www.snowbasin.com

Snowbird Ski & Summer Resort
Snowbird, UT
Phone: (800) 232-9542
Website: www.snowbird.com

Solitude Ski Resort
Salt Lake City, UT
Phone: (801) 534-1400
Website: www.skisolitude.com

Sundance
Sundance, UT
Phone: (801) 225-4107
Website: www.sundance-utah.com

The Canyons
Park City, UT
Phone: (435) 649-5400
Website: www.thecanyons.com

Vermont

Ascutney Mountain Resort
Brownsville, VT
Phone: (802) 484-7711
Website: www.ascutney.com

Bolton Resort
Richmond, VT
Phone: (802) 434-2131

Bromley
Manchester Center, VT
Phone: (802) 824-5522
Website: www.bromley.com

Burke Mountain Resort
East Burke, VT
Phone: (802) 626-3305
Website: www.burkemountain.com

Haystack Ski Area
West Dover, VT
Phone: (802) 464-3333
Website: www.mountsnow.com

Jay Peak Ski Resort
Jay, VT
Phone: (802) 988-2611
Website: www.jaypeakresort.com

Killington Resort
Killington, VT
Phone: (802) 422-3333
Website: www.killington.com

Magic Mountain Ski Area
Londonderry, VT
Phone: (802) 824-5645

Middlebury College Snow Bowl
Middlebury, VT
Phone: (802) 388-4356

Mount Snow Resort
Mount Snow, VT
Phone: (802) 464-3333
Website: www.mountsnow.com

Okemo Mountain Resort
Ludlow, VT
Phone: (802) 228-4041
Website: www.okemo.com

Quechee Ski Area
Quechee, VT
Phone: (802) 295-9356

Smugglers' Notch Resort
Jeffersonville, VT
Phone: (800) 451-8752
Website: www.smuggs.com

Stowe Mountain Resort
Stowe, VT
Phone: (802) 253-3500
Website: www.stowe.com/smr

Sugarbush Resort
Warren, VT
Phone: (802) 583-6300
Website: www.sugarbush.com

Suicide Six Ski Area
Woodstock Inn & Resort
Woodstock, VT
Phone: (800) 448-7900
Website: www.woodstockinn.com

Virginia

Bryce Resort
Basye, VA
Phone: (800) 821-1444
Website: www.bryceresort.com

Massanutten Ski Resort
Harrisonburg, VA
Phone: (800) 207-MASS
Website: www.massresort.com

The Homestead Ski Area
Hot Springs, VA
Phone: (540) 839-1766

Wintergreen Resort

Wintergreen Resort
Wintergreen, VA
Phone: (804) 325-2200
Website:
www.WintergreenResort.com

Washington

49 Degrees North Ski Area
Chewelah, WA
Phone: (509) 935-6649
Website: www.ski49n.com

Loup Loup Ski Area
Omak, WA
Phone: (509) 826-2720

Mission Ridge
Wenatchee, WA
Phone: (509) 663-6543
Website: www.missionridge.com

Mt. Baker
Bellingham, WA
Phone: (360) 734-6771

Mt. Spokane Ski Area
Mead, WA
Phone: (509) 238-2220
Website: www.mtspokane.com

Ski Bluewood
Dayton, WA
Phone: (509) 382-4725
Website:
www.skiwashington.com/resorts/
SkiBluewood.shtml

Stevens Pass
Skykomish, WA
Phone: (206) 812-4510
Website: www.stevenspass.com

The Summit At Snoqualmie
Snoqualmie Pass, WA
Phone: (425) 434-7669
Website: www.summit-at-sno-
qualmie.com

West Virginia

Canaan Valley Resort
Davis, WV
Phone: (304) 866-4121
Website: www.canaanresort.com

Silver Creek Resort
Snowshoe, WV
Phone: (304) 572-5252
Website: www.snowshoemtn.com

Snowshoe Mountain Resort
Snowshoe, WV
Phone: (304) 572-5252
Website: www.snowshoemtn.com

Timberline Four Seasons Resort
Davis, WV
Phone: (304) 866-4801
Website:
www.timberlineresort.com

Winterplace Ski Resort
Ghent, WV
Phone: (304) 787-3221
Website: www.winterplace.com

Wisconsin

**'The Mountain Top' At Grand
Geneva Resort**
Lake Geneva, WI
Phone: (414) 248-8811

Alpine Valley Resort
East Troy, WI
Phone: (414) 642-7374

Ausblick Ski Area
Sussex, WI
Phone: (414) 246-3090

Cascade Mountain Ski & Snowboard Area
Portage, WI
Phone: (608) 742-5588
Website:
www.cascademountain.com

Christmas Mountain Village
Wisconsin Dells, WI
Phone: (608) 254-3971

Devil's Head Resort & Convention Center
Merrimac, WI
Phone: (608) 493-2251

Heiliger Huegel Ski Club
North Lake, WI
Phone: (414) 628-3202

Highlands of Olympia Ski & Snowboarding Hill
Oconomowoc, WI
Phone: (414) 567-2577

Mt. La Crosse
La Crosse, WI
Phone: (608) 788-0044

Nordic Mountain Ski Area
Hancock, WI
Phone: (920) 787-3324

Rib Mountain Ski Area
Wausau, WI
Phone: (715) 845-2846

Sunburst Ski Area
Kewaskum, WI
Phone: (414) 626-8404

Telemark Ski Area
Cable, WI
Phone: (715) 798-3999

Trollhaugen Ski Area
Dresser, WI
Phone: (715) 755-2955
Website: www.trollhaugen.com

Tyrol Basin Ski & Snowboard Area
Mt. Horeb, WI
Phone: (608) 437-4135
Website: www.tyrolbasin.com

Wilmot Mountain, Inc.
Wilmot, WI
Phone: (414) 862-2301

Wyoming

Antelope Butte Ski Area
Dayton, WY
Phone: (307) 655-9530
Website: www.quickpage.com/A/
Antelopeski

Grand Targhee Ski & Summer Resort
Alta, WY
Phone: (307) 353-2300
Website: www.grandtarghee.com

Hogadon Ski Area
Casper, WY
Phone: (307) 235-8499

Jackson Hole Mountain Resort
Teton Village, WY
Phone: (800) 443-6931
Website:
www.jacksonhole.com/ski

Powder Pass Ski Area
Buffalo, WY
Phone: (307) 366-2600

Sleeping Giant Ski Area
Cody, WY
Phone: (307) 587-4044

Snow King Resort
Jackson, WY
Phone: (800) 522-KING
Website: www.snowking.com

Appendix C

Skiing Glossary

Acro-skiing: This freestyle event, once known as ballet skiing, is like figure skating on skis, with competitors judged on grace and difficulty, rather than speed.

Aerials: In this freestyle event, a skier is launched from a specially designed ramp, and flies 50 feet or more in the air while performing twisting, turning and flipping maneuvers, and then lands on a steep, softened landing hill.

Alpine skiing: Another term for downhill skiing.

Antifriction device (AFD): A Teflon pad or mechanical slider on the binding designed to reduce friction between the boot sole and the binding to ensure consistent release.

Après-ski: Literally after skiing — this refers to the activities at the end of the day when skiers go to restaurants and bars to socialize.

Base: The average depth of snow on a mountain.

Base material: The smooth material, usually polyethylene, on the bottom of your skis that makes your skis slide.

Bevel: Filing or grinding a ski edge at a small angle (usually about one degree) relative to the base for better grip or, more commonly, easier turn initiation.

Base lodge: A building at the base of the slopes, open to all skiers, where you can find a variety of skier services, from food to lift tickets, or you can simply take a break from the slopes.

Base Structure: The microscopic texture, characterized by fine longitudinal grooves, ground into a ski base to improve its glide.

Bowl: An open area above a mountain's tree line with no defined trails. Bowl skiing is often, but not always, for more advanced skiers.

Bunny slope: The most gently sloping hill on a mountain, where beginner lessons are held.

Camber: The gentle arch that can be seen in an unweighted ski when it's resting on a flat surface.

Cap: The uppermost layer of most skis, which wraps around the sides and top. Sometimes this is an important structural element, and sometimes merely an aesthetic covering.

Carving: A type of ski turn in which the ski moves almost exclusively forward along the length of its edge with little or no lateral skidding. Carves can often be identified by the narrow, slot-like tracks made by the skier.

Chatter: Instability caused by the ski bouncing over a hard uneven surface instead of sliding.

Corduroy: A slang term for freshly groomed snow, which it resembles.

Corn snow: A condition, usually found in the spring, characterized by large, loose granules of snow that freeze together at night, and then melt apart again during the day.

Cross-country: Self-propelled skiing on a generally flat surface, usually through wooded areas, using special skis, boots, and poles.

Cruising: Skiing at moderate to high speed while making medium to long radius turns.

Damping: A ski's ability to quiet vibration, making for a smoother ride and better grip on the snow.

DIN setting: An adjustable setting on a skier's bindings that influences how much torque must be applied to a boot to release it from the binding. The setting depends on a skier's height, weight, and skiing style.

Double: A lift in which each chair seats two people.

Downhill: A high-speed race, contested in the Olympics and other major competitions. Racers reach speeds up to 80 miles per hour in some stretches.

Edge: A metal strip on either side of the ski base that enables the ski to grip on hard snow.

Extreme Skiing: A subgenre of the sport in whick skiers challenge themselves on very steep terrain and/or by jumping off cliffs, either in competition or for still photos or videos. Sometimes called *free skiing*.

Fall line: The straightest line down a mountain, characterized by the path that water would take down a particular slope.

Flex: The relative stiffness or softness of a ski against a bending or twisting force.

Frozen granular: A hard surface of old snow formed by granules freezing together after a rain or warm temperatures.

Glade skiing: Downhill skiing in wooded areas, usually between trails, where untracked snow can often be found between trees. This type of skiing is for advanced and expert skiers only.

Gondola: A lift that features enclosed cars, in which a group of six or more skiers sit or stand while riding to the top of the mountain.

Groomed: Refers to a slope that has a smoothed, softened snow surface. The final result resembles wide-wale corduroy.

Halfpipe: A U-shaped snow structure built for freestyle snowboarding. Snowboarders travel back and forth up the sides of the halfpipe, often performing tricks as they get airborne off the edge.

Hard pack: When natural or machine-made snow becomes very firmly packed because of grooming or wind exposure, but has never melted and recrystallized.

Heli-skiing: Skiing in which the participants in search of untracked powder are transported by helicopter to an area otherwise inaccessible by lifts.

Ice: A hard, glazed, usually translucent surface created either by freezing rain, ground water seeping up into the snow and freezing, or by the rapid freezing of snow saturated with water from rain or melting.

Lift capacity: The number of people who can ride up the mountain on a lift in one hour. For example, a lift capacity of 2,600 means that a lift can transport 2,600 skiers per hour at maximum speed, although you should keep in mind that lifts rarely run at maximum speed.

Lift corral: A maze of ropes or partitions designed to funnel skiers onto a lift in an orderly fashion.

Lift line: Skiers waiting one behind the other in a lift corral to board a chair lift.

Loose granular: This surface results after powder or packed powder thaws, refreezes, and recrystallizes. It can also be created by machine grooming of frozen or icy snow.

Machine-groomed granular: Loose granular snow that has been repeatedly groomed by power tillers so that the texture is halfway between loose granular and packed powder.

Mashed potatoes: A slang term for wet, heavy snow.

Moguls: Bumps on an ungroomed ski run that are formed naturally by the turns of earlier skiers on the slope.

NASTAR: An acronym for National Standard Racing. These competitions, open to all skiers, are runs on standardized courses on which skiers are timed, and their results compared to a national standard.

Never-ever: An individual who has never skied before, usually referring to someone who signs up for a first-time ski lesson.

Nordic combined: This Olympic event combines a 90-meter ski jump followed by a 15K cross-country ski race.

Off-piste: Terrain, usually ungroomed, within ski area boundaries, that doesn't consist of a conventional trail.

Out of bounds: Terrain outside the boundaries of the ski area. In these areas, which are not patrolled, you can encounter avalanche conditions, impassable terrain, and other dangerous conditions.

Packed powder: Powder snow, either natural or machine-made, that has been packed down by skier traffic or grooming machines. The snow is no longer fluffy, but it is not so extremely compacted that it is hard.

Parabolic ski: A term used to describe the specific sidecut geometry on certain skis manufactured by Elan, sometimes incorrectly used to describe any shaped ski.

Powder: Cold, new, loose, fluffy, dry snow that has not been compacted and is usually the product of fresh, natural snowfall at a low temperature.

Quad: A chair lift carrying four people that comes in two basic varieties. A high-speed detachable quad has two separate cables. At the beginning and end of the ride, the chair moves to a slow-moving cable for safe and easy loading and unloading. But in between, the chair is switched to a very fast-moving cable for speedy trips. A fixed-grip quad has only a single cable.

Rope tow: A continuously moving rope that pulls skiers up the mountain as they slide along on their skis. Rope tows usually are found on novice trails.

Run: One "lap" of a lift or mountain, riding to the top and skiing back to the bottom.

Schussing: Skiing straight down a slope without making turns, often in a full tuck position.

Shaped ski: A ski with a particularly deep sidecut.

Shovel: The widest part of the ski found just behind the tip.

Sidecut: The difference between the tip and the waist of the ski, which is visible in the ski's hourglass shape.

Slalom/Giant slalom: A two-run race in which racers must ski around narrowly spaced spring-loaded gates. The best combined time for two runs wins.

Snowboarding: Descending a slope on a small, single board, wider and shorter than a ski, using techniques derived from surfing or skateboarding.

Snowcat: A large truck with tank-like treads used for grooming and occasionally transporting skiers to a backcountry destination.

Spring conditions: A snow reporting term, which is the late season equivalent of variable conditions, often with the addition of bare spots or a discolored surface from melting and traffic.

Surface lift: Lifts such as rope tows and t-bars that pull the skier up the mountain while they slide on their skis.

Super G: The newest racing discipline, a one-run race in which skiers negotiate a course that includes more turns than a downhill course but is faster than a giant slalom.

Ski in, Ski out: Lodging located close enough to the slopes that guests can conveniently walk or ski to a nearby trail or lift.

Ski Patrol: An on-snow emergency squad charged with assisting and transporting injured skiers, controlling avalanches, and eliminating other dangerous conditions and enforcing the rules of safe skiing.

Skidding: A style of turning, usually employed by beginners and intermediate skiers, in which the ski is allowed slide sideways across the snow in an attempt to control speed.

Snowmaking: Using a system that combines air and water under pressure to make artificial snow, especially during the early season or when levels of natural snowfall are low.

Tail: The rearmost section of a ski, behind the skier's boot, which is wider than the waist but narrower than the shovel.

T-bar: A surface lift that pulls skiers up the mountain on their skis by means of a bar placed behind the skiers' legs. Two skiers go at a time, one leaning on one section of the upside-down T.

Tip: The upturned front portion of a ski.

Torsional stiffness: A ski's resistance to twisting.

Trail ratings: A national system by which U.S. ski areas apply ability-related designations to individual trails. Green circle trails are the easiest, blue squares are more difficult, and black diamond trails are the most difficult.

Tree line: The altitude above which trees do not grow on the mountain, giving skiers an unobstructed expanse on which to ski. See *Bowl*.

Triple: A lift in which each chair seats three people.

Tuning: Optimizing the performance of a pair of skis by flattening the bases and/or sharpening the edges, and applying wax.

Variable conditions: A snow reporting term that means that a variety of surfaces may be encountered.

Vertical drop: The height of a mountain, as expressed by the difference between the altitude at the top and the altitude at the base.

Waist: The narrowest part of the ski, usually located near or just behind the center of the boot.

Wax: A compound applied to a ski base — called hot wax when it's melted on — that allows the ski to glide more easily on the snow.

Wet granular: Loose or frozen granular snow that has become wet after rainfall or high temperatures.

Windpack: A firm, but sometimes breakable surface formed on snow that's exposed to wind.

Index

fitness
  about, 189
  avoiding injuries, 189–190
  soreness, 194, 196
  stretching, 193–194
  training, 190–193
fitting boots, 14–15, 25–32
flamingo exercise, 138, 139
flashlight, 229
flat lighting, 173
flats, 169–171
fleece
  care of, 76
  insulation layer, 65–67
flex, 23, 25, 39, 315
flex adjuster, 23
flexibility, ski lessons, 130
flights, booking, 252–254
float, 42
flying early, 252–253
fog, 172
fogging goggles, 92
follow me drill, 146
food for car, 229
forward flex, boots, 25
forward lean adjustment, boots, 23
foul-weather hats, 89
free skiing, 263–265
frequent skiing for free skiing, 264
friends, skiing with, 264
front-entry boots, 23–24
frostbite
  first aid, 199
  signs, 198
frozen granular snow, 166, 315
fuel, 229
Fur Elise drill, 146

• G •

game improvement skis, 45
gear. *See* equipment
Georgia ski areas, 297
giant slalom, 150
gimmicks for free skiing, 263
glade skiing, 315
gliding, 41
gloves
  about, 83, 103–104
  component style gloves, 84
  insulated nylon gloves, 84
  mittens, 84
  mountaineering style gloves, 84
  spring gloves, 84–85
  waterproof gloves, 85
goals of ski lessons, 130
goggles, 90–92
  fit, 92
  fogging, 92
  lens color, 91
gondolas, 243, 315
Gore-Tex, 69
gouge filling, ski maintenance, 58
Grand Targhee, 282
green circles on trails, 162–163, 180
grip of poles, 11, 55–56
groomed snow, 315
grooming reports, 164–166
group ski lessons
  about, 125–126
  children, 216
GS skis, 47

• H •

halfpipe, 315
hamstring muscles, 191
hamstring stretch, 194
hand-me-down skiwear for children, 211
hands in front exercise, 140–141

YOUR ONLINE RESOURCE

WWW.DUMMIES.COM

Discover Dummies Online!

The Dummies Web Site is your fun and friendly online resource for the latest information about ...*For Dummies*® books and your favorite topics. The Web site is the place to communicate with us, exchange ideas with other ...*For Dummies* readers, chat with authors, and have fun!

Ten Fun and Useful Things You Can Do at www.dummies.com

1. Win free ...*For Dummies* books and more!
2. Register your book and be entered in a prize drawing.
3. Meet your favorite authors through the IDG Books Author Chat Series.
4. Exchange helpful information with other ...*For Dummies* readers.
5. Discover other great ...*For Dummies* books you must have!
6. Purchase Dummieswear™ exclusively from our Web site.
7. Buy ...*For Dummies* books online.
8. Talk to us. Make comments, ask questions, get answers!
9. Download free software.
10. Find additional useful resources from authors.

Link directly to these ten fun and useful things at
http://www.dummies.com/10useful

SURF THE NET

WWW.DUMMIES.COM

For other technology titles from IDG Books Worldwide, go to
www.idgbooks.com

Not on the Web yet? It's easy to get started with *Dummies 101*®: *The Internet For Windows*®*98* or *The Internet For Dummies*,® 6th Edition, at local retailers everywhere.

IDG BOOKS WORLDWIDE

Find other ...*For Dummies* books on these topics:

Business • Career • Databases • Food & Beverage • Games • Gardening • Graphics • Hardware
Health & Fitness • Internet and the World Wide Web • Networking • Office Suites
Operating Systems • Personal Finance • Pets • Programming • Recreation • Sports
Spreadsheets • Teacher Resources • Test Prep • Word Processing

IDG BOOKS WORLDWIDE BOOK REGISTRATION

Register This Book and Win!

We want to hear from you!

Visit **http://my2cents.dummies.com** to register this book and tell us how you liked it!

✔ Get entered in our monthly prize giveaway.

✔ Give us feedback about this book — tell us what you like best, what you like least, or maybe what you'd like to ask the author and us to change!

✔ Let us know any other *...For Dummies*® topics that interest you.

Your feedback helps us determine what books to publish, tells us what coverage to add as we revise our books, and lets us know whether we're meeting your needs as a *...For Dummies* reader. You're our most valuable resource, and what you have to say is important to us!

Not on the Web yet? It's easy to get started with *Dummies 101*®: *The Internet For Windows*® *98* or *The Internet For Dummies*®, 6th Edition, at local retailers everywhere.

Or let us know what you think by sending us a letter at the following address:

...For Dummies Book Registration
Dummies Press
7260 Shadeland Station, Suite 100
Indianapolis, IN 46256-3917
Fax 317-596-5498

BESTSELLING BOOK SERIES